THE SAFETY OF THE KINGDOM

Government Responses to Subversive Threats

J. Michael Martinez

Carrel Books may be purchased in bulk at special discounts for sales promotion, corporate gifts, fund-raising, or educational purposes. Special editions can also be created to specifications. For details, contact the Special Sales Department, Carrel Books, 307 West 36th Street, 11th Floor, New York, NY 10018 or carrelbooks@skyhorsepublishing.com.

Carrel Books® is a registered trademark of Skyhorse Publishing, Inc.®, a Delaware corporation.

Visit our website at www.carrelbooks.com.

10 9 8 7 6 5 4 3 2 1

Library of Congress Cataloging-in-Publication Data is available on file.

Cover design by Owen Corrigan

ISBN: 978-1-63144-024-3
Ebook ISBN: 978-1-63144-033-5

Printed in the United States of America

For Nero Blake Carter, my youngest grandson (so far)—with hopes he will love his country and his papa, warts and all, when he is old enough to appreciate both.

Wherein you would have sold your king to slaughter,
His princes and his peers to servitude,
His subjects to oppression and contempt
And his whole kingdom into desolation.
Touching our person seek we no revenge;
But we our kingdom's safety must so tender,
Whose ruin you have sought, that to her laws
We do deliver you.

—William Shakespeare, *King Henry V,* Act II, Scene ii

TABLE OF CONTENTS

INTRODUCTION AND ACKNOWLEDGMENTS

This book is to some extent a sequel to my earlier book, *Terrorist Attacks on American Soil: From the Civil War Era to the Present*. The earlier work sought to understand the typology of terrorist attacks in the United States from the 1850s through the 9/11 episode and the lessons to be learned in preparing for future attacks. This book takes up the question of how the US government typically responds to terrorist attacks and, in the absence of an attack, the fear of foreign and subversive elements that may harm the nation. In some cases, the government "overreaction" leads to a series of abuses that amplifies the severity of the original threat. The objective here is not to select every instance of government reaction to threats, but to examine representative cases.

The horrendous events of September 11, 2001, highlighted the nature of terrorism unlike all but a handful of major catastrophes in American history. It is a date no one will ever forget—akin to the Japanese attack on Pearl Harbor on December 7, 1941, and President Kennedy's assassination on November 22, 1963. It is only natural that citizens and their political leaders have struggled to respond to such events.

After a terrorist episode occurs, the question invariably arises: what should government do to eliminate or reduce the likelihood of a future attack? Often the initial reaction is supported at the outset, only to become a matter of debate when the shock of the original event wears off. Slightly more than six weeks after the 9/11 attacks in the United States, for example, Congress passed and President George W. Bush signed into law the Uniting and Strengthening America by Providing Appropriate Tools Required to Intercept and Obstruct Terrorism Act of 2001, commonly referred to as the USA PATRIOT Act (USAPA).

The USAPA provides the federal government with enhanced authority to prevent future terrorist attacks. The act allows federal agencies to request stored information from third-party providers, including telephone companies and Internet service providers; makes fundamental changes in the application and execution of search warrants; and authorizes agencies to share information that was restricted in the past. The statute was popular in 2001 as Americans struggled to make sense of the horrors they had witnessed. In subsequent years, the USAPA lost much of its political support.

I started working on this project in the spring and summer of 2013. During my initial stages of research and writing, the Boston Marathon bombings and Edward Snowden's disclosure of classified information related to the National Security Agency's covert surveillance program dominated the news. As I entered the final stages of preparing the manuscript for publication, a jury in Boston, Massachusetts, found Dzhokhar Tsarnaev guilty on thirty charges related to the Boston Marathon bombings, which killed three people and wounded more than two hundred and sixty others. Such high-profile cases highlight the ongoing salience of terrorism as well as the debate over an appropriate governmental response. At the heart of this debate is the perennial trade-off between freedom and authority. The debate casts these concepts as antithetical values so that an increase in one value necessarily requires a corresponding decrease in the other.

At one end of the spectrum is absolute freedom, which can be defined as a complete absence of constraints on individual behavior. In a state of absolute freedom, no government exists. A person can do whatever he or she wants. At the other end of the spectrum, a totalitarian state can be created so there is no individual freedom whatsoever. Most US citizens desire a balance—a middle approach. A mixed polity—that is, a regime where people, acting through their elected representatives, make some political decisions, but unelected experts also contribute to policy-making—is the preferred form of government for a people who profess to love individual freedom but also desire a strong state that meets many needs, especially for national defense, protecting free markets, and ensuring equality of opportunity (although the

definition of the latter term is debated). The US political system calls to mind Winston Churchill's famous comment that a democracy is the worst form of government—except, of course, for all the others.

Since September 11, 2001, many books and articles have been published about terrorism and America's response to the problem of "non-state actors" that engage in violence. Rather than focus on the initial acts that qualify as terrorism and subversion, however, this book focuses on government responses to terrorism and perceived subversion. Sometimes the responses are effective, and sometimes they trigger a backlash that leads to abuses at the hands of government agents.

As I embarked on my research and writing, I harbored high hopes and soaring ambitions. I would discuss every case in American history and uncover every episode where government sought to ensure the safety of its citizens but sometimes went astray. I quickly realized that such ambitious plans were unworkable. If I were to tackle every episode, the resultant book would become a 1,000+ page tome. Comprehensive works have their place, but often their heft makes them inaccessible. Choices would have to be made. Therefore, I selected what I thought were representative cases from across a broad expanse of American history, beginning with the Alien and Sedition Acts and ending with 9/11. In most instances, the choices were obvious owing to the importance of the issue and the availability of research material. In other cases, I used my judgment to select what I thought were interesting and illustrative examples.

Acknowledgments

My name is printed on the cover of this book, but I realize that no one writes a long work without considerable assistance from others. First and foremost, I appreciated the tremendous assistance I received from Niels Aaboe, executive editor at Skyhorse Publishing. Niels and I worked together on a previous book when he was with Rowman & Littlefield some years ago, and, as always, it was a pleasure to renew our professional association. I also appreciated the efforts of the many fine folks at Carrel Books/Skyhorse, especially Leigh Eron, who worked behind the scenes to bring this work into print.

Numerous archivists and researchers provided assistance, especially Kimberly David at the Library of Congress. Ms. David assisted me on several books in the past. The interlibrary loan staff at the Horace W. Sturgis Library, Kennesaw State University, also assisted in locating sources, just as they have done on most of my previous works. I also received valuable marketing advice from Liz Kula of webdesignsbyliz. com. Liz created my website at www.jmichaelmartinez.com and kept it updated. Colleagues at Dart Container Corporation and Kennesaw State University have supported my writing as well.

As always, my family and friends have been terrific sources of support and TLC. In alphabetical order, I extend thanks to the late Charles DuBose and his wife, Glenda; Shirley Hardrick; Wallace and Leila Jordan; Laura Mead and her children; Phil and Carolyn Mead and their children; Martha and Dick Pickett; Dr. William D. Richardson, my mentor who now chairs the political science department at the University of South Dakota; Chuck Redmon; Keith W. Smith, an old law school buddy; Barbara Wise and her children and grandchildren; and Bob and Peggy Youngblood. Thanks also to family members who are fellow writers—Chris Mead (cousin), Loren B. Mead (uncle), Walter Russell Mead (cousin), Robert Sidney Mellette (cousin), William W. Mellette (uncle), and Jim Wise (cousin).

Needless to say (but I will say it, anyway), all errors or omissions in fact or interpretation are my responsibility alone.

Chapter 1

THE ALIEN AND SEDITION ACTS

I have sworn upon the altar of God eternal hostility against every form of tyranny over the mind of man.

—THOMAS JEFFERSON,
LETTER TO DR. BENJAMIN RUSH, SEPTEMBER 23, 1800[1]

Americans who look back through the dark pages of history often are perplexed by the behavior of forebears who championed measures clearly at odds with the prevailing myth of the republic as a proverbial shining city on a hill. Yet the 1790s, the first full decade that the United States existed under the new US Constitution, teemed with danger and intrigue. The nation was less than a generation removed from the American Revolution, and its perpetual existence was hardly assured. For citizens fearful of an avaricious European power asserting its dominance over the American landscape, measures to lessen or avoid foreign subversion appeared prudent and necessary to the national interest. Concerns over alien, corrosive elements led to the first major backlash against subversion in the country's history: passage of the Alien and Sedition Acts.[2]

Background

The laws were the result of a long train of events. Tensions, especially with Great Britain, reached a crisis early in the 1790s. The British still occupied forts in the Great Lakes region and continually impressed Americans into service as British sailors a decade after the Treaty of Paris had ended the war between Britain and her former colonies. By repeatedly encouraging Native American attacks against settlers in the

western territories and interfering with trade in the West Indies, the English also threatened the well-being of citizens eking out a living on the frontier. The first US president, George Washington, was not a man to back away from a fight, but he recognized that a bellicose attitude toward the British could lead to disastrous consequences. Ill-prepared for war and mindful of the necessity of resolving ongoing disputes, his administration, propelled by a prominent Anglophile, Alexander Hamilton, negotiated a treaty that ensured at least a temporary rapprochement with Great Britain. Formally titled the Treaty of Amity, Commerce, and Navigation, Between His Britannic Majesty and the United States of America, the agreement, hammered out by a well-known lawyer and statesman, John Jay, solved one set of problems while triggering others.[3]

The nation of France, a perennial British adversary, interpreted the Jay Treaty as a threat to French interests in the New World. In response to the apparent normalization of Anglo-American relations, French officials seized American ships and confiscated the cargo. The Federalist Party, now headed by a new president, John Adams, reacted with alacrity at any perceived French threat. Had calm, deliberative reason taken hold, the dispute probably could have been resolved through normal channels of diplomatic discourse. Yet relations with France were so strained that each side attributed bad faith to the actions of the other.[4]

President Adams convened a special session of Congress in May 1797 to urge his brethren to prepare for war with France. His action ignited an acrimonious debate between his supporters in the Federalist Party and their rivals, the Democratic-Republicans, usually referred to as Republicans. The former believed that French forces represented a distinct threat to American interests and must be met with military preparedness. They suggested that internal subversion also was a threat because sympathetic Francophiles were known to live and work in the United States. A Massachusetts congressman, Harrison Gray Otis, warned that "an army of soldiers would not be so dangerous to the country, as an army of spies and incendiaries scattered throughout the Continent."[5]

Republicans countered that the Adams administration was exaggerating the crisis to reap the political benefits of public hysteria. They cautioned that the administration's actions would confuse dissent with treason. The notion of a loyal opposition is a crucial feature of a healthy republic. When a group fears that its members will be prosecuted for speaking the truth to power, disaffected voices fall silent. If the American system of government is constructed on a foundation of bargaining and negotiation, the regime becomes unstable when one or more parties are dissuaded from engaging in the rough-and-tumble world of political debate and compromise.[6]

Conscious of the turmoil he had helped to create, John Adams sought to chart a prudent course amid waves of turbulence and contention. If it came to an armed confrontation, the president was under no illusions about the nation's vulnerability. Recalling how his predecessor had avoided war with Great Britain in 1794 by sending envoys overseas to iron out disagreements, Adams agreed to dispatch representatives to France. Unfortunately, the effort, although presumably designed to preserve the peace, exacerbated tensions.[7]

The crisis escalated into the notorious XYZ affair in 1797 and 1798. Led by Charles Cotesworth Pinckney, the president's emissaries John Marshall and Elbridge Gerry arrived in France in October 1797 and requested a meeting with Charles Maurice de Talleyrand, the French foreign minister. Standard protocol dictated that foreign representatives present their credentials to the appropriate official, in this case Talleyrand. Typically, the exchange was a pro forma affair. In this instance, however, the foreign minister was irked about improved U.S.-British relations and suspicious of the Americans following a speech by President Adams that Talleyrand deemed overly hostile to his nation's interests. In the flurry of back-and-forth negotiations, Talleyrand demanded a loan to the French government and a bribe for himself. Such unsavory methods were all-too-commonplace in European diplomacy at the time, but news of the affair ignited a firestorm of protest in the United States. "Millions for defense, but not one cent for tribute" became a rallying cry among citizens incensed by the French effrontery.[8]

Thus began a quasi-war, which Adams sardonically labeled "the half war with France." Among other things, his administration established an embargo on trade with the French, formally withdrew from existing treaties, and authorized American ships on the high seas to assail French vessels. As the nation armed, talk of conspiracies circulated with frightening regularity. In addition to fears of a French war, administration officials worried that civil war might erupt between Americans who supported the British and those who allied themselves with the French.[9]

The Alien and Sedition Acts

It was this fear over foreign influences threatening the health of the fledgling nation that led Congress to pass, and President John Adams to sign, four laws known as the Alien and Sedition Acts. The laws restricted naturalization procedures, authorized the detention of foreign nationals if war broke out with their respective countries, authorized the deportation of noncitizens suspected of plotting against the United States, outlawed "conspiracies" that criticized government policies, and prohibited false or malicious writing against Congress or the president.[10]

The statutes were written out of concern for national security, but the objectives of the Alien Acts were different from the objectives of the Sedition Act. The three Alien Acts were aimed at curbing subversive activity by foreign elements that might work toward nefarious ends behind the scenes. The first statute, known as the Naturalization Act of 1798, increased the time for immigrants to become US citizens from five to fourteen years.[11] Under the Alien Enemies Act, if the nation declared war against another country, citizens from the belligerent country who were physically present in the United States could be detained, confined, or deported, as necessary, to ensure they were not engaged in subversive plots. The law passed with bipartisan support and engendered relatively little controversy.[12] The Alien Friends Act, however, proved to be far more contentious. An "emergency" measure authorized the president of the United States to seize, detain, and deport any noncitizens the president determined to be dangerous to the welfare of the country. No hearing was required and the

President John Adams signed the infamous Alien and Sedition Acts into law.
Courtesy of the Library of Congress

president was not obliged to seek approval or counsel from anyone before he acted. Unlike the Alien Enemies Act, the Friends Act did not include a requirement that the person seized and deported be a citizen of a country at war with the United States. Although the law was set to expire on President Adams's last day in office, critics regarded the broad statute as a dangerous precedent and likely

to enhance executive power at the expense of the other branches of government.[13]

If the Alien Acts sought to curtail subversion practiced under the cover of darkness, the Sedition Act was designed to prevent subversion undertaken in the light of day. Critics of the administration or its policies would not be permitted to engage in "seditious speech" without bearing legal consequences. The law passed along a straight party vote. Because the Federalists controlled both houses of Congress, they enacted the statute over Republican objections. In response to criticism that the law violated First Amendment freedom of speech, supporters argued that it modified common law definitions of sedition by imposing a requirement that malicious intent be an element of the crime. Truth was a recognized defense and a jury could determine whether a particular instance of speech rose to the level of sedition. In the view of one Federalist, the Sedition Act, far from being the burdensome law suggested by ardent Republicans, was "a wholesome and ameliorating interpreter of the common law."[14]

Some historians have concluded that the acts were an overreaction to the French government's hostility toward the new American republic while others have viewed the punitive measures as a convenient pretext, little more than a thinly-veiled effort by President Adams's Federalist Party to undermine Thomas Jefferson's Republican Party. Although Adams did not use the new Alien Acts to persecute his enemies, the Sedition Act was especially worrisome to proponents of free speech because it could be wielded as a weapon, in effect nullifying the First Amendment. Anyone who criticized the government could be prosecuted for treasonous activities—a potentially potent weapon for Federalists to silence their Republican critics, to say nothing of the chilling effect even in the absence of formal prosecution. One historian characterized the measure as "perhaps the most grievous assault on free speech in the history of the United States."[15]

In retrospect, the folly of such xenophobic legislation is not difficult to comprehend, but the tenor of the times suggested that enemies lurked around every corner. With new immigrants reaching the nation's shores every day, the possibility that subversion might imperil the regime haunted many an elected official and party leader. The land

was awash with Frenchmen, to say nothing of "wild Irishmen" and other suspect nationalities. Who knew what mischief strange peoples might propagate when their loyalties were divided and their motives impure?

That the Federalists would have authored the odious measures seemed anomalous, for the party was known to be friendly toward immigrants. Early in the 1790s, the Federalist Party had welcomed the tired, poor, huddled masses as potential recruits. Land speculators among the Federalist ranks especially envisioned a nation of transplanted Europeans eager to buy up land and spread the gospel of Americana. As the decade progressed, however, attitudes regressed. All sorts of revolutionary ideas and peoples flocked to the New World, and with them came a backlash against the infusion of foreign cultures and values. The orderly, hierarchical society that was supposed to flourish in the wake of a transformed citizenry was displaced by a chaotic horde of unwashed masses that reveled in distinctiveness. If the plan was to assimilate these new inhabitants into a uniquely American ethos, many immigrants, anxious to retain a separate ethnic heritage, refused to get with the program. Add to this disturbing trend of alien customs and habits the fervor of the French Revolution, attacks by British and French forces on American vessels and frontier outposts, and dark rumors circulating about conspiracies lurking on the fringes of American society, and the seeds were planted for a government overreaction.[16]

Fear of aliens, while perhaps overblown, can be understood as a consequence of uncertainty and feelings of powerlessness combined with steadily increasing immigration rates. Yet the desire to implement a Sedition Act requires an additional leap of faith. Apologists contended that the Federalist understanding of democratic theory was consistent with enactment of a seditious libel statute because these men of an elitist bent did not believe the legislation threatened core values. To modern sensibilities, the give-and-take among persons of different beliefs and ideologies is essential to the perpetuation of a healthy government based on the consent of the governed. The marketplace of ideas, as it was called in later days, is crowded with concepts that do not always reflect perspicacity or tasteful sentiments, but that

nonetheless advance the cause of human freedom by allowing participants to present their grievances and debate efficacious public policy. Freedom of speech is a crucial component of a robust democratic government because citizens are engaged in the discussion. A law that curtails free speech is a law that undermines regime values.

The Federalists took issue with the idea that all manner of citizens should engage in public policy debates. They argued that disputes about the appropriate course of action necessarily occur among representatives chosen to present (or re-present) the views of their constituents within the formal organs of government. Because so much of the public debate among the citizenry results in cacophonous noise and ushers in civic chaos and disorder, spirited conversation among the masses not only fails to fulfill the goals of a democratic system, but may ignite violence and lead to the breakdown of harmonious relations. According to this view, stifling speech through a statute does not undermine the concept of a democratic government. It ensures that order is maintained and possibly violent communications are quashed before they can trigger violence and thereby harm the republic.

It was a curious interpretation, and not in accord with a mainstream perspective on the virtues of democratic government. Even in the early days of the American regime, a large number of citizens already subscribed to the credo that this new nation, unlike the old, stodgy governments of Europe, was a place where persons could settle and make their way free from ancient encumbrances and anti-democratic entanglements. The United States was a shining beacon by which peoples of a modest station could come and carve out an improved existence. To penalize the expression of their ideas was anathema, a decidedly undemocratic proposition. If the sea of liberty was boisterous and subject to turbulent squalls, so be it. A price must be paid to enjoy the blessings of liberty.[17]

The Republicans adopted this libertarian creed in their response to the Alien and Sedition Acts. Never reluctant to criticize his political enemies, Thomas Jefferson was quick to denounce the statutes as unwise and dangerous. Writing to his faithful protégé James Madison, Jefferson attacked the new laws as "so palpably in the teeth of the Constitution as to shew they mean to pay no respect to it." As he

took his objections public, Jefferson might have faced prosecution for his pointed comments, but he was never hailed into court. Perhaps the political repercussions of prosecuting a sitting vice president who served in the same administration that had pushed for passage of the acts were too much for even the staunchest Federalist to stomach. In any case, Jefferson was fortunate to escape prosecution.[18]

The Lyon-Griswold Incident

Other detractors did not share in the vice president's good fortune. Several prominent Republicans, notably John Daly Burk, William Duane, Anthony Haswell, James Callender, and Matthew Lyon, were tried for sedition during this time. The latter, a Republican congressman from Vermont, is remembered as a forceful, colorful character, especially for his conduct during a scuffle that broke out on the floor of the US House of Representatives in 1798.[19]

The episode originated with an epithet hurled by Connecticut Congressman Roger Griswold, a Federalist, who referred to Lyon as a scoundrel. Such profanity, while commonplace in underground mutterings, was shocking when expressed in public. If Griswold's purpose was to initiate a contentious battle of linguistic jousting, he had selected exactly the right opponent. A cantankerous, hot-headed gentleman, Lyon needed no pretext to engage in verbal battle with representatives of the party in power. He had arrived in Congress hell-bent on containing the growing Federalist menace, which he viewed as a contagion that would infect the land unless men of courage stepped forward to check its spread. Attacked in the pages of Federalist rags and denigrated as "ragged Matt, the democrat," a wild "beast" whose lineage was suspect, Lyon was already on edge when he met Griswold during a brief congressional recess on January 30, 1798.

The incident began as a simple exchange of insults. Lyon was boasting that he was a friend to the common man and needed to venture into Connecticut to turn the people into Democratic-Republicans. Overhearing the harangue, Griswold remarked that Lyon had better strap on his wooden sword if he came to Connecticut, a humiliating reference to Lyon's supposedly less-than-exemplary service during the American Revolution. The standard Federalist myth held that Lyon

had been cashiered for cowardice while serving on General Horatio Gates's staff in New York and had been forced to wear a wooden sword as punishment. Lyon had always vehemently denied the affair, but he remained irate whenever anyone questioned his military service or his moral rectitude. When Griswold insulted his honor that fine winter's day, an incensed Lyon acted without hesitation or regret. He spat in the man's face.

Witnesses intervened to prevent fisticuffs on the spot, but the matter was far from concluded. Griswold and his supporters moved to have Lyon expelled from the House for "gross indecency." Two weeks later, on February 15, 1798, Griswold lost his patience with the endless delays. He might have challenged his rival to a duel, but he believed it beneath his station to defend his honor from the actions of

Vermont Representative Matthew Lyon (a critic of the Adams administration) brandishes tongs while he brawls with Connecticut Representative Roger Griswold (an Adams supporter), who wields a club, on the floor of the US House of Representatives in 1798. Lyon was later convicted of violating the Sedition Act for his incendiary anti-Adams rhetoric. Courtesy of the Library of Congress.

a beastly reprobate. Instead, he confronted Lyon in the House chamber and caned the man repeatedly. Lyon responded by snatching up a pair of tongs and vigorously defending himself. Horrified onlookers characterized the ruckus as more appropriate to a tavern than to the halls of Congress. A famous political cartoon titled "Congressional pugilists" made the rounds shortly thereafter accompanied by a satirical ditty: "He in a trice struck Lyon thrice / Upon his head, enrag'd sir, / Who seiz'd the tongs to ease his wrongs, / And Griswold thus engag'd, sir."[20]

With both men participating in the unbecoming behavior, Congress chose not to censure either legislator. The leadership seemingly obeyed the old legal adage that to one who is willing, no injury occurs. Both partisans had engaged in the physical altercation.

For all the humor arising from his newfound notoriety, Lyon did not laugh for long. He soon found himself on trial under the Sedition Act for his bitter criticism of the Adams administration. After a short trial where his guilt was all but a foregone conclusion, the congressman was convicted on October 10, 1798, sentenced to four months in jail, and slapped with a $1,000 fine. While imprisoned, he won reelection to the House, an impressive feat given his dire circumstances. Yet his constituents loved him not in spite of his legal wrangling, but because of it. For all of his shortcomings, Lyon became a hero among Republicans for his impassioned and flamboyant, if not altogether dignified, defense of free speech.[21]

Backlash

If the Federalists had expressed misgivings about the new law and had chosen to pursue a policy of lax enforcement, matters might have been less volatile for everyone concerned. Yet the administration appeared eager to enforce the new measures. Secretary of State Timothy Pickering led the charge. His zeal for attacking enemies of the Federalist Party, which he viewed as enemies of the state, became legendary. He was an indefatigable advocate in his quest to root out Republicans who might infect the republic with their love of all things French. Scouring the Republican newspapers each day, Pickering was determined to prosecute any administration critics, and he would

use the full might of the state to do so. His supporters hailed the man as "the Scourge of Jacobinism" even as his detractors labeled him a "Federalist ogre." Pickering proved to be a talented persecutor. When all was said and done, the secretary ensured that twenty-five Republicans were arrested. Under Pickering's watch, the Federalists issued fifteen indictments for seditious libel, and ten cases proceeded to trial. Each of the ten trials resulted in a conviction.[22]

Yet if the goal was to break the back of Republican critics, Pickering's witch hunt was an abysmal failure. He jailed several prominent editors and forced two Republican newspapers out of business, but he did not envision the backlash that occurred. The Federalists' decision to prepare for a possible war against France had proven to be popular among many citizens, but the Adams administration soon found its public support eroding. In the wake of passage of the Sedition Act, public criticism grew substantially. A petition submitted from twelve hundred Northampton County, Pennsylvania, citizens typified the reaction among many people who feared that prosecuting political opponents would be "inimical to the genius of a republican government." Pickering apparently hoped to improve Adams's reelection chances by stifling dissent among the opposition press. Instead, he inadvertently stiffened their resolve and encouraged citizens to react negatively to the sedition charges.[23]

The Kentucky and Virginia Resolutions

It was an age of extremes. While the Federalists embarked on a witch hunt to consolidate political power and assuage their followers' concerns about conspiracies lurking around every corner, the Republicans reacted viscerally, championing policies that were as misguided in their own way as the Federalist agenda. The two major Republican Party leaders, Thomas Jefferson and James Madison, were not satisfied to leave the political tussling to their proxies or the citizenry. To demonstrate their mistrust of centralized federal authority, they penned the famous Kentucky and Virginia resolutions, albeit anonymously. The resolutions were troubling. Responding to the Lyon prosecution as well as attacks on other prominent critics of the Adams administration, the resolutions were extraordinary documents that

THOMAS JEFFERSON,
3ʳᵈ PRESIDENT OF THE UNITED STATES.

PHILADELPHIA.
Published by C.S.WILLIAMS, N.E. corner of Market & 7ᵗʰ St.

Thomas Jefferson led the charge to repeal the Alien and Sedition Acts when he became president in 1801. Before that time, he authored the Kentucky Resolution arguing against expanding federal power at the expense of the states. Courtesy of the Library of Congress.

essentially authorized states to nullify acts of the federal government if the states believed those laws (such as the Alien and Sedition Acts) were unconstitutional. Originating with the principal author of the Declaration of Independence and the man heralded as the father of the US Constitution, respectively, the manifestos provided incredible insight into the political debates of the day. A quarter of a century would pass before the identities of the authors would be known, but

the influence of the resolutions on subsequent events in American history was unmistakable and profound.

The Kentucky legislature enacted two resolutions, one on November 16, 1798, which Jefferson authored. The second dated from December 3, 1799, but the author was never established. Madison wrote the Virginia resolution, which the state passed on Christmas Eve in 1798. The resolutions argued that the US Constitution was not designed to elevate the federal government above the states as a uniform, or unifying, entity. Instead, the Constitution was a compact among the states agreeing to surrender limited sovereignty in exchange for benefits to all states, such as military defense against foreign enemies. When the federal government enacts measures that violate the Constitution or infringe on the authority of the states, the states can declare the laws null and void. Under the controversial "Principles of 98," the states, not the federal government, can determine whether the laws are constitutional.[24]

Reaction to the resolutions was immediate and vehement. The aging lion George Washington commented in retirement that if the doctrines articulated in the laws were "systematically and pertinaciously pursued," the consequences would "dissolve the union or produce coercion." Years later, James A. Garfield, a future president of the United States, reflected on the long-term causes of the civil war that broke out in 1861. In Garfield's view, the resolutions "contained the germ of nullification and secession, and we are today reaping the fruits." Even the authors of the resolutions appeared to back away from the logical ramifications of their arguments. Yet if Jefferson and Madison, after flirting with the concept of secession, ultimately back away, they set the stage for the nullification and secession crises that would occur in the years to come, especially beginning in the 1830s, when the slavery issue assumed center stage in American political life.[25]

The Nullification Crisis of 1832 was to some extent the logical progeny of the Kentucky and Virginia resolutions. The crisis originated after South Carolina enacted an Ordinance of Nullification declaring that two federal tariffs—one from 1828 and another in 1832—were unconstitutional and therefore not binding on the states. The state's authority to nullify federal laws was not readily apparent in the US

Constitution, but state leaders argued that such an interpretation was fully consistent with the Kentucky and Virginia resolutions. If the Constitution were a compact among states, the states could modify the terms and conditions when the compact no longer suited their needs.

President Andrew Jackson responded forcefully to reject the state's construction of state and federal relations. "The ordinance is founded, not on the indefeasible right of resisting acts which are plainly uncon-stitutional, and too oppressive to be endured, but on the strange posi-tion that any one State may not only declare an act of Congress void, but prohibit its execution—that they may do this consistently with the Constitution—that the true construction of that instrument permits

JAMES MADISON,
FOURTH PRESIDENT OF THE UNITED STATES.

James Madison, pictured here, penned the Virginia Resolution, a withering attack on the Alien and Sedition Acts. Courtesy of the Library of Congress.

a State to retain its place in the Union, and yet be bound by no other of its laws than those it may choose to consider as constitutional," he stated in a December 1832 proclamation. "I consider, then, the power to annul a law of the United States, assumed by one State, incompatible with the existence of the Union, contradicted expressly by the letter of the Constitution, unauthorized by its spirit, inconsistent with every principle on which It was founded, and destructive of the great object for which it was formed."[26]

From retirement, James Madison distinguished the Kentucky and Virginia resolutions from the South Carolina ordinance in 1832. "Altho' the Legislature of Virginia declared at a late session almost unanimously, that S. Carolina was not supported in her doctrine of nullification by the Resolutions of 1798, it appears that those resolutions are still appealed to as expressly or constructively favoring the doctrine." In Madison's view, a government could not operate under conditions where a state could countermand the actions of the central authority. To allow such dissension would invite chaos. According to Madison, "It follows, from no view of the subject, that a nullification of a law of the US can as is now contended, belong rightfully to a single State, as one of the parties to the Constitution; the State not ceasing to avow its adherence to the Constitution. A plainer contradiction in terms, or a more fatal inlet to anarchy, cannot be imagined." He explained that the purpose of the Virginia Resolution had not been to allow a state to nullify a law. Instead, the purpose was to encourage cooperation among states to seek a redress of their grievances through recognized constitutional means such as an amendment. Whether this later interpretation was true to the spirit of the original resolution can be debated, but by the 1830s, Madison understood the dangers inherent in championing a state rights position on constitutional interpretation.[27]

Aside from the nullification crisis of 1832, the notion that the US Constitution was merely a compact among independent states that exercised sovereignty over the Union would hold enormous repercussions in American history, especially in the subsequent works of John C. Calhoun and the arguments of southern secessionists leading to the American Civil War in 1861. Moreover, the image of an obdurate,

overbearing central government oppressing its citizens at the whim of a party in power would prove to be stubbornly persistent. Each generation would seek to balance the power of government to ensure its perpetuation with the freedom of the individual to hold beliefs and practice behaviors that were not always welcomed by leaders or, for that matter, a majority of the citizenry.[28]

As for the Alien and Sedition Acts, John Adams's name was forever tarnished by his administration's support for legislation hostile to freedom of thought and expression. Adams lost the election of 1800 for a variety of reasons, including his support for such unpopular laws. With the exception of the Alien Enemies Act, which remains in effect as of this writing, the Alien and Sedition Acts expired beginning in 1800, consigning the odious measures to the dustbin of history. Yet the repercussions of overreacting to fears of subversive threats would endure as a central feature of American government and law.[29]

Conclusion

The passage of the Alien and Sedition Acts provides a lesson in the dangers of overreacting to fears of subversion. Although the safety and perpetuation of the nation were not assured in the 1790s, the decision to enact laws that would stymie free expression exacerbated an already volatile situation, heightening suspicions and deepening the partisanship between competing factions. A pattern developed that would continue throughout the life of the republic: in response to a genuine or perceived threat, decision-makers hastily cobble together a solution to address the problem. In the heat of the moment, the solution offers a course of action that creates its own set of challenges and threats apart from the original threat. If alien characters appear to imperil the health of the state, their speech and activities must be monitored and possibly curtailed. If strange ideas promise to infect the body politic, the ideas must be eradicated and the resultant cleansing will protect the status quo ante. The irony is that the reaction is often worse than the original threat in terms of its negative effect on the values cherished by supporters of a republican form of government.

Yet even with the benefit of hindsight, the Alien and Sedition Acts cannot be uniformly condemned without considering the

political and historical context. In any regime, the pressure on decision-makers to act with dispatch cannot be discounted. If a republic ideally exists as a government founded on the principle of rule by the consent of the governed, elected officials must respond to constituent demands. If consensual government is to hold any meaning, it must allow citizens input into decision-making—even if the decisions they champion are misguided or driven by prejudice and passion. Citizens who feel that their values and livelihoods are under attack naturally will urge their representatives to take swift, decisive action. If the incumbents will not respond, voters will visit the ballot box and select deputies who will do their bidding in due course. Because savvy officials recognize the need to appease their constituents, they frequently act quickly lest they pay a heavy electoral price. That is not to say that elected leaders should respond by enacting laws that are foolhardy or unwise, but often they act rapidly in response to constituent demands. Rapid law-making under pressure in crisis times typically leads to legislation that engenders its own set of negative results.

More to the point, human nature dictates that a response is necessary in the face of a threat. In an ideal world, decision makers would allow sufficient time to pass before acting to allow a cooling-off period that could ensure deliberative, reasoned discussion and debate. Would that all decision-making could wait for the calm calculus of reason to prevail. In a less-than-perfect world, officials must act both to prevent future threats from materializing and to assuage the fears of the citizenry.

That persons fearful of lingering plots and conspiracies would seek to avenge a previous assault and forestall a subsequent attempt is hardly surprising. Human beings are predisposed to see patterns even when they do not exist. Some scholars refer to Type I and Type II errors in cognition. In the former case, a person will perceive a false positive. In other words, a threat seems to exist but no threat actually exists. This situation can be contrasted with a Type II error or a false negative where a person believes that no threat exists when, in fact, it does. Human beings have learned that in situations of enormous stress and doubt, the consequences of making a Type I error are less

damaging than making a Type II error. If a person assumes there is a pattern, such as a plot or conspiracy, and the pattern does not exist, the person prepares to meet the threat but is not directly harmed as a result. Making a Type II error ensures that the person is unprepared if the threat materializes. Depending on the nature of the threat, the person (or nation) may be harmed irreparably.[30]

Yet a Type I error, despite the lack of direct consequences, is not without its problems. When a nation enacts laws to limit the damaging speech and actions of would-be conspirators, the laws may undermine the values of the populace and the principles of the nation. Especially in cases when the conspiracy was minimal or non-existent, the reaction invariably harms the life of the republic to a far greater extent than did the original threat. The challenge is to know when a genuine threat exists and how to meet it without undermining regime values. Balancing the freedom of the individual against the authority of the nation-state is enormously complex and never-ending, yet it is a quest that must be undertaken as long as the republic exists.

Chapter 2

LINCOLN AND THE SUSPENSION OF HABEAS CORPUS

To state the question more directly, are all the laws but one to go unexecuted, and the Government itself to go to pieces lest that one be violated?

—ABRAHAM LINCOLN,
MESSAGE TO CONGRESS IN SPECIAL SESSION, JULY 4, 1861[31]

Abraham Lincoln had not yet become the iconic figure revered by generations of Americans when he faced a "fire in the rear" during the US Civil War. The fire was born of frustration with the war and the administration's seemingly inept management of the affair. During the early days of the new president's tenure in March and April 1861, the standoff between opposing forces, North and South, was supposed to end quickly. Former US Senator James Chestnut Jr. sardonically offered to drink all the blood that would be shed in the conflict, confident the differences could be resolved, as they so often had been in the past, through an eleventh-hour compromise praised by no one and yet enjoyed by all. Even if fighting erupted, surely the bloodshed would not drag on for more than a few days or weeks at most.[32]

Yet this time no legislative miracle was in the offing. Henry Clay, the political magician who somehow had pulled a rabbit from his hat more than once during three decades in high office, was long dead. His colleagues in the Great Triumvirate, Daniel Webster and John C. Calhoun, likewise rested in their graves at the dawn of the 1860s. Even if those master legislators had lived, they probably could not have forestalled armed conflict save through compromises that one party or

the other would have deemed untenable. Time and tempers had passed beyond the point of reasoned solutions.[33]

When the shooting began thirty-nine days into the Lincoln administration, no one imagined the scope and duration of what would follow. The heady days between the firing on Fort Sumter and the Battle of Bull Run saw Union supporters and rebels alike confident that a glorious future lay just around the bend. Everyone was an ardent supporter of his respective cause. When it became clear that neither side would earn an easy victory and a long, hard struggle lay ahead, the less resolute citizens vehemently criticized their leaders' efforts. Some disaffected souls organized antiwar factions aimed at ending the conflict short of total victory.[34]

Lincoln and the Challenges of the 1860s

Lincoln had known before he assumed the mantle of executive power that the fragile peace between the North and South was on the verge of collapse. The 1850s had been a time of increasing tension between the sections. In the years leading up to his election as president in 1860, a series of events had eroded what little trust and good will existed between competing sectional factions. Yet the new president was far from despondent as he prepared to take his oath of office. Many times throughout the nineteenth century, extending back at least as far as 1819—and even to the constitutional convention of 1787 if the debate over the decision to count slaves as three-fifths as productive as free whites was considered—incendiary rhetoric had been exchanged, each side threatening the other with violence and disunion. Yet somehow cooler heads had prevailed and a resolution had been found. Lincoln knew the hour was late, but he refused to believe that war was inevitable.[35]

He had spent much of his life in public service crafting a middle position. The abolitionists in the North called for immediate emancipation of the slaves and a fundamental reordering of southern society. Although their numbers were small, the antislavery men possessed an uncanny talent for stirring up trouble and amplifying their voices. To southern ears, these radical interlopers spoke for a wide variety of northern interests. By contrast, southern Fire-Eaters expressed their

disdain for the federal government and its encroachment on the powers of the states. In their view, the erosion of hallowed federalism principles was part of a deep conspiracy among power-hungry abolitionists
who would free black slaves and make white slaveholders vassals to the
northern moneyed-interests.[36]

Although he was not an abolitionist, Lincoln had expressed his
distaste for slavery on numerous occasions. Perhaps most famously (or
infamously, in the opinion of his southern brethren), he had delivered
a political harangue in Springfield, Illinois, on June 16, 1858. Known
as his "house divided" speech, it had galvanized persons of both sides
of the slavery debate with its powerful language. At the time, he was a
candidate for the US Senate, and many of his supporters worried that
the searing words would harm his candidacy. Lincoln lost the election,
although it is difficult to know how much the speech contributed to the
result. In those days, state legislators chose US senators. Republican
candidates won the popular vote, but Democrats took more seats, 54
to 46, which meant that Lincoln lost the Senate post.[37]

"A house divided against itself cannot stand," he had said, allud-
ing to the Christian Bible. "I believe this government cannot endure,
permanently half *slave* and half *free*. I do not expect the Union to be
dissolved—I do not expect the house to *fall*—but I *do* expect it will
cease to be divided. It will become *all* one thing or *all* the other."[38]

Years later, slaveholders believed the speech meant that Lincoln
as president intended to interfere with slavery and perhaps emancipate
their property. Yet for all his personal antipathy toward the peculiar
institution, Lincoln the chief executive did not believe he possessed
the authority to interfere with the constitutional arrangement absent
extraordinary circumstances. When the war began, he did not believe
that the circumstances allowing for an eradication of slavery yet
existed. At best, he thought that the federal government could arrest
its spread into the territories and preserve the status quo—hardly a
ringing endorsement of the abolitionist position.[39]

Yet nuances were lost on southern ears. Southerners viewed
Lincoln's position and the antislavery stance as a distinction without a
difference. The election of a Republican president meant that the institution of slavery was imperiled. It was only a matter of time before the

new chief executive and his minions renewed the assault on slavery that had occurred throughout the 1850s. Lincoln thought he could assuage southern fears with careful, precise language in his inaugural address, but he misunderstood the haunted southern psyche. "In *your* hands, my dissatisfied fellow-countrymen, and not in *mine*, is the momentous issue of civil war," he said. "The Government will not assail *you*. You can have no conflict without being yourselves the aggressors." It was an indication of how far passion had strained the bonds of affection that southerners simply could not accept such assurances as anything other than hollow rhetoric and empty promises.[40]

Events deteriorated precipitously during the time between the election of November 1860 and Lincoln's inauguration in March 1861. If war was not a foregone conclusion, it certainly loomed large on the American landscape. And so Lincoln stepped into the presidency at a critical moment in history. Saboteurs and would-be secessionists seemed to lurk around every corner, imperiling the republic. Riding the train toward Washington, D.C. on the way to his inauguration, Lincoln learned that he might be assassinated by southern sympathizers when he reached Baltimore, Maryland. Despite his political judgment that showing weakness would play into the hands of his enemies, the president-elect bowed to the wishes of his security detail and canceled his public appearance in the city. After slipping quietly into Washington, D.C. under the cover of night, Lincoln came under a barrage of criticism. Democrats howled at the new man's cowardice. Lincoln regretted the circumstances of his arrival, but at least he would be inaugurated without presenting a convenient target for an assassin.[41]

If the Lincoln of 1861 was primarily a conservative politician seeking to find a way to ameliorate the situation facing him, his critics saw in him a budding dictator. The "Peace Democrats," a northern party faction intensely critical of the Republican administration, won the nickname the "Copperheads" during the summer of 1861 when an anonymous writer in the *Cincinnati Commercial* compared the group to snakes in the Bible. Genesis 3:14 says, "And the Lord God said unto the serpent, Because thou hast done this, thou *art* cursed above all cattle, and above every beast of the field; upon thy belly shalt thou

go, and dust shalt thou eat all the days of thy life." Lincoln supporters viewed these men of little faith as no better than reptiles slithering in the grass, quasi-traitors awaiting an opportunity to strike at the body politic.[42]

What originated as a term of derision soon became a badge of honor for northern Democrats who opposed the war. To demonstrate their approval of the appellation, Peace Democrats clipped the Goddess of Liberty from Copperhead coins and pinned the image to their lapels. They saw themselves as a vocal minority speaking the truth to power regardless of the costs. In time, they came to understand the sacrifices that would be required. Whether the group amounted to a minor problem for the administration or represented a genuine threat to the northern prosecution of the war remains a matter of dispute.[43]

During the early days of the war, the Copperheads appeared to be out of step with mainstream public opinion as Lincoln enjoyed wide support. Their occasional outbursts were irritants, to be sure, but hardly cause for concern. The American system of government was built on a foundation of dissent expressed by a loyal opposition that felt compelled to highlight the party-in-power's deficiencies. Even in wartime, a healthy debate on public policy, including the conduct of military operations, is a fundamental component of a healthy republic.[44]

As war-weariness set in and the public mood soured, the question arose as to whether Copperheads were loyal opponents or something worse. Their vehement denunciations of the administration began to appear in some quarters as sinister and detrimental to northern morale. Despite the risks of antagonizing the Lincoln administration, the faction grew increasingly disenchanted with the man occupying the Executive Mansion as 1861 gave way to 1862 and eventually 1863. Joining with many Americans, they were appalled at the battlefield carnage and the administration's inability or unwillingness to end the fighting. They also chafed at the president's plodding, apparently rudderless wartime leadership. Upset with the Emancipation Proclamation and its promise of "nigger equality," they believed that Lincoln intended to make himself a dictator and, in the process, rewrite the social customs and traditions that had governed life since the inception of the republic.[45]

The Great Writ of Liberty

As far as the Copperheads were concerned, nothing demonstrated the president's nefarious purposes better than his suspension of the writ of habeas corpus. A cherished feature of Anglo-American jurisprudence, "habeas corpus"—literally, "you have the body"—is a shortened form of the Latin phrase "habeas corpus ad subjiciendum," a writ directed to an authority that detains an individual. The writ, or court order, requires that the detainee be produced, in person, before a judge. The writ does not delve into the guilt or innocence of a detainee. The purpose is to ensure that an individual is not held in custody indefinitely without being subjected to a formal legal process. In some nations, a citizen is picked up, brought into custody, and promptly disappears into a labyrinthine system of government jails, never to be seen or heard from again. The American Founders sought to ensure that Americans would not be subjected to such an extreme government penalty.[46]

The "great writ of liberty" was considered so important to the common law tradition that the Founders addressed the issue in the most sacred of political documents. In Article I, Section 9, of the US Constitution, they stated, "The privilege of the writ of habeas corpus shall not be suspended, unless when in causes of rebellion or invasion of the public safety may require it." Relying on this provision, President Lincoln believed that the Constitution allowed him to act decisively—especially since the legislative branch was not available in an immediate crisis.[47]

Suspending the writ of habeas corpus was not a matter to be taken lightly. In "Federalist 84," Alexander Hamilton wrote that certain protections, including the great writ, "are perhaps greater securities to liberty and republicanism" than almost any other protections included in the US Constitution. The writ was a necessary means of safeguarding the citizenry from government abuses because "the practice of arbitrary imprisonments" has been, "in all ages, the favorite and most formidable of instruments of tyranny."[48]

Fear of tyranny was one thing, but worries about a government undermined by enemies, foreign and domestic, required extraordinary measures. When the rebels fired on Fort Sumter on April 12, 1861, thus initiating a violent act of rebellion against the US government,

President Abraham Lincoln, shown here in November 1863, suspended the writ of habeas corpus during the American Civil War. Courtesy of the Library of Congress.

Congress was not in session. Fearful that the rebellion could spiral out of control if he did not act immediately, Lincoln suspended habeas corpus in Maryland on April 27, 1861, in response to reports that mobs of pro-southern rabble-rousers intended to destroy railroad service between Annapolis and Philadelphia. The suspension was limited at that time, but as the war progressed, the president would expand his authority in the interests of national security.[49]

For pro-southern forces, the loss of the great writ was an ominous development. A president who could exercise extraordinary powers to put down the rebellion could be expected to act with dispatch as soon as a threat was perceived. The Constitution explicitly allowed

the federal government to suspend the writ, but the nature and extent of the suspension was a matter of legal debate. It would not be long before the US Supreme Court, as the final arbiter of constitutional interpretation, weighed in on the matter.[50]

As Union solders rounded up suspected traitors, they captured a secessionist, cavalryman John Merryman, suspected of burning bridges and sabotaging telegraph lines during the April melee. Taken into military custody and sent to Fort McHenry for detention, Merryman wasted no time in filing for a writ of habeas corpus in the federal courts. The irony of a man who would destroy the Union seeking to avail himself of its legal protections was lost on no one, least of all the chief justice of the US Supreme Court, Roger Brooke Taney. It was left to the chief justice to render judgment in a case before the high court, *Ex Parte Merryman*.[51]

Because Supreme Court justices sat as circuit court judges at the time, Merryman's lawyers presented the writ directly to the chief justice without involving other members of the court. Taney was outraged by what he viewed as an abuse of power. He ordered that General George Cadwalader, commanding officer at Fort McHenry, to appear the next day and show cause why Merryman had been detained. Cadwalader dispatched a colonel to tell the chief justice that he had suspended habeas corpus and would not produce the prisoner as ordered. Taney issued a writ of attachment ordering a US marshal to seize Cadwalader and forcibly haul him into court. Unfortunately for the marshal, US soldiers refused to allow him entry into Fort McHenry. The angry chief justice vowed to render a written opinion within a week.[52]

Chief Justice Taney's reaction to the suspension of habeas corpus was not a surprise. By the 1860s, he had become a proponent of the southern position, largely reflected in his majority opinion in *Dred Scott v. Sandford*, which held that a black man possessed no legal rights a court was bound to respect. Taney has been judged harshly by history, but he was not quite the caricature of popular lore. He was born into a well-to-do Maryland family in 1777 and reared in a society where Negro slavery was presupposed to be an immutable fact of life. He chose a career in law and politics, once even defending an abolitionist minister against charges of inciting a slave insurrection. As a

member of the US Supreme Court, he later voted to free the slaves on trial in the celebrated *Amistad* case. The figure that one day would be identified as a vocal apologist for slavery was known early in his career as a northern man.[53]

The young Roger Taney was a Federalist but eventually navigated to the Democratic Party and aligned himself with Andrew Jackson. In 1831, Old Hickory appointed him attorney general, and Taney gamely joined the president in opposing reauthorization of the Second Bank of the United States. In response, the US Senate refused to confirm Taney as secretary of the treasury when Jackson nominated his ally for the position in 1834. Later, the Senate refused to confirm the thoroughgoing Jacksonian as an associate justice of the US Supreme Court. The defeats, as it turned out, were minor setbacks. Upon the death of Chief Justice John Marshall, Jackson deftly maneuvered to take advantage of a change in Senate membership to reward his loyal adherent with the premier position on the high court. Taney had served as chief for a quarter of a century by the time the *Merryman* case appeared on his docket.[54]

As promised, the chief justice announced the *Merryman* decision shortly after his exchange with General Cadwalader. On May 26, 1861, Taney held that only Congress can suspend the writ of habeas corpus. He observed that the authority to suspend the writ appears in Article I of the US Constitution, which governs the authority of Congress. If the Founders had intended for the president to exercise such power, presumably the provision would have appeared in Article II, which governs the presidency. Taney also reviewed the English law on habeas corpus, finding that the House of Commons had curtailed legislative authority to issue the writ and prohibited the sovereign from suspending the writ altogether. Because the Bill of Rights acted as an additional limit on federal power, the chief justice concluded that Lincoln had overstepped his bounds as president. Therefore, his action was unconstitutional.[55]

Lincoln recognized, as did Taney's patron, Andrew Jackson, before him, that a world of difference exists between a court issuing an opinion and the court enforcing an order. The president simply ignored the ruling. In another time, the dispute between an activist

president and a restraintist chief justice no doubt would engender controversy and plaintive wails about a constitutional crisis. In 1861, however, the republic faced a much larger constitutional crisis than a war of words between representatives of different government branches. Public opinion was clearly in Lincoln's favor at the time. The president knew he could act without fearing a loss of approval. In the short run, he was correct.[56]

By the time that Congress convened on July 4, 1861, Lincoln's actions had become controversial. Two days earlier, the president had authorized General Winfield Scott to expand the scope of his order suspending habeas corpus.[57] Realizing he must explain his actions to a legislative body that would review all presidential activities undertaken in its absence, Lincoln sent a message to Congress. After outlining the crisis facing the incoming administration, he justified his decision to suspend habeas corpus as essential to the preservation of the Union. "Finding this condition of things and believing it to be an imperative duty upon the incoming Executive to prevent, if possible, the consummation of such an attempt to destroy the Federal Union, a choice of means to that end became indispensable," he explained. As he did throughout his presidency, Lincoln cast the conflict in broad terms. "And this issue embraces more than the fate of these United States. It presents to the whole family of man the question whether a constitutional republic or democracy—a Government of the people, by the same people—can or cannot maintain its territorial integrity against its own domestic foes." The new president had resolved to answer the question affirmatively. He would not allow the Union to dissolve on his watch. A constitutional republic would endure.[58]

After calling up seventy-five thousand militia—"the response of the country was most gratifying, surpassing in unanimity and spirit the most sanguine expectation," Lincoln reminded his audience—the commander in chief realized that other steps were necessary to contain the insurrection. "Soon after the first call for militia it was considered a duty to authorize the commanding general in proper cases according to his discretion, to suspend the privilege of the writ of habeas corpus, or in other words to arrest and detain, without resort to the ordinary processes and forms of law, such individuals as he might deem

dangerous to the public safety." The president recognized that such a step should not be taken without due deliberation. "This authority has purposely been exercised but very sparingly. Nevertheless the legality and propriety of what has been done under it are questioned and the attention of the country has been called to the proposition that one who is sworn to 'take care that the laws be faithfully executed' should not himself violate them. Of course some consideration was given to the questions of power and propriety before this matter was acted upon."[59]

Having established a context and assuring Congress that he was mindful that his administration must not degenerate into tyranny, the president expressed in no uncertain terms the high stakes involved. He set out to address two questions. First, he discussed whether the writ of habeas corpus could be suspended in the first place. Second, he answered the question of whether the president or Congress was empowered to suspend the writ.

With respect to the first question, Lincoln expressed no doubt that the writ could be suspended in times of crisis:

> The whole of the laws which were required to be faithfully executed were being resisted and failing of execution in nearly one-third of the States. Must they be allowed to finally fail of execution, even had it been perfectly clear that by the use of the means necessary to their execution some single law, made in such extreme tenderness of the citizen's liberty that practically it relieves more of the guilty than of the innocent, should to a very limited extent be violated? To state the question more directly, are all the laws but one to go unexecuted and the Government itself go to pieces lest that one be violated? Even in such a case would not the official oath be broken if the Government should be overthrown, when it was believed that disregarding the single law would tend to preserve it? But it was not believed that this question was presented. It was not believed that any law was violated. The provision of the Constitution that "the privilege of the writ of habeas corpus shall not be suspended unless when in cases of rebellion

or invasion the public safety may require it," is equivalent to a provision—is a provision—that such privilege may be suspended when in cases of rebellion or invasion the public safety does require it. It was decided that we have a case of rebellion, and that the public safety does require the qualified suspension of the privilege of the writ which was authorized to be made.[60]

It was a powerful rejoinder to his critics. Lincoln had to take immediate, drastic steps lest the republic be fatally assailed by hostile forces. It would make no sense to allow a government to fall victim to its enemies in a misguided effort to honor all of its laws all of the time.

He then spoke to the second crucial issue: whether the president or Congress could suspend habeas corpus. "Now, it is insisted that Congress and not the Executive is vested with this power. But the Constitution itself is silent as to which, or who, is to exercise the power; and as the provision was plainly made for a dangerous emergency, it cannot be believed the framers of the instrument intended that in every case the danger should run its course until Congress could be called together, the very assembling of which might be prevented, as was intended in this case, by the rebellion."[61]

The message accomplished the president's goals. First, he clearly and convincingly spelled out his policy regarding the rebellion. He also justified his past actions by placing them into a constitutional and historical context. Acting as commander in chief, he had taken the necessary and appropriate steps to safeguard the perpetual American Union. Congress had an important role in addressing the crisis, but the president was the primary authority on the front lines.

Lincoln did not specifically address the *Merryman* decision, but, in any case, subsequent events obviated Chief Justice Taney's ruling. First, in February 1862, the president ordered the prisoners rounded up during the April 1861 raids released. In addition, the legislative branch stepped into the breach. Recognizing that the president as commander in chief was best situated to put down a rebellion, Congress, acting under its constitutional authority, passed the Habeas Corpus Suspension Act of 1863, which allowed the president to suspend the "writ of liberty," as necessary, to combat the crisis facing the Union.

Lincoln used the new law to justify suspending the writ through-out the Union in cases involving prisoners of war, spies, traitors, or military personnel. He argued that broad wartime powers were nec-essary to put down the rebellion. The suspension remained in effect until Lincoln's successor, Andrew Johnson, revoked the authority on December 1, 1865, more than seven months after the war ended.[62]

Copperheads on the Rise

As the Copperheads viewed the situation, the tyrannical Lincoln must be resisted or one of two calamitous outcomes would occur—either the North would lose the war after thousands of additional soldiers were slain in battle, or else King Abraham I would destroy a republi-can form of government and install himself on the throne of a king. His loyal subjects would be the newly emancipated slaves who would blindly obey his every command.[63]

THE COPPERHEAD PARTY.—IN FAVOR OF *A VIGOROUS PROSECUTION OF PEACE!*

This editorial cartoon from the February 28, 1863, edition of *Harper's Weekly* magazine depicts the "peace" faction of the Northern Democratic Party as venomous "Copperhead" snakes striking at the heart of the nation (symbolized by the figure of Columbia wielding a sword and holding the Union as a shield). Although Ohio politician Clement Vallandigham was a leading Copperhead, he was not caricatured here. Courtesy of the Library of Congress.

The face of the Copperheads belonged to Clement Laird Vallandigham, a charismatic Democratic congressman from Ohio. He was a smooth one, this silver-tongued orator who often sought and captured public attention. The man possessed a seemingly innate ability to command a room, and he expressed no compunction about forcefully expressing an opinion on any subject whether he knew anything about it or not.[64]

First elected to the state legislature at the age of twenty-five, he had progressed through the ranks to win election to the US House of Representatives in 1858. Even before the war had started, Vallandigham used his public platform to attack the Republican Party. As early as 1855, he had praised the Kansas-Nebraska Act as "that most just, most Constitutional, and most necessary measure." The act called for the creation of the territories of Kansas and Nebraska, reversing decades of legislative initiatives aimed at balancing the admission of Free States and Slave States into the Union. Under the Missouri Compromise of 1820, slavery was outlawed north of the 36° 30' line, and Missouri was designated a Slave State, although territory to the north and west of its border was deemed to be free. Congress struck a similar balance with the adoption of the Compromise of 1850. The Kansas-Nebraska Act threatened to destroy the Missouri Compromise by promoting the concept of popular sovereignty, a doctrine allowing residents of the territories to decide for themselves whether they would allow human bondage within their borders. Northern men such as Lincoln attacked the law as "squatter sovereignty." Rather than ameliorate the sectional divide, the Kansas-Nebraska Act exacerbated tensions.[65]

Clement Vallandigham thrived on tension and controversy. Throughout his career, he appeared to revel in every opportunity to cast aspersions on his political enemies and express his support for the Democratic Party, which he viewed as the one entity that could save the Union. On February 20, 1861, he stood up in the House and offered a speech titled "The Great American Revolution." According to the congressman, the Republicans had driven the country to the edge of a dangerous precipice by using belligerent language to characterize the sectional divide. In Vallandigham's opinion, abolitionist sentiment was driving the northern position as antislavery forces

hijacked the Republican Party. He did not denigrate the southern Fire-Eaters who uttered dire pronouncements about the fate of the Union if northerners elected a Republican president or attempted to use force against federal forts in southern territory. He sought salvation from the Democrats who valued peace at any price.[66]

Vallandigham also publicly supported the Crittenden Compromise, a proposal set forth by Kentucky Senator John J. Crittenden in December 1860 to amend the US Constitution to protect slavery in places where it existed and to prohibit its spread. The compromise called for a constitutional provision forbidding future amendments from changing the agreed-upon terms. Southerners found the proposal acceptable, but Republicans refused to kowtow to the Slave Power, which they believed the proposal required. The Crittenden Compromise was not the answer to the divisions between the northern and southern sections, nor was Clement Vallandigham the man to prevent the outbreak of hostilities. The plan failed.[67]

Vallandigham's public profile grew as a result of his Copperhead activities. Encouraged, he continued to raise a hue and cry over the administration's defects and poor conduct of the war. Even after he was redistricted out of his House seat after 1862, he held forth on Lincoln's numerous shortcomings, especially the decision to issue a preliminary emancipation proclamation. He resolved to run for governor of Ohio to secure another public platform from which to preach his incendiary sermon.[68]

In a January 1863 speech titled "The Constitution-Peace-Reunion," Vallandigham heatedly attacked the Lincoln administration, which the congressman described as "one of the worst despotisms on earth." Having lost the last election, he abandoned any restraints in blasting the powers that be. He was angry that even as the war on the battlefield was faltering, the president saw fit to issue an edict on behalf of slaves. Observing the state of affairs at the start of another year of war, Vallandigham remarked that the "war for the Union was abandoned" while the "war for the Negro openly begun." It was a masterpiece of indignation highlighted by the departing congressman's call for both sides to end the war and demobilize their forces.[69]

It would not be difficult to dismiss Vallandigham as a demagogue that democratic governments always seem to attract were it not for the fact that much of what he said could be characterized as legitimate dissent. Setting aside his intemperate language, this occasionally infuriating gadfly raised provocative issues that needed to be addressed in a free, open society even in crisis times. Vallandigham's response to the administration's admittedly extreme actions was to contend that political power justified by pleas of necessity can lead to a slippery slope where expediency supplants principle. When stripped of all its inflammatory, florid verbiage, Vallandigham's core arguments contained substantial merit.[70]

In addition, he was not alone in his assessment. The Copperheads had appeared to be a fringe group at the outset of the war, but as the nation's fortunes appeared increasingly bleak throughout late 1862 and into 1863, the group's message resonated in far-flung corners of the republic. It is inevitable that a wartime administration enjoys widespread public support at the outset when flags are unfurled, marching bands take to the field, and dreams of everlasting glory are commonplace. As the conflict deepens and the reality of a protracted campaign sets in, the public mood changes. With each military setback and every casualty reported from the front, yesterday's patriots potentially become today's detractors. The Copperheads simply positioned themselves to take advantage of the deteriorating circumstances.[71]

Following the defeat at the Battle of Chancellorsville in 1863, Lincoln reputedly exclaimed, "My God! My God! What will the country say?" The Copperheads knew exactly what the country would say—or should say. It was time for a change in leadership and a reversal of strategy. Rather than tear the country apart in the service of the dictatorial Lincoln's demands on behalf of the abolitionists and against the wishes of a majority of the people, the executive should negotiate a peace to stanch the bloodshed and allow the Confederates to go on their way. With the current president devoted to a suicidal course of action and willing to employ whatever unconstitutional powers he could dredge up to pursue his misguided policy, it was only a matter of time before the republic imploded.[72]

The Copperhead position has been discredited by the vast majority of historians in the decades since the war ended, but at the time it was not necessarily an outlandish point of view. In fact, as long as they remained purely speech, the Copperheads could be forgiven their occasional excesses. By providing an alternate view of crucial public policy questions, the group arguably was performing a powerful educative function. The question remains, however, whether their activities evolved from being irksome criticism to becoming downright sinister and perhaps dangerous to the health and welfare of the nation.[73]

In most cases, self-identified Peace Democrats talked about forcing the administration to end the war on any terms, but their dedication to forcing a compromise was sporadic and ineffectual. In extreme cases, however, the Copperheads were prepared to oppose the Union war effort through force. A faction from the 1850s, the Knights of the Golden Circle, eventually morphed into the Order of American Knights during the 1860s. By 1864, the faction was known as the Order of the Sons of Liberty, and Vallandigham was the group's nominal head. Several members of the Order of the Sons of Liberty, including Harrison H. Dodd, publicly advocated the violent overthrow of Border State governments. Copperhead-led riots and even a plot to spring Confederate prisoners of war from Illinois encampments could be laid at the feet of Copperhead elements.[74]

Against this backdrop of intense criticism and deepening intrigue, Lincoln continually searched for a means to end the war. As part of his strategy, he assigned General Ambrose Burnside to command the Department of Ohio in March 1863. A West Point graduate and a distinguished gentleman who sported long sideburns and spoke with a mellifluous voice, he certainly looked the part of the successful general. Alas, looks can be deceiving. Burnside had risen through the ranks owing to his paper credentials and his connections with important military figures such as General George B. McClellan, but his abilities were limited. Burnside recognized his limitations. He had offered to retire to private life following a humiliating defeat at the Battle of Fredericksburg, but Lincoln could not afford to let the man go. With so few trained officers in uniform, the Union leadership relied on men that might otherwise have been sent packing.[75]

For all of his deficiencies, Burnside could not be faulted for lacking zeal. Although in command of an army that was not expected to be terribly proactive, the general remained eternally vigilant to the lurking enemies, real and imagined. Cognizant of the Union's shaky support in some areas under his command, on April 13, 1863, Burnside took it upon himself to declare martial law and issue General Order No. 38 criminalizing any actions or speech "declaring sympathies for the enemy." By issuing such an order, the general unconsciously mimicked the Sedition Act from an earlier epoch. Criticism of the administration or the war effort would not be tolerated, and Burnside established himself as the arbiter of what constituted criticism.[76]

He did not have to look far to find a treasure trove of anti-government speech, starting with Clement Vallandigham, now on his quest to become governor of Ohio. The ambitious politician had been disappointed in April 1863 when he failed to garner popular support for his gubernatorial bid. He needed a new platform to recapture public attention. Given the public antipathy toward the supposedly dictatorial excesses of the Lincoln administration in some quarters, Vallandigham saw an opportunity and he took it. He publicly attacked General Order No. 38.[77]

On May 1, 1863, Vallandigham appeared in Mount Vernon, Ohio, before a crowd estimated at between fifteen thousand and twenty thousand people. The scene was reminiscent of a state fair with wagons, floats, and horses stretched along a four-mile parade route. It was tailor-made for Vallandigham's flamboyant style of demagoguery, and he made the most of his opportunity. Denouncing General Order No. 38 as a "base usurpation of arbitrary authority," he railed against "King Lincoln" and his minions. With the Emancipation Proclamation only four months old, Vallandigham cited it as an example of Lincoln's propensity to overreach. The proclamation had transformed the war from a struggle to preserve the Union to a crusade to free blacks. In Vallandigham's words, it was "a wicked, cruel, and unnecessary war, one not waged for the preservation of the Union, but for the purpose of crushing out liberty and to erect a despotism; a war for the freedom of the blacks and the enslavement of the whites." Toeing the Copperhead Party line, he charged that the executive deliberately

had prolonged the fighting. "If the administration had not wished otherwise," he said, "the war could have been honorably terminated long ago."[78]

The Arrest and Trial of Clement Vallandigham

Public criticism of General Order No. 38 had its intended effect. Union solders acting under orders from General Burnside arrested Vallandigham four days after the fiery speech. The scene occurred at 2:40 a.m. when more than one hundred troops appeared at the former congressman's house in Dayton, Ohio. Observing the soldiers ensconced on his lawn, the great Copperhead refused to surrender. The soldiers broke down the door and forced their way inside, arresting Vallandigham in his bedroom. Over his vehement protests, they escorted the prisoner to a train bound for Cincinnati, Ohio. There he would be tried before a military commission. Burnside's decision to arrest the irritating administration critic would ignite one of the great political controversies of the Civil War.[79]

Union General Ambrose E. Burnside, shown here in uniform, ignited a firestorm of press attention when he arrested Clement Vallandigham on charges of disloyalty to the Union. Courtesy of the Library of Congress.

An indignant Vallandigham appeared before a five-member military commission for his arraignment. When asked to enter a plea, he refused to participate, denying the tribunal's jurisdiction in the matter. The commission members instructed the judge advocate to enter a "not guilty" plea and proceed with trial, which commenced the following day.[80]

Despite his objection to the proceedings, Vallandigham presented a public defense. He contended that he had been arrested not for a crime of illegal conduct, but for exercising his free speech rights. This travesty of justice must not be allowed to stand because "the alleged 'offense' is not known to the Constitution of the United States, or to any law thereof." He eloquently defended the rights of a vocal minority to criticize persons in power without fear of retribution by explaining the character of his speech:

> It is words spoken to the people of Ohio in an open and public political meeting, lawfully and peaceably assembled, under the Constitution and upon full notice. It is words of criticism of the public policy of the public servants of the people, by which policy it was alleged that the welfare of the country was not promoted. It was an appeal to the people to change that policy, not by force, but by free elections and the ballot-box. It is not pretended that I counseled disobedience to the Constitution, or resistance to laws and lawful authority. I never have. Beyond this protest I have nothing further to submit.[81]

Despite this stirring defense of free speech, the verdict in the two-day trial was never in doubt. As expected, the military commission convicted the defendant for his speech of May 1. Specifically, the commission found that Vallandigham's "opinions and sentiments he well knew did aid, comfort, and encourage those in arms against the Government, and could but induce in his hearers a distrust of their own Government, sympathy for those in arms against it." Had the commissioners not been afraid of transforming the prisoner into a martyr, they might have sentenced him to death by firing squad. Instead, the tribunal recommended that he "be placed in close confinement in

some fortress of the United States, to be designated by the commanding officer of this Department, there to be kept during the continu-
ance of the war."[82]

General Burnside agreed with the commission's recommendations and selected Fort Warren in Boston Harbor as a suitable site
for Vallandigham's imprisonment. He soon found, however, that the
case had become a cause célèbre among critics of the war. For persons
critical of the military despotism they believed to be on the horizon,
the arrest and trial before a military commission of a prominent critic
was evidence that Lincoln's objective was to destroy the constitutional republic and install himself on the throne of a new empire. Even
to moderates who were not predisposed to see conspiracies lurking
around every corner, the administration's actions were worrisome.[83]

Vallandigham wasted no time in filing the requisite habeas corpus
appeal in federal district court. He argued that he was entitled to a
trial by jury in a civilian court and all the rights associated with such a
proceeding. The military commission had not afforded him due process of law because he was not indicted by a grand jury or tried before
a petit jury of his peers, nor was he allowed to confront the witnesses,
enjoy the right to have compulsory process for witnesses in his behalf,
or satisfactorily challenge the evidence. Judge Humphrey H. Leavitt
denied the petition, explaining that the "court cannot shut its eyes to
the grave fact that war exists, involving the most eminent public danger, and threatening the subversion in destruction of the constitution
itself. In my judgment, when the life of the republic is in peril, he mis-
states his duty and obligation as a patriot who is not willing to concede
to the constitution such a capacity of adaptation to circumstances as
may be necessary to meet a great emergency, and save the nation from
hopeless ruin. Self-preservation is a paramount law."[84]

In his sworn statement before the original military commission,
General Burnside explained his reasons for ordering Vallandigham's
arrest. "If I were to find a man from the enemy's country distributing
in my camps speeches of their public men that tended to demoralize
the troops or to destroy their confidence in the constituted authorities
of the Government I would have him tried and hung if found guilty,
and all the rules of modern warfare would sustain me," he stated.

"Why should such speeches from our own public men be allowed?" As a man supposedly dedicated to public service, Vallandigham bore a special responsibility for supporting the armed forces in a time of war. "The press and public men in a great emergency like the present should avoid the use of party epithets and bitter invectives and discourage the organization of secret political societies which are always undignified and disgraceful to a free people, but now they are absolutely wrong and injurious; they create dissensions and discord which just now amount to treason."[85] At the conclusion of his statement, General Burnside appealed to the public to understand his position and ratify his actions. "I beg to call upon the fathers, mothers, brothers, sons, daughters, relatives, friends and neighbors of the soldiers in the field to aid me in stopping this license and intemperate discussion which is discouraging our armies, weakening the hands of the Government and thereby strengthening the enemy."[86]

The Aftermath

Lincoln had not been informed that Burnside was going to arrest Vallandigham beforehand, and the political fallout embarrassed the president. In fact, Lincoln read about the event in the newspaper. The president harbored no love for Clement Vallandigham, but Lincoln's political instincts were much better honed than his general's clumsy attempts to cite political reasons to support military action. The suspension of habeas corpus had been aimed at allowing the army to arrest suspected saboteurs, deserters, and spies who could be counted on to wreak havoc on Union property and imperil the lives of soldiers and citizens alike. Lincoln had not intended to suppress dissent, no matter how distasteful he found the criticism to be. Yet General Burnside had taken the initiative, and Lincoln faced a public relations dilemma as a consequence. It was not the first time the president was confronted with a political imbroglio created by a military leader, and it would not be the last.[87]

Despite the political firestorm, the president chose to support his field commander. In a telegraph dated May 29, Lincoln informed Burnside, "All the cabinet regretted the necessity of arresting, for instance, Vallandigham, some perhaps, doubting, that there was a

real necessity for it but, being done, all were for seeing you through with it." He had no stomach for releasing Vallandigham and thereby empowering his Copperhead critics. Already known for his willingness to interfere into military affairs when he believed it was necessary to compel action from a recalcitrant general officer, Lincoln also recognized it was dangerous to second-guess military commanders, especially those in the field who were required to make quick decisions under conditions of great stress. If he micromanaged every aspect of the war, his military leaders might hesitate to engage in bold maneuvers when the times required swift, decisive action.[88]

At the same time, the president knew that holding Vallandigham in prison for the duration of the war would magnify the man's importance. In the immediate aftermath of the arrest, Democratic newspapers attacked the administration and championed Vallandigham as a virtuous man of principle who dared to stand up to an autocrat that desired nothing so much as the enslavement of a free people. The longer he remained a political prisoner, the longer Vallandigham would inflict damage on the administration. He was more dangerous languishing behind bars than he was traveling about and spewing his invective to like-minded individuals.[89]

The president's concerns were well-founded. In June, a month after Vallandigham's arrest, the Ohio Democratic Convention nominated its newly established favorite son for governor. The plan had worked brilliantly. Before his May 1 speech, Vallandigham believed his political career was at a standstill. He desperately needed to energize his supporters. Thanks to General Burnside's orders, the former congressman could look to a future political career as a champion of free speech and democratic government.[90]

To blunt the criticism and remove Vallandigham from prison, Lincoln commuted the sentence and banished his nemesis to the rebellious states on May 19. "Must I shoot a simple minded soldier boy who deserts," he mused, "while I must not touch a hair of a wily agitator who induces him to desert?" The answer, he implied, was no. If Vallandigham was such a firm supporter of the southern cause, Lincoln would deliver the "agitator" to the rebels and allow them to figure out what to do with him.[91]

On May 5, 1863, Clement Vallandigham, an Ohio politician who led the anti-war "Copperhead" faction of the Democratic Party and frequently criticized the Lincoln administration, was arrested for his "habit of declaring sympathies for the enemy." After Vallandigham's petition for habeas corpus was denied, Lincoln ordered the "wily agitator" deported to the Southern Confederacy. Courtesy of the Library of Congress.

Lincoln's attempt to forge a middle ground was conceptually elegant, but it did little to quell the outrage among his critics. Predictably, the Democrats cried foul from the pages of their newspapers. Wilbur F. Storey, a well-known Copperhead editor of the *Chicago Times,* spilled so much ink in blasting the administration that General Burnside suppressed further publication until Lincoln interceded to revoke the order.[92]

Even the Republican press mostly was unsympathetic. Although the editors expressed no lost love for the Copperheads or Vallandigham, they bemoaned the blunder as a means of emboldening the Peace Democrats and increasing their support among Americans who wavered in their support for the administration. Battlefield reverses could be explained away, but an executive that suppressed free speech

and democratic institutions was sure to lose popular support even among his well-wishers.[93]

Indeed, protests erupted in many northern cities. Perhaps the most stinging rebuke came from a group in Albany, New York, that issued the "Albany Resolves" on May 16, 1863, questioning whether Lincoln intended to fight the rebels or "destroy free institutions." The resolves insisted that the president repudiate the military's arbitrary arrest of citizens and publicly pledge not to try civilians before military commissions. The presiding officer of the meeting, Erastus Corning, forwarded the resolves to Lincoln with a request that he give the document his "earnest consideration."[94]

The president did exactly that. In a reply dated June 12, he set forth his position. "Habeas corpus does not discharge men who are proved to be guilty of defined crime," he explained. In Lincoln's view, "its suspension is allowed by the Constitution on purpose that men may be arrested and held who cannot be proved to be guilty of a defined crime. . . . This is precisely our present case—a case of rebellion, wherein the public safety does require the suspension."[95]

As for the specific charges lodged against Clement Vallandigham, Lincoln contended that the arrest and conviction were not based on a desire to chill free speech. It was the man's actions and not his words that landed him in prison. He had damaged the army, not the administration, by undermining the Union war effort:

> It is asserted, in substance, that Mr. Vallandigham was, by a military commander, seized and tried "for no other reason than words addressed to a public meeting, in criticism of the course of the Administration, and in condemnation of the Military orders of the general." Now, if there be no mistake about it, if this assertion is the truth and the whole truth; if there was no other reason for the arrest warrant, then I concede that the arrest was wrong. But the arrest, as I understand, was made for a very different reason. Mr. Vallandigham avows his hostility to the WAR on the part of the Union, and his arrest was made because he was laboring, with some effect, to prevent the raising of troops, to encourage desertions from the army, and to

leave the rebellion without an adequate military to suppress it. He was not arrested because he was damaging the political prospects of the administration, or the personal interests of the Commanding General, but because he was damaging the army, upon the existence and vigor of which the life of the Nation depends. He was warring upon the military, and this gave the military constitutional jurisdiction to lay hands upon him.[96]

The president reiterated his thinking in a reply to the Ohio Democratic Convention on June 29. After carefully outlining his position on suspending habeas corpus—"by the Constitution the benefit of the writ of habeas corpus itself may be suspended when in cases of rebellion or invasion the public safety may require it" and "The Constitution contemplates the question as likely to occur for decision, but it does not expressly declare who is to decide it"—he explicitly addressed the Vallandigham question:

The military arrests and detentions which have been made, including those of Mr. Vallandigham, which are not different in principle from the other, have been for prevention, and not for punishment—as injunctions to stay injury—as proceedings to keep the peace—and hence, like proceedings in such cases, and for like reasons, they have not been accompanied with indictments, or trials by juries, nor in a single case, by any punishment whatever beyond what is purely incidental to the prevention. The original sentence of imprisonment in Mr. Vallandigham's case was to prevent injury to the military service only, and the modification of it was made as a less disagreeable mode to him of securing the same prevention.[97]

While the public debate about Vallandigham's treatment and the reasons for his arrest and trial raged, US soldiers complied with the president's order, transporting the prisoner to Murfreesboro, Tennessee, and handing him over to the Confederates. Vallandigham reportedly told his new captors, "I am a citizen of Ohio, and of the

United States. I am here within your lines by force, and against my will. I therefore surrender myself to you as a prisoner of war."[98]

Southerners seemed as perplexed about the proper method of handling Vallandigham as the northern men had been. Jefferson Davis had no more use for a "fire in the rear" than did Abraham Lincoln. After a brief confinement, Vallandigham traveled around the Confederacy expressing his support for an armistice to end the war and pave the way for a compromise. His Confederate hosts assured him in no uncertain terms that any compromise would have to recognize southern independence. Since Lincoln repeatedly insisted that he would never recognize the Confederate States of America as a legitimate, sovereign government, the Copperhead position, at least as Vallandigham expressed it, was untenable.[99]

Riding a wave of public sympathy, the exiled Vallandigham captured the Democratic nomination for governor of Ohio. It was the high point of his campaign. After wearing out his welcome in the Southland, the gubernatorial candidate caught a blockade-runner from Wilmington, North Carolina, to Canada via Bermuda. From Canadian shores he ran for office *in absentia*. Unfortunately for Vallandigham, as Union military successes increased and the political brouhaha over his arrest, conviction, and exile decreased, he lost his public platform. He was a man without a country and a candidate without a compelling message to attract voters. As a consequence, he lost the general election.[100]

Before he finished strutting and fretting his hour upon the stage and was heard no more, Vallandigham had one more card to play. He appealed his conviction to the US Supreme Court. It was a last desperate measure to keep this cause alive, but the case was no more successful than its predecessor. The high court determined that it could not grant relief. "Whatever may be the force of Vallandigham's protest, that he was not triable by a court of military commission," Justice James M. Wayne wrote for the court majority, "it is certain that his petition cannot be brought within the 14th section of the act; and further, that the court cannot, without disregarding its frequent decisions and interpretation of the Constitution in respect to its judicial power,

originate a writ of certiorari to review or pronounce any opinion upon the proceedings of a military commission."[101]

He was told he would be arrested if he re-entered the United States in express violation of Lincoln's order of banishment, but Vallandigham risked a second arrest by sneaking back onto American soil wearing a disguise in 1864. When he learned of the episode, Lincoln wisely chose to ignore it. Although he instructed his men to keep a watch on Vallandigham's whereabouts, Lincoln understood that the former congressman no longer enjoyed a public platform from which to espouse his views. A second confrontation would only play into the man's schemes.[102]

Vallandigham was hailed as a hero among die-hard Peace Democrats. One intrepid newspaperman confidently predicted that the Ohioan would be elected the next president of the United States. Despite the hyperbole, Vallandigham was not well-positioned to capture the presidential nomination in 1864, but he helped draft the party's platform calling for a cessation of hostilities short of victory. This plank proved to be disastrous for the Democrats, and it helped to assure Lincoln's triumph over the Democratic candidate, General George B. McClellan. After presenting numerous problems for Lincoln in 1863, Vallandigham inadvertently assisted the president in accomplishing his goals in 1864.[103]

A political creature by nature, Vallandigham remained active in Democratic Party affairs after the war. He became a vocal critic of the Radical Republicans in Congress, bitterly criticizing their efforts to provide for the welfare of the freedmen during Reconstruction. Despite his disappointment with federal Reconstruction policy, Vallandigham counseled his fellow Democrats to bide their time, taking care to win elections as political support for the current policy faded. The "New Departure" policy was supposed to distance the postwar Democratic Party from the failed Copperhead strategy of the war years. It was sage advice designed to create future opportunities for a revival of his political career. Alas, it was not to be. Vallandigham stood for election to the US Senate in 1868, but he lost. Afterward, he returned to the private practice of law.[104]

Vallandigham died in Lebanon, Ohio, at the age of fifty in June 1871 as the result of an unfortunate accident. He was defending a

man suspected of killing a person in a barroom fight. Vallandigham's theory of the case was that the decedent had accidentally shot himself when he tried to remove a pistol from his clothing. To demonstrate the point, Vallandigham reenacted the scene with a pistol he thought was unloaded. It was not. The pistol fired into his stomach and he died the next day. It may have been a poor consolation to learn that his demonstration proved to be inarguably persuasive and the defendant won an acquittal.[105]

As for the question of whether citizens could be tried before a military tribunal after the suspension of habeas corpus, the Vallandigham affair was not the only case to arise during the 1860s. After the war ended, several pro-Confederate operatives were tried before a military tribunal for crimes perpetrated against the Union. Sentenced to be hanged, they appealed to the US Supreme Court. In a famous 1866 case, *Ex Parte Milligan,* the high court ruled that when Congress suspended the writ of habeas corpus in 1863, the president was not authorized to approve the use of military tribunals where the civil courts were open and operational. Of course, by the time the Supreme Court ruling was announced, the crisis had ended.[106]

As for the suspension of the great writ, Lincoln was all-too-conscious of the controversy surrounding his decision to suspend habeas corpus. With few precedents to rely on, the president asked his attorney general, Edward Bates, to render an opinion. Bates' opinion, researched and written by a subordinate, was anything but clear. The precedents simply were not precise.

With few historical examples to guide him, Lincoln suspended the writ eight times during his tenure in office, but he was always careful to explain his reasoning with reference to the powers provided in the US Constitution. Lincoln argued that he possessed extraordinary powers in times of crisis, but he was not above the Constitution. His powers were implicit in the document and yet always rooted in the laws of the republic. History seems to have agreed. Whatever the legality of his actions at the time, Abraham Lincoln has been deemed a great man and a wise, benevolent wartime leader.[107]

THE ESPIONAGE ACT OF 1917 AND THE SEDITION ACT OF 1918

I think all men recognize that in time of war the citizen must surrender some rights for the common good which he is entitled to enjoy in time of peace. But, sir, the right to control their own government according to constitutional forms is not one of the rights that the citizens of this country are called upon to surrender in time of war.

—SENATOR ROBERT M. FOLLETTE SR.,

FROM THE FLOOR OF THE US SENATE, OCTOBER 6, 1917[108]

War changes nations and people in ways unimaginable before hostilities commence. When fighting breaks out, political leaders sometimes feel compelled to suppress dissent because negative comments about the government or its military supposedly embolden the enemy and undermine national morale. Yet the notion of a loyal opposition that dares to speak the truth to power is the hallmark of a republican form of government. Stifling dissent presents a danger to the republic that sometimes equals the threat posed by foreign belligerents. Distinguishing between legitimate criticism and speech that creates a clear and present danger to the safety and security of the regime can be difficult in peacetime. During wartime, the task is complicated by inflamed passions as well as rational and irrational fear of the enemy.

The US response to the Great War, as it was called before people knew global conflicts would require numbering, presented a clear example of the damage caused by government responses to fears of foreign elements. The war years were worrisome for many Americans.

They watched, horrified, as casualty figures rolled in from across the Atlantic. The European War of 1914 to 1918 was directly or indirectly responsible for 37 million deaths. Of that total, more than one hundred seventeen thousand were Americans. Although the number of American dead paled in comparison to the millions of Europeans who perished, the carnage nonetheless shocked the citizenry. Why had the nation's solders paid so high a price? Surely muddy, blood-soaked acreage in Belgium, France, and Germany was not worth the lives of a generation of young men who did not even live on the European continent.[109]

When war erupted in 1914, US President Woodrow Wilson pledged to keep his nation free from foreign entanglements that for many citizens seemed far removed from American interests. For a time, he honored his commitment. Wilson's campaign slogan during his 1916 reelection bid, "he kept us out of war," helped the president to eke out a narrow victory. Yet the tide was too strong to resist. After a German U-boat destroyed the British ship the *Lusitania* in 1915, killing 128 Americans onboard, public outrage increased. Additional attacks in the years that followed heightened tensions and turned public opinion against Germans living in Europe as well as those living in the United States.[110]

On April 2, 1917, President Wilson requested a declaration of war during an address before a joint session of Congress. He characterized Germany's indiscriminate use of submarines to sink ships coming to England and France as "warfare against mankind." Always an idealist, Wilson boldly stated his war aims: "The world must be made safe for democracy," he said. "Its peace must be planted upon the tested foundations of political liberty. We have no selfish ends to serve. We desire no conquest, no dominion. We seek no indemnities for ourselves, no material compensation for the sacrifices we shall freely make. We are but one of the champions of the rights of mankind. We shall be satisfied when those rights have been made as secure as the faith and the freedom of nations can make them." At the conclusion of his speech, the president couched his message in florid language that did little to prepare his fellow countrymen for the horrors that would follow. "To such a task we can dedicate our lives and our fortunes, everything that

we are and everything that we have, with the pride of those who know that the day has come when America is privileged to spend her blood and her might for the principles that gave her birth and happiness and the peace which she has treasured. God helping her, she can do no other." Two days later, the US Senate voted in favor of war, 82 to six. On April 6, the US House of Representatives agreed by a 373-to-50 vote. The United States had formally entered into the First World War.[111]

The Espionage Act of 1917

Shortly after the United States entered the war, federal authorities expressed concerns that spies and subversives might interfere with military operations. Congress eventually enacted, and President Wilson signed, the Espionage Act of 1917, which made it a crime, among other things, "To convey information with intent to interfere with the operation or success of the armed forces of the United States or to promote the success of its enemies." This vaguely worded provision left much discretion to US attorneys in local jurisdictions to prosecute cases involving persons they deemed to be undesirable. Enforcement varied widely throughout the country.[112]

President Woodrow Wilson signed the Espionage Act of 1917 as well as the 1918 amendments. Courtesy of the Library of Congress.

The act was an extraordinary measure. After the Sedition Act of 1798 expired in 1801, no federal law in the United States prohibited seditious expression or the dissemination and publication of information harmful to national defense until the Espionage Act won passage in 1917. For all of Abraham Lincoln's allegedly tyrannical impulses, he never benefited from overarching legislation that curtailed freedom of expression during the Civil War. President Lincoln argued that his piecemeal actions to censor the press and suspend the writ of habeas corpus were justified by the exigencies of a rebellion. As commander in chief of the armed forces, he possessed immense authority to suppress an insurrection. He could act in ways that normally would be unconstitutional, but his power was not unchecked. After peace prevailed, a president's power would diminish, and the normal constitutional checks and balances would be in force.[113]

The Espionage Act was crafted to apply, at least in theory, during the war as well as after the cessation of hostilities. Designed to meet a national emergency, the statute was not limited by the nature or extent of the emergency. Unlike Lincoln's use of extraordinary power under temporarily extraordinary circumstances, the Espionage Act would expand federal authority, specifically the authority of the president, to such an extent that suppression of dissent could become an ordinary duty of government.

To their credit, the sponsors limited the original bill's provisions regarding a free press by noting that "nothing in this section shall be construed to limit or restrict any discussion, comment, or criticism of the acts or policies of the Government." The statement appeared to ground the Espionage Act within the confines of the First Amendment, but the statement before it introduced a level of ambiguity to the law. The president of the United States was authorized to prevent publication of objectionable material if, in his view, it was "of such a character that it is or might be useful to the enemy."[114]

Some presidents might be reluctant to employ such broad measures, but when it came to using political power, Woodrow Wilson was not a timorous man. During his annual report to Congress in December 1915, well before he asked for a declaration of war, Wilson outlined his position on subversives who undermined the nation. "I

am sorry to say that the gravest threats against our national peace and safety have been uttered within our own borders," he told legislators. "There are citizens of the United States, I blush to admit, born under other flags but welcomed under our generous naturalization laws to the full freedom and opportunity of America, who have poured the poison of disloyalty into the very arteries of our national life; who have sought to bring the authority and good name of our Government into contempt, to destroy our industries wherever they thought it effective for their vindictive purposes to strike at them, and to debase our politics to the uses of foreign intrigue." In the president's view, "we are without adequate federal laws to deal with" subversion practiced by disloyal persons. He asked the Congress to rectify the oversight. "I urge you to enact such laws at the earliest possible moment and feel that in doing so I am urging you to do nothing less than save the honor and self-respect of the nation." In an ominous warning to foreign and subversive elements, the president inveighed:

> Such creatures of passion, disloyalty, and anarchy must be crushed out. They are not many, but they are infinitely malignant, and the hand of our power should close over them at once. They have formed plots to destroy property, they have entered into conspiracies against the neutrality of the Government, they have sought to pry into every confidential transaction of the Government in order to serve interests alien to our own. It is possible to deal with these things very effectually. I need not suggest the terms in which they may be dealt with.[115]

The lack of specificity would provide the president with the flexibility and discretion necessary to bend federal power to his will.

When Congress debated whether to provide the president with broad powers of press censorship, opposition appeared from all sides. Major newspapers decried the attempt to snuff out honest criticism of government policies. Members of Congress argued against a measure that might be interpreted as abridging the First Amendment. One prescient congressman, Simeon Fess of Ohio, remarked, "In time of war we are very apt to do things" that are unwise. Everyone recalled

Thomas Jefferson's famous phrase, "The basis of our governments being the opinion of the people, the very first object should be to keep that right; and were it left to me to decide whether we should have a government without newspapers or newspapers without a government, I should not hesitate a moment to prefer the latter." Congress resoundingly defeated the press censorship provision of the original bill.[116]

Another controversial proposal in the bill empowered the US Postmaster General to exclude from the mails any material he deemed to be "of a treasonable or anarchistic character." Because "treasonable" and "anarchistic" were broad terms open to different, possibly competing, interpretations, the postmaster would be authorized to open the mail, read the contents, and decide on whatever basis—partisan preferences, racial or class biases, or simply a whim—to prosecute an offender. Members of Congress eventually altered the text to prohibit "any matter advocating or urging treason, insurrection or forcible resistance to any law of the United States." Although the phrase remained broad and subject to competing interpretations, the final version narrowed the postmaster's authority because the material would have to advocate illegal action. Presumably, "treasonable" and "anarchistic" statements written as general desires absent an express call to action would be permissible, although it was not clear whether such niceties would be recognized.

A third provision outlawed making false reports or statements "with intent to interfere with the operation or success" of the nation's military and also willfully causing "disaffection in the military or naval forces of the United States." Once again, the use of a broad term—"disaffection"—worried some legislators because it could be misused. A newspaper reporter or a citizen writing a letter to a member of the armed forces expressing concern that the war effort was not going well might be assailed for engendering disaffection. The loyal opposition, in an earnest desire to rectify problems in military operations, must not be prosecuted for calling attention to defects. In response to this concern, the architects of the legislation amended the provision to prohibit actions that would "cause or attempt to cause insubordination, disloyalty, mutiny, or refusal of duty." By substituting this list for "disaffection," the bill sponsors

believed they were protecting persons who criticized the war effort in a good faith attempt to remedy deficiencies versus the subversive character who deliberately spread rancor and encouraged disloyalty among the nation's fighting men.[117]

For all the criticism it later received, the Espionage Act was not a hastily drafted statute enacted in the hysteria of the moment. Members of Congress debated the law for nine weeks and carefully considered the chilling effect that such a measure might have on free speech. Had the original bill passed intact, the law would have been far more destructive to First Amendment values than the final version. For its part, the Wilson administration had lobbied for legislation that would empower the president to punish disloyalty with few, if any, legal safeguards. The bill that passed both houses of Congress was a distinct disappointment. The president had asked Congress to provide him with broad authority, and he believed that the measure fell short of his request.[118]

The Committee on Public Information (CPI)

During the same month that the United States entered the war and Congress debated the Espionage Act, Wilson and his advisors created an independent agency known as the Committee on Public Information (CPI). "I hereby create a Committee on Public Information, to be composed of the Secretary of State, the Secretary of War, the Secretary of the Navy, and a civilian who shall be charged with the executive direction of the Committee," a terse Executive Order 2594 directed on April 13. "As Civilian Chairman of this Committee, I appoint Mr. George Creel. The Secretary of State, the Secretary of War, and the Secretary of the Navy are authorized each to detail an officer or officers to the work of the Committee."[119]

The CPI was to serve as the administration's propaganda arm. George Edward Creel, the president's choice as the agency head, was a former journalist, police commissioner of Denver, and staunch Woodrow Wilson supporter. Although some journalists claimed to be neutral observers who objectively reported stories, Creel famously admitted that "an open mind is not part of my inheritance. I took in prejudices with mother's milk and was weaned on partisanship."[120]

He proved to be as good as his word. Creel believed that his mission was to drum up support for the war effort even if that meant taking liberties with the facts. The CPI set out to promote citizen loyalty and demonize the enemy. He understood that spreading his message through newspapers was effective, but not everyone read the paper. To reach the unwashed masses, Creel devised the concept of the Four-Minute Men, a volunteer group composed of thousands of men who traveled around the country making pro-war speeches, especially outside movie theaters. In addition, the CPI created a news division and a films division. The Division of Pictorial Publicity augmented the agency's messaging by distributing photographs of German brutalities.

A motion picture was an especially effective means of delivering patriotic messages. The CPI Film Division sponsored early war films such as *Pershing's Crusaders* and *Our Colored Fighters*. The former was a documentary showing President Wilson's address to Congress and the background of the war as well as General "Black Jack" Pershing's arrival in Europe to head the American war program. The latter was another documentary, in this case highlighting the 15th New York Infantry Regiment, an all-black unit nicknamed "Harlem Hellfighters." The army dispatched the Hellfighters to France to serve the war effort. In light of the base treatment of black soldiers during the war, a film glorifying Negro fighters was an anomaly for the era.

The CPI's later films focused on German atrocities and moved away from the strict documentary style, which informed audiences, but did not always manipulate public opinion. If George Creel was dedicated to anything, however, it was keeping Americans in a state of patriotic fervor, which meant using whatever means were necessary to shock them. In the 1918 film *The Kaiser: The Beast of Berlin*, the film-makers depicted Germany's Kaiser Wilhelm II as greedy and savage. The film played to packed houses as theater managers urged patrons to "raise the roof" with hisses and boos at appropriate intervals. In some places, signs outside the movie theater urged passersby to express their hatred for the Hun. The Kaiser was hanged in effigy outside several screenings and a sign advertised that "All pro-Germans will be admitted free." As anticipated, no one accepted the offer.[121]

The CPI forged a brilliant propaganda campaign. Aside from promoting anti-German films and printed material, the organization insisted that Americans prove their loyalty. The attorney general asked citizens to perform their patriotic duty by reporting the suspicious activities of their neighbors to appropriate authorities. A voluntary citizen group composed of conservative businessmen, the American Protective League (APL), was adept at filing reports on all manner of allegedly subversive activity. With more than 200,000 members, the APL ensured that rumor, gossip, and innuendo were afforded great weight. Other groups, including the Boy Scouts of America, contributed to the hysteria by spying on members of the community.[122]

The zeal of these and many other "patriotic" organizations eventually caused some Americans to question whether the excesses of the federal government caused as much damage to the polity as the enemy's bullets. One leading critic of the administration, Wisconsin's Progressive US Senator Robert M. La Follette Sr., took to the floor of the US Senate on October 6, 1917, to speak on the subject of "Free Speech in Wartime." "I have in my possession numerous affidavits establishing the fact that people are being unlawfully arrested, thrown into jail, held incommunicado for days, only to be eventually discharged without even having been taken into court, because they have committed no crime," the senator claimed. "Private residences are being invaded, loyal citizens of undoubted integrity and probity arrested, cross-examined, and the most sacred constitutional rights guaranteed to every American citizen are being violated." La Follette worried that the government no longer recognized the constraints on the use of power found in the Constitution. The excuses offered—in a time of war the government must exercise extraordinary authority—was but a rationalization, and a weak one at that, for pursuing repressive measures against persons espousing unpopular opinions. As La Follette explained:

> It appears to be the purpose of those conducting this campaign to throw the country into a state of terror, to coerce public opinion, to stifle criticism, and suppress discussion of the great issues involved in this war. I think all men recognize that

in time of war the citizen must surrender some rights for the common good which he is entitled to enjoy in time of peace. But, sir, the right to control their own government according to constitutional forms is not one of the rights that the citizens of this country are called upon to surrender in time of war.[123]

Despite occasional criticism of the administration's robust prosecution of disloyal citizens, during the war most Americans expressed little outrage over their government's activities. Attorney General Thomas Watt Gregory's encouragement of the APL and similar groups eventually earned public opprobrium, especially after the organizations attacked "slackers," or citizens who had not registered for the draft. Nonetheless, the Wilson administration had created an effective war machine based on public hysteria and fear.[124]

Amendments: The Sedition Act of 1918

Although the Espionage Act was interpreted broadly by pro-administration prosecutors, in 1918 the Justice Department believed that it needed greater authority to punish persons who sought to undermine the war effort. Attorney General Gregory cleverly argued that enacting tough laws that provided the federal government with broad powers to protect American interests during wartime would prevent frightened citizens from taking the law into their own hands. Citing a recent incident in which a mob lynched a German-American reputed to be disloyal to the United States, he blamed the action on fearful citizens who did not believe that the laws were strong enough to control subversives. Amending the Espionage Act would assure citizens their government planned aggressive action on their behalf.[125]

Gregory tapped into a rising tide of intolerance, some of which had been created by the CPI propaganda machine and some of which resulted from stories about the carnage in the trenches. The mood in the country had soured in the year since the Espionage Act was enacted. April 1917 had been an uncertain time, but Americans were confident they could march into Europe and clean up the terrible mess the Allies had made of the war. Patriotic speeches were in the air, and optimism tinged with apprehension appeared to be the consensus. As

casualty figures arrived along with the broken bodies of young men wounded and killed in action, the air of confidence from 1917 degenerated into xenophobia and war-weariness.

In the poisoned atmosphere, the amendments sailed through the US House of Representatives by a vote of 293 to one, although opposition arose in the Senate. Henry Cabot Lodge of Massachusetts, a frequent critic of the Wilson administration, expressed fears about further infringement on free speech. Recognizing that criticism of the administration's draconian initiatives was sometimes viewed as a betrayal of the United States, the senator lamented, "I have become a little weary of having senators get up here and say to those of us who happen to think a word had better be changed" that "we are trying to shelter treason." Senator Hiram Johnson of California argued that the Espionage Act did not need to be amended because it already contained sufficiently broad authority. Echoing Lodge's concerns about opponents demonizing anyone who defended freedom of expression, Johnson remarked that "what has transpired again and again in this Chamber" and "all over this land" is that "any man who did not subscribe instanter to any doctrine, however subversive of this Republic and of its fundamental principles," has by "that very token" been charged with "disloyalty."[126]

Whether Gregory's reasoning ultimately was persuasive or war hysteria was so great that passage was a foregone conclusion, the Senate eventually voted 48 to 26 to amend the law in May 1918. The Sedition Act of 1918 made it a crime to use any "disloyal, profane, scurrilous, or abusive language about the form of government of the United States . . . or the flag of the United States, or the uniform of the Army or Navy" or to thwart the war effort. The two laws, enacted to keep the United States safe during wartime, were used to convict 877 individuals in the postwar period between 1919 and 1920.[127]

Court Cases

In light of the controversial nature of the Espionage Act and its broad application by the Wilson administration, it was no surprise that the statute became the basis for numerous lawsuits during and immediately following the war. In most cases, conservative judges and members of

the bar expressed little or no compunction in punishing actions and speech they deemed to be injurious to the war effort. In a few rare cases, federal judges upheld a broad interpretation of First Amendment freedom of speech.

Masses Publishing Company v. Patten was one notable case in which a judge upheld freedom of expression. The case involved a publication known as *The Masses,* described as "a monthly revolutionary journal." The magazine was designed for intellectuals of a progressive bent, but after the United States entered the First World War, it became well-known for its antiwar sentiments. In June 1917, immediately following passage of the Espionage Act, New York City Postmaster Thomas G. Patten, acting on instructions from Postmaster General Albert S. Burleson, prohibited *The Masses* from distributing its upcoming issue via the US mail owing to material that Patten deemed objectionable. The magazine's editors filed suit in the US District Court for the Southern District of New York seeking an injunction prohibiting the ban.[128]

The case came before Judge Learned Hand, a progressive jurist who spent a long and storied career as a federal district court judge and who later became a judge of the Second Circuit Court of Appeals. During his fifty-two years on the federal bench, Hand developed a reputation as a fierce champion of free speech and something of a judicial philosopher. His elegantly crafted, tightly reasoned opinions became models of legal clarity and style, influencing generations of lawyers and judges. *Masses* became one of Hand's most famous early cases defending free speech from those in power who would stifle dissent.[129]

Prosecutors pointed to four cartoons, three articles, and a poem that contained antiwar messages. Nothing in the magazine specifically urged readers to violate the Espionage Act. The messages expressed support for draft resisters and questioned the administration's decision to enter the war, but it was not a clarion call for the citizenry to oppose the government. Nonetheless, Section 3 of the act punished persons who "shall wilfully make or convey false reports or false statements with intent to interfere with the operation or success of the military or naval forces of the United States or to promote the success of its enemies and whoever when the United States is at war, shall wilfully

cause or attempt to cause insubordination, disloyalty, mutiny, refusal of duty, in the military or naval forces of the United States, or shall wilfully obstruct the recruiting or enlistment service of the United States, to the injury of the service or of the United States. . . . " The question was whether the offending material in *The Masses* met this standard and, if so, whether Section 3 violated First Amendment freedom of expression.[130]

Judge Hand could have relied on the broad language in the statute to determine that general expressions of disapproval likely would cause disloyalty among persons who read the material. Instead, he proposed a narrower standard. The appropriate test was whether the words in the offending material amounted to a "direct incitement" to engage in illegal action. In his view, the dispositive issue was not whether "the indirect result of the language might be to arouse a seditious disposition, for that would not be enough."[131] The crucial question was whether "the language directly advocated resistance to the draft." Since nothing in *The Masses* called for direct action against the war effort or advocated illegal activity, Hand upheld the right of *The Masses* to be disseminated through the US mail and issued the injunction.[132]

War fever had infected the land, and rational appeals were not in vogue. The court of appeals overruled Hand's opinion in November 1917. Passed over for an appointment to the appellate court, at least in part because of his liberal views on free expression, Judge Hand reflected on his *Masses* opinion in a letter to prominent New York lawyer Charles Burlingham. "The case cost me something, at least at the time," he admitted, but "I have been very happy to do what I believe was some service to temperateness and sanity."[133] As for *The Masses*, seven of the publication's editors faced indictments for violating the Espionage Act. Without access to the mails, circulation plummeted and the magazine was out of business by year's end.[134]

Decades later, the *Masses* opinion would be hailed as a jurisprudential masterpiece, a seminal case that established Judge Hand's reputation as a jurist of the first order. In the meantime, the US Supreme Court wrestled with the same issues in the statute. One member of the court, Justice Oliver Wendell Holmes Jr. would change his opinion as

cases came before the court and as he and Judge Hand corresponded on the importance and vitality of the First Amendment.

The first major case to reach the high court, *Schenck v. United States,* involved the general secretary of the Philadelphia Socialist Party, Charles Schenck. The party's executive committee, which included Schenck and another member, Elizabeth Baer, had authorized between 15,000 and 16,000 leaflets to be printed and mailed to men who were eligible to be inducted into military service during the war. The leaflets encouraged the recipients to "assert your rights," contending that a person conscripted into the army is no better than a convict or a slave. The leaflet went on to charge, "If you do not assert and support your rights, you are helping to deny or disparage rights which it is the solemn duty of all citizens and residents of the United States to retain." Among other things, the leaflet urged readers to join the Socialist Party, contact their members of Congress to protest conscription, and "petition for repeal of the act." Schenck was tasked with responsibility for overseeing the printing and distribution of the leaflets.[135]

The defendants were arrested and indicted on three counts. The first count charged a conspiracy to violate the Espionage Act of 1917 "by causing and attempting to cause insubordination, &c., in the military and naval forces of the United States, and to obstruct the recruiting and enlistment service of the United States, when the United States was at war with the German Empire. . . ." A conspiracy count requires one or more overt acts in furtherance of the conspiracy, and the printing as well as the distribution of the leaflets met the requirement. Although only a few inductees received the leaflets and no one claimed to have been influenced by the message, the intent of the defendants was the crucial issue, not the effect of their actions. The second count of the indictment alleged a conspiracy to commit an offense against the United States by using the US mails to transmit material deemed to be "nonmailable" under the Espionage Act. The third count was the actual use of the mails to transmit the objectionable materials. Schenck and Baer were convicted at trial. They appealed, arguing that the First Amendment forbade Congress from enacting a law abridging freedom of speech or press. When the case arrived in the US Supreme

Court, Justice Oliver Wendell Holmes Jr. wrote the majority opinion for a unanimous court.[136]

Justice Holmes explained that war presents exigencies that cannot be ignored in determining whether the First Amendment protects speech. "We admit that, in many places and in ordinary times, the defendants, in saying all that was said in the circular, would have been within their constitutional rights. But the character of every act depends upon the circumstances in which it is done." A fundamental step in any free speech analysis is to decide whether the circumstances justified unfettered speech. "The most stringent protection of free speech would not protect a man in falsely shouting fire in a theatre and causing a panic," Holmes famously remarked. He then set forth the "clear and present danger" test:

> The question in every case is whether the words used are used in such circumstances and are of such a nature as to create a clear and present danger that they will bring about the substantive evils that Congress has a right to prevent. It is a question of proximity and degree. When a nation is at war, many things that might be said in time of peace are such a hindrance to its effort that their utterance will not be endured so long as men fight, and that no Court could regard them as protected by any constitutional right.[137]

In short, because the defendants' actions had created a clear and present danger during a time of war by criticizing the draft, their convictions were upheld.

Critics observed that urging citizens to protest lawfully against the draft does not present a clear and present danger. If Schenck and Baer had advocated draft resistance or argued in favor of immediate action contrary to the United States in a time of war, a clear and present danger would have existed. Holmes's test appeared substantively different from the "bad tendency" approach favored by some courts, which suggested that speech causing a generally negative view of government action could be abridged. Holmes argued for a more imminent threat. Yet in developing his new test, Holmes seemed to rely on

the "bad tendency" approach in affirming the convictions since the threat in *Schenck* was not imminent.[138]

The high court also announced opinions in two cases exactly a week after announcing *Schenck*. The first, *Frohwerk v. United States*, involved Jacob Frohwerk, an editor who published twelve antiwar editorials from July 6 through December 7, 1915, in a German-language newspaper in Kansas City, Missouri, the *Missouri Staats Zeiung*. Frohwerk was arrested and charged with violating the Espionage Act of 1917. The trial court convicted Frohwerk and sentenced him to a fine and imprisonment. On appeal, Frohwerk argued that the law violated his First Amendment free speech rights.[139]

Once again writing for a unanimous Supreme Court, Justice Holmes reiterated his reasoning from *Schenck v. United States*. Citing that case, he explained why the defendant was properly convicted:

> It may be that all this might be said or written even in time of war in circumstances that would not make it a crime. We do not lose our right to condemn either measures or men because the country is at war. It does not appear that there was any special effort to reach men who were subject to the draft, and if the evidence should show that the defendant was a poor man, turning out copy for Gleeser, his employer at less than a day laborer's pay, for Gleeser to use or reject as he saw fit, in a newspaper of small circulation, there would be a natural inclination to test every question of law to be found in the record very thoroughly before upholding the very severe penalty imposed. But we must take the case on the record as it is, and, on that record, it is impossible to say that it might not have been found that the circulation of the paper was in quarters where a little breath would be enough to kindle a flame, and that the fact was known and relied upon by those who sent the paper out.[140]

Holmes did not mention the "clear and present danger" test by name, but it was clear that the statement "a little breath would be

enough to kindle a flame" was sufficient grounds for upholding a conviction.

The second case involved Eugene V. Debs, a perennial thorn in the side of American political leaders for decades. A co-founder of the Industrial Workers of the World (the IWW, also known as the Wobblies), a radical labor union, Debs ran for president five times as a presidential candidate for the Socialist Party of America. In the 1912 election, he garnered almost a million votes. He was well-known for his fiery oratory and frequent criticism of American policies, including the decision to enter into the Great War.[141]

Debs v. United States, announced on the same day as the *Frohwerk* opinion, resulted from a speech that Debs made to a crowd of 1,200 people on June 16, 1918, after visiting with three Socialists imprisoned in Canton, Ohio.

> I realize that, in speaking to you this afternoon, there are certain limitations placed upon the right of free speech. I must be exceedingly careful, prudent, as to what I say, and even more careful and prudent as to how I say it. I may not be able to say all I think; but I am not going to say anything that I do not think. I would rather a thousand times be a free soul in jail than to be a sycophant and coward in the streets. They may put those boys in jail—and some of the rest of us in jail—but they cannot put the Socialist movement in jail. Those prison bars separate their bodies from ours, but their souls are here this afternoon. They are simply paying the penalty that all men have paid in all the ages of history for standing erect, and for seeking to pave the way to better conditions for mankind.[142]

He concluded by urging his listeners to unite and oppose the oppressive forces of capitalism. "Get into the Socialist Party and take your place in its ranks," he railed. "Help to inspire the weak and strengthen the faltering, and do your share to speed the coming of the brighter and better day for us all."[143]

Debs was arrested, tried, and convicted for violating the Espionage Act. In affirming the conviction, Justice Holmes determined that "the

main theme of the speech was Socialism, its growth, and a prophecy of its ultimate success. With that we have nothing to do, but if a part or the manifest intent of the more general utterances was to encourage those present to obstruct the recruiting service and if in passages such encouragement was directly given, the immunity of the general theme may not be enough to protect the speech." In fact, the jury decided that Debs had crossed the line from merely glorifying an ideology to undermining the war effort. In Holmes's view, "the jury were most carefully instructed that they could not find the defendant guilty for advocacy of any of his opinions unless the words used had as their natural tendency and reasonably probable effect to obstruct the recruiting service, etc., and unless the defendant had the specific intent to do so in his mind." The jury had found Debs guilty of violating the law, and because no compelling legal errors were alleged, Holmes refused to second guess that determination.[144]

In the months following the trio of opinions in *Schenck, Frowerk*, and *Debs*, several prominent members of the legal community reached out to Justice Holmes regarding his free speech analyses in those cases. Judge Learned Hand corresponded with Holmes. The justice also discussed the issues with law professors Ernst Freund from the University of Chicago and Zechariah Chafee Jr. from Harvard Law School as well as the noted British political theorist and economist Harold Laski. The scholars gently prodded the justice to extend free speech protections. As a result of these discussions, Holmes reexamined his views on the First Amendment. His opinion in *Abrams v. United States*, a 1920 case, illustrated how far his thinking had evolved in a short time.[145]

The case originated, as many such cases do, with the actions of a group of unpopular defendants. Jacob Abrams, Harold Lachowsky, Samuel Lipman, Jacob Schwartz, and Mollie Steimer had fled Czarist Russia to avoid persecution by the authoritarian Czar Nicholas II. When Nicholas II was in power, he served as an ally of the United States in the Great War. After the Bolsheviks removed the czar in 1917 during the Russian Revolution, the new government signed a peace treaty with Germany. No longer required to fight the Russians along an Eastern Front, Germany could consolidate its forces on the Western Front and present a stronger defense against the Western allies. Desperate to

open a new Eastern Front, the United States dispatched US Marines to Murmansk and Vladivostok. Other nations joined in this Siberian Expedition, as it was called. Abrams and his colleagues believed that the US action was not legitimately aimed at gaining a strategic advantage. Rather, it was a thinly veiled effort to reverse the Russian Revolution.[146]

Furious at the government's actions, the group produced a leaflet decrying President Wilson's "cowardly silence" about his real intentions for intervening into Siberia and condemning the action because it "reveals the hypocrisy of the plutocratic gang in Washington." At its conclusion, the leaflet read, "Awake! Awake, you Workers of the World! REVOLUTIONISTS." A second leaflet, written in Yiddish, again extolled the reader to recognize the duplicity of the US government. "Workers, Russian emigrants, you who had the least belief in the honesty of our government," it read, referring to the American polity, "must now throw away all confidence, must spit in the face the false, hypocritic, military propaganda which has fooled you so relentlessly, calling forth your sympathy, your help, to the prosecution of the war." The leaflet charged that money collected for Liberty Bonds to support the war effort was being used not only to fight Germany, but also "the Workers Soviets of Russia." The leaflet concluded with a clear call to action: "Workers, our reply to the barbaric intervention has to be a general strike! An open challenge only will let the government know that not only the Russian Worker fights for freedom, but also here in America lives the spirit of Revolution."[147]

Military police arrested the authors of the leaflets and charged them with violating the Sedition Act of 1918. From the outset, the trial was patently biased against the defendants. The judge did not attempt to hide his disgust, commenting as he sentenced the defendants to lengthy prison sentences that the "only thing they know how to raise is hell."[148]

When the *Abrams* case came before the US Supreme Court in the fall of 1919, seven justices voted to affirm the conviction. Justice John H. Clarke wrote for the majority. Acknowledging the importance of free speech in the debate about issues of public concern, Justice Clarke explained why the defendants in *Abrams* had moved beyond mere speech. "This is not an attempt to bring about a change

of administration by candid discussion, for no matter what may have incited the outbreak on the part of the defendant anarchists, the manifest purpose of such a publication was to create an attempt to defeat the war plans of the government of the United States, by bringing upon the country the paralysis of a general strike, thereby arresting the production of all munitions and other things essential to the conduct of the war." General criticism of government is not punishable, but "the plain purpose of their propaganda was to excite, at the supreme crisis of the war, disaffection, sedition, riots, and, as they hoped, revolution, in this country for the purpose of embarrassing and if possible defeating the military plans of the government in Europe." For that reason, the defendants' convictions were supported by the evidence.[149]

Justice Holmes, joined by Justice Louis D. Brandeis, dissented. Although his thinking about free speech had evolved since his earlier opinions, Holmes was not prepared to repudiate his position. "I never have seen any reason to doubt that the questions of law that alone were before this Court in the Cases of *Schenck, Frohwerk,* and *Debs* were rightly decided," he wrote. Context is important, but the immediacy of the threat is the crucial issue. "But as against dangers peculiar to war, as against others, the principle of the right to free speech is always the same," he observed. "It is only the present danger of immediate evil or an intent to bring it about that warrants Congress in setting a limit to the expression of opinion where private rights are not concerned."[150]

Holmes did not believe that the leaflets under consideration in *Abrams* presented "a clear and imminent danger." The nexus between the production and distribution of the offending materials and damage to the war effort was far too attenuated. "Now nobody can suppose that the surreptitious publishing of a silly leaflet by an unknown man, without more, would present any immediate danger that its opinions would hinder the success of the government arms or have any appreciable tendency to do so," he wrote.[151]

Toward the conclusion of his opinion, Holmes eloquently summarized the dangers inherent in suppressing free speech:

> But when men have realized that time has upset many fighting faiths, they may come to believe even more than they believe

the very foundations of their own conduct that the ultimate good desired is better reached by free trade in ideas—that the best test of truth is the power of the thought to get itself accepted in the competition of the market, and that truth is the only ground upon which their wishes safely can be carried out. That at any rate is the theory of our Constitution. It is an experiment, as all life is an experiment. Every year if not every day we have to wager our salvation upon some prophecy based upon imperfect knowledge. While that experiment is part of our system I think that we should be eternally vigilant against attempts to check the expression of opinions that we loathe and believe to be fraught with death, unless they so imminently threaten immediate interference with the lawful and pressing purposes of the law that an immediate check is required to save the country.[152]

If it was not quite a reversal of his previous opinions, Holmes's *Abrams* dissent certainly indicated a new-found willingness to tolerate potentially subversive speech. He had written of a "clear and present danger" in *Schenck,* yet he could not bring himself to adhere to the standard he had set. By the time he penned his dissent in *Abrams* eight months later, the justice had wholeheartedly embraced his own principle. Subsequent cases demonstrated Holmes's willingness, joined by Justice Brandeis, to apply the "clear and present danger" test while a majority of the court relied on the "bad tendency" test. Together, the two justices dissented in a series of cases that eventually established a rule for First Amendment free speech protection later in the twentieth century.[153]

The division of opinion between the two tests became clear in subsequent decisions. In *Schaefer v. United States,* a case involving the editors of two German-language newspapers, the Philadelphia *Tageblatt* and the Philadelphia *Sonntagsblatt,* who translated news from English-language newspapers while demonstrating a pro-German bias, a majority of the court determined that three of the five defendants had violated the Espionage Act whereas no evidence existed against the two others connecting them with the offending publication. Justice

US Supreme Court Justice Oliver Wendell Holmes Jr. wrote a series of opinions concerning free speech in the Espionage Act of 1917 as well as the 1918 amendments. Courtesy of the Library of Congress.

Brandeis, joined by Justice Holmes, dissented from upholding a conviction against any defendants, arguing that "an intolerant majority, swayed by passion or by fear, may be prone in the future, as it has often been in the past to stamp as disloyal opinions with which it disagrees. Convictions such as these, besides abridging freedom of speech, threaten freedom of thought and of belief."[154]

In *Pierce v. United States,* four self-professed Socialists from Albany, New York, circulated a pamphlet questioning President Wilson's statements about the country's reasons for entering the Great War. In the Socialists' opinion, the United States did not enter the conflict to make the world safe for democracy, as Wilson claimed, but rather the country sought to protect its interests by exploiting commercial possibilities in developing nations. A majority of the US Supreme Court upheld the defendants' convictions for violating the Espionage Act because the defendants' statements were "grossly false." Justice Brandeis, again joined by Justice Holmes, argued against upholding the convictions because opinions vary as to why people and nations act. "The cause of a war—as of most human action—is not single. War is ordinarily the result of many cooperating causes, many different conditions, acts, and motives," Brandeis wrote. "Historians rarely agree in their judgment as to what was the determining factor in a particular war, even when they write under circumstances where detachment and the availability of evidence from all sources minimizes both prejudice and other sources of error. . . ."[155]

In *Gilbert v. Minnesota,* another contemporaneous case, the defendant, Joseph Gilbert, made a speech violating a state law against sedition. The Minnesota statute read, in part: "It shall be unlawful for any person in any public place, or at any meeting where more than five persons are assembled, to advocate or teach by word of mouth or otherwise that men should not enlist in the military or naval forces of the United States or the State of Minnesota." Gilbert was arrested after he charged, "We are going over to Europe to make the world safe for democracy, but I tell you we had better make America safe for democracy first." Later in the speech, he asserted, "We were stampeded into this war by newspaper rot to pull England's chestnuts out of the fire

for her. I tell you if they conscripted wealth like they have conscripted men, this war would not last over forty-eight hours. . . ."[156]

Convicted of violating the statute and sentenced to a year in jail, a $500 fine, and a requirement to pay court costs, Gilbert appealed. Justice McKenna, writing for a majority of the US Supreme Court, affirmed the conviction. According to McKenna, the effect of the defendant's words was to discourage his listeners from enlisting in the armed forces. Gilbert could not argue he was unaware of the seditious nature of his speech because "he was informed in affairs and the operations of the government, and every word that he uttered in denunciation of the war was false, was deliberate misrepresentation of the motives which impelled it and the objects for which it was prosecuted. He could have had no purpose other than that of which he was charged. It would be a travesty on the constitutional privilege he invokes to assign him its protection."[157]

Justice Holmes concurred in the result, but Brandeis again filed a dissent. "The right to speak freely concerning functions of the federal government is a privilege or immunity of every citizen of the United States," he wrote. Although the statute was a state law, federalism considerations did not interfere with a citizen's rights to speak freely about important public policy matters.[158]

The Supreme Court cases illustrated repeatedly the importance of context in determining the permissible parameters of free speech. Despite Holmes's and Brandeis's willingness to tolerate offensive speech that does not advocate immediate action against the interests of the US government in wartime, a majority of the jurists believed that seditious speech is dangerous well before an immediate call to action is made. The Espionage Act of 1917 and the 1918 amendments were subject to broad interpretation during the Great War, but the question was whether they would be narrowly construed or repealed altogether in a time of peace.[159]

Postwar Hysteria: The Red Scare and the Palmer Raids

After the war ended late in 1918, victorious soldiers returned to the United States. They and their fellow citizens longed for a return to lives of safe routines. It was not to be. The wartime economy had

been booming, but the sudden influx of many tens of thousands of workers into the marketplace triggered an economic crisis, which in turn provoked skirmishes between management and labor. Aside from domestic strife, the world beyond American shores was a frightening place. With the spread of Communism in Europe following a revolution in Russia and the rise of the anarchist movement across the globe, the American way of life seemed to be under sustained attack. Citizens expected their government to do something to protect them from the rising tide of Bolshevik radicalism and global anarchism. As the newly minted US attorney general, A. Mitchell Palmer became the Wilson administration's leading crusader against the threat of the red menace.[160]

Palmer was a Pennsylvania Democrat who came to the administration in its waning years. During three terms in the US House of Representatives, he aligned himself with the party's progressive wing and won the attention of President Wilson. Wilson urged Palmer to run for the US Senate in the 1914 election, and the congressman agreed. After he lost, Palmer announced his retirement from public life, although he continued to work in favor of Democratic Party ideals. Palmer's second act in public life came when President Wilson tapped the Pennsylvanian to succeed retiring Attorney General Thomas Watt Gregory early in 1919. Gregory had been one of the architects of the Espionage Act as well as a zealous enforcer of the law. In 1918, Gregory proudly declared, "It is safe to say that never in its history has this country been so thoroughly policed." Not everyone regarded this boast as a positive feature of the Wilson administration. Even the president recognized that Gregory had become a political liability, widely criticized for his heavy-handedness in pursuing persons the administration deemed undesirable. Moreover, critics believed that Wilson had overloaded his cabinet with southerners. Installing a progressive northern man in the nation's top law enforcement position would allow the president to complete his final two years with a fresh start in the Justice Department. A. Mitchell Palmer appeared to be the right man for the right job at the right time.[161]

Early in his tenure, Palmer seemed reluctant to pursue suspected radicals assiduously. Perhaps he wished to avoid the excesses that had

characterized Gregory's reign, or he may have been unsatisfied with the quality of information he received through formal and informal channels. Before accepting his new position, Palmer had rejected information provided by the American Protective League because too often it was based on hearsay, rumor, and innuendo. After stepping into his new position, he even ordered the release of thousands of German aliens the US government had rounded up during the war.[162]

Palmer changed his views after several events persuaded him that aggressive action was needed. In April 1919, supporters of the infamous Italian anarchist Luigi Galleani mailed a bomb to Palmer's house as well as to the homes of other prominent federal, state, and local officials, including Supreme Court Justice Oliver Wendell Holmes Jr. and Postmaster General Albert S. Burleson. Well known businessmen and newspaper editors also received packages. At least thirty-six devices were sent. Some of the packages detonated, but alert federal officials located the remaining bombs before they harmed their intended targets.

The attorney general had escaped injury, but worse was yet to come. Around 11:15 p.m. on the evening of June 2, 1919, a bomb detonated inside his home. Palmer and his family had retired upstairs shortly before the device exploded, which prevented the family from being injured or killed. Assistant Secretary of the Navy Franklin D. Roosevelt, who lived nearby, agreed to help search through the wreckage. The two men discovered a dead body and anarchist literature, suggesting the bomb had exploded prematurely and killed one of the terrorists. Eight incendiary devices exploded simultaneously in eight cities across the country that night.[163]

Citizens demanded action, as did the US Congress. A subcommittee of the US Senate Judiciary Committee declared that the Bolshevik menace was the "greatest current danger facing the Republic." In October of that year, the Senate demanded that Palmer explain his failure to round up suspected radicals and either put them on trial or immediately deport them. By that time, Palmer had already established the General Intelligence Division (GID) within the Department of Justice and directed a youthful Bureau of Investigation employee, J. Edgar Hoover, to gather information on radicals. Hoover wasted no

time in assembling a lengthy dossier on more than 200,000 people suspected of engaging in radical activities. The GID reported on a variety of activities, most of which were innocuous. Owing to sensationalized and exaggerated claims, however, Americans more than ever believed they were in danger. They demanded that their government take immediate action to safeguard the homeland from subversive elements. The government was only too happy to comply with their wishes.[164]

In November 1919 and January 1920, Palmer, having learned a valuable lesson about the political risks of pursuing a measured, deliberative approach to law enforcement when the public is upset, authorized a series of nationwide police actions where "radicals" were arrested and detained without the benefit of warrants and trials. The actions were performed supposedly under authority granted by the Espionage Act of 1917 and the Sedition Act of 1918. The so-called "Palmer Raids" led to approximately 10,000 arrests, of which 3,500 people were detained and several hundred people deported. Emma Goldman, the well-known anarchist, was among the deportees shipped to the Soviet Union.[165]

President Wilson's attorney general, A. Mitchell Palmer, led a series of raids against suspected enemies of the state. Courtesy of the Library of Congress.

Palmer the progressive converted to Palmer the paranoid. He pursued his campaign against radicalism with a vigor that even Thomas Watt Gregory could not match. The attorney general denounced subversives who would undermine the American way of life in a series of public appearances in 1919 and 1920. Appearing before the US House of Representatives Rules Committee on June 1, 1920, Palmer assured the congressmen that he and his men were up to the task of fighting the enemy. And he was convinced he could ferret out the enemy using whatever law enforcement techniques were necessary. "If there be any doubt of the general character of the active leaders and agitators amongst these avowed revolutionists, a visit to the Department of Justice and an examination of their photographs there collected would dispel it," he charged. "Out of the sly and crafty eyes of many of them leap cupidity, cruelty, insanity, and crime; from their lopsided faces, sloping brows, and misshapen features may be recognized the unmistakable criminal type."[166]

Initially, many citizens praised the attorney general as a hero. Yet public support can be a fickle mistress. As the year stretched on, attitudes softened. A series of court challenges, a blistering report by the American Civil Liberties Union titled *Report upon the Illegal Practices of the United States Department of Justice* detailing the department's unwillingness to obey constitutional dictates, and criticism even among members of the Wilson administration transformed Palmer from a noble public servant into a power-hungry, would-be demagogue. Called into service to clean up his predecessor's penchant for overreaching, he had become the face of a presidential administration that persecuted individuals and groups for expressing unpopular ideas even when those ideas did not represent a genuine threat to the polity.[167]

Conclusion

Citizens expect their government to keep them safe from all threats, foreign and domestic, especially in wartime. Historians with the benefit of hindsight can find fault with policies that ultimately encroach on civil liberties, but policymakers do not enjoy such luxuries in times of crisis. They must balance competing values—individual freedom and

government authority—and often they must do so as public hysteria reaches a fever pitch.

All questions involving government involve a complex balancing act of competing values. While a maximum level of liberty appears inviting, it may lead to chaos and disorder. In a state of absolute liberty, government does not exist. A person can do whatever he or she wants, which is an invitation to engage in mischief detrimental to the well-being of others. A majority of mainstream Western thinkers since the Enlightenment have viewed a state of absolute liberty with disdain, for it appears to invite chaos and disorder. According to social contract theory, rational beings agree to surrender a measure of liberty to create a state. The central question is: how much individual freedom should be surrendered in exchange for the authority of the state? Individual freedom and state authority are antithetical ideals: an increase in one decreases the other.

Citizens must be cautious in empowering a government to act. If they are not careful, they create a totalitarian state where most or all political and economic decisions are made by forces beyond their control. This was the great fear of the American Founders—they were fixated on the problem of "too much power in too few hands"—and so they created a system of federalism, separated powers, and checks and balances. A mixed polity is the result, a government where people, acting through the elected representatives, make some political decisions, but unelected experts also make decisions within their areas of expertise.[168]

Yet political decisions are not reached in a vacuum, and political relationships are not fixed. Crisis times call for crisis solutions. The goal is not to exacerbate the problem by creating a new crisis that is worse than the original crisis itself. This point was illustrated vividly during the Great War by artist William Allen Rogers in a cartoon he sketched following enactment of the Sedition Act in 1918. "Now for a Round-up" shows Uncle Sam, as a symbol of the United States government, chasing down "Spy," "Traitor," "IWW" (International Workers of the World, a radical international union), "German money," and "Sinn Fein," an Irish Republican political party. The banner "Sedition Law Passed" is visible in the background. The artist

This political cartoon shows Uncle Sam gathering up traitors and spies after Congress enacted the Sedition Act of 1918. Courtesy of the Library of Congress.

clearly was concerned that the nation, in its quest to protect citizens from subversives, would err too far on the side of consolidated power and intolerance.[169]

Rogers was right to be worried. The Wilson administration reacted to public fears in a predictable fashion: seeking congressional approval to strengthen federal laws against subversion, the executive

branch vigorously sought to root out genuine threats to the republic. A president who will not listen to the citizenry's concerns is a leader who cannot hope to succeed. Woodrow Wilson hoped to succeed, and he was attuned to public perception. Yet his administration was not satisfied to respond to public needs and desires. Rather than merely react to the mood of the citizenry, his men manipulated public opinion. They stoked understandable concerns and transformed them into mass hysteria. Americans who normally regarded others with tolerance suddenly evinced a deep suspicion of alien forces and individuals, seeing conspiracies lurking around every corner. Fringe public figures and oddball characters espousing absurd political ideologies would usually be ignored in peacetime unless they posed a direct and immediate threat, but at the height of the war they were classified as enemies of the state and prosecuted in a broad interpretation of the law.[170]

Free speech has never been a fixed or static concept. It frequently becomes a casualty of war when safety and security require, or seem to require, a unified voice. As Justice Robert Jackson once wrote in a different context: "Those who begin coercive elimination of dissent soon find themselves exterminating dissenters. Compulsory unification of opinion achieves only the unanimity of the graveyard. It *seems trite* but necessary to say that the First Amendment to our Constitution was designed to avoid *these* ends by avoiding *these* beginnings."[171]

The concept of free speech means that unpopular, even offensive, messages can and probably will be expressed within the marketplace of ideas. To suppress speech that does not present a clear and present danger, to use Justice Holmes's phrase, is to take a dangerous step toward consolidated power, the dreaded "too much power in too few hands." The irony is that a nation that violates its values in the quest to protect those values can harm itself as much as, or more than, a foreign enemy. This lesson is not often learned, or, if it is learned, it is easily forgotten.[172]

Chapter 4

THE SMITH ACT OF 1940

We have heard a lot of talk here about abusing the poor alien. The gentlemen who have been talking that way cannot complain about this section. We have laws against aliens who advocate the overthrow of this Government by force, but do you know that there is nothing in the world to prevent a treasonable American citizen from doing so?

—CONGRESSMAN HOWARD W. SMITH,

JULY 29, 1939[173]

The Great War was supposed to end all wars. In 1928, a decade after the combatants signed an armistice, nations previously involved in the conflict ratified the General Treaty for Renunciation of War as an Instrument of National Policy, commonly called the Kellogg-Briand Pact, pledging not to engage in armed confrontation as a means of resolving "disputes or conflicts of whatever nature or of whatever origin they may be, which may arise among them." Despite such idealistic assurances, wars raged unabated across the globe.[174]

When a new world war erupted in Europe in 1939, Americans feared that the conflagration might cross the Atlantic. The world was changing rapidly, and no one knew when the next crisis would arise. As Nazi Germany initiated a war in Europe, the Japanese empire appeared ascendant. Many noncitizens, including persons from nations that might soon be at war with the United States, were streaming into the country. Lawmakers grew fearful that these alien entities might undermine national security. In response to growing fears about the spread of dangerous ideas and persons who might drag the nation into the conflict, the US Congress passed the Alien Registration Act, commonly known as the Smith Act, in 1940.[175]

Members of Congress had expressed concern about the growing problem of tracking noncitizen aliens inside the country for years, but the impetus for passing the Smith Act involved not a foreign threat, but a radical labor organizer named Harry Bridges who already resided inside the United States. An immigrant from Australia, Bridges had set up shop after his arrival in the country in 1920. He was known to associate with Communists in his vocal campaign to improve the conditions of factory workers. Government officials first attempted to deport Bridges in 1938 under the auspices of the Espionage Act of 1917 and the Sedition Act of 1918, but to no avail. Those laws required that a deportee be currently affiliated with an organization that advocated the overthrow of the government. Bridges had severed his official Communist ties by that time. James M. Landis, dean of the Harvard Law School, served as a special master in the government's deportation case. During a hearing in January 1940, Landis concluded that Bridges could not be deported under existing law because past affiliations were not actionable. Secretary of Labor Frances Perkins sustained Landis's opinion.[176]

The Context of the Statute

If subversives such as Harry Bridges were to be dealt with effectively, a new, broader law was needed. Enter Howard W. Smith, a congressman from Virginia. Initially a New Deal supporter, the conservative Democrat became convinced that the National Labor Relations Board (NLRB), created by the Wagner Act of 1935, was staffed by left-leaning subversives. He spent much of his thirty-six-year career in the House of Representatives battling "alien" forces, whether they were leftist public administrators, radical labor organizers or, later, black civil rights advocates. In 1940, alarmed at Harry Bridges's activities and the major deficiencies in current law, Smith introduced the Alien Registration Act. The measure passed the House of Representatives on June 22, 1940, by a vote of 382 to 4. Coincidentally, the House acted on the same day Germany forced the French government to sign an armistice following the Nazi invasion a month earlier. The US Senate approved the bill that same week, and President Franklin D. Roosevelt signed it into law on June 29.[177]

Congressman Howard W. Smith (left), principal sponsor of the Smith Act, which was named for him, talks with National Labor Relations Board member William M. Leiserson during a break from a congressional hearing in 1939. Courtesy of the Library of Congress.

Roosevelt publicly expressed strong support for protecting civil liberties, but his actions did not always match his rhetoric. He was not immune to the tenor of the times, and he recognized that government must ensure the safety of its citizens even if it meant he had to step beyond constitutional boundaries upon occasion. Reacting to critics who feared that the law might punish free speech, the president demurred, observing that its provisions did not "constitute an improper encroachment on civil liberties in the light of present world conditions." He might have vetoed the measure on constitutional grounds, but the president acquiesced in its passage. He was preparing the nation for the possibility that the war consuming much of Europe might require American intervention. Whatever else could be said of him, FDR was a crafty political operative. It was helpful to empower

the federal government to battle against subversives when and if the time came to enter the war.[178]

The Smith Act criminalized the actions of anyone who "prints, publishes, edits, issues, circulates, sells, distributes, or publicly displays any written or printed matter advocating, advising, or teaching the duty, necessity, desirability, or propriety of overthrowing or destroying any government in the United States by force or violence, or attempts to do so; or . . . organizes or helps or attempts to organize any society, group, or assembly of persons who teach, advocate, or encourage the overthrow or destruction of any such government by force or violence; or becomes or is a member of, or affiliates with, any such society, group, or assembly of persons, knowing the purposes thereof." The act also allowed the deportation of an alien who was a member of a subversive group or affiliated "at any time" with such an organization since arriving in the United States. This provision was designed to get around the "Harry Bridges problem" of pursuing a radical who had already severed formal ties with an offending organization. To ensure that government officials knew the whereabouts of aliens on American soil, the statute required noncitizens to register under oath and provide information on "(1) the date and place of entry of the alien into the United States; (2) activities in which he has been and intends to be engaged; (3) the length of time he expects to remain in the United States; (4) the criminal record, if any, of such alien; and (5) such additional matters as may be prescribed by the Commissioner, with the approval of the Attorney General."[179]

The Smith Act strengthened federal law because it could be used against someone who was a member of a subversive organization at the time he or she entered the country. Armed with this tough new legal authority, the government again instituted deportation proceedings against Harry Bridges. Charles B. Sears, a prominent lawyer and former judge from New York, served as the hearing officer. After reviewing evidence that Bridges had been affiliated with a subversive group when he entered the United States in 1920, in September 1941 Sears recommended immediate deportation. Bridges appealed the opinion, and the Board of Immigration Appeals (BIA) unanimously reversed the decision.[180]

In this photograph, International Longshore and Warehouse Union (ILWU) President Harry Bridges testifies before the House Merchant Marine Committee on May 10, 1939. Courtesy of the Library of Congress.

In 1942, as the Roosevelt administration was becoming increasingly worried about seditious speech in the wake of the country's entry into World War II, Attorney General Francis Biddle overruled the BIA and ordered Bridges deported. As Biddle explained in his memoirs, he believed deporting Bridges was necessary, but he was concerned that the Soviets, ostensibly American allies in the fight against Nazi Germany, might be upset by the deportation. Biddle visited the White House to tell President Roosevelt of his decision before announcing it publicly. "I did not ask his advice, but spoke in some detail of the reasons for my action," Biddle recalled. The president listened intently, adding, "I'll bet that the Supreme Court will never let him be deported."[181]

In leading the administration's prosecutions under the Smith Act, Francis Biddle was placed in an awkward position. He was hardly a reactionary on matters of free speech. In fact, he had warned against "the disgraceful hysteria of witch hunts" and promised to be vigilant in protecting civil liberties. Raised as a progressive, he later joined the American Civil Liberties Union (ACLU).

President Roosevelt fretted that Biddle, with all this talk of civil liberties, was not tough enough to prosecute subversives if the president appointed him permanently to the top post at the Justice Department. Although he questioned the constitutionality of the Smith Act, Biddle understood what was required to land his position. Roosevelt repeatedly needled his man: "when are you going to indict the seditionists?" The acting attorney general recognized he could not ignore pointed inquiries from the president of the United States. Although he later expressed regret for authorizing Smith Act prosecutions, at the time he was pliable. Biddle remained concerned about potential excesses in prosecuting seditious speech, and he was well aware of the government's willingness to prosecute undesirables during World War I. Accordingly, he sought to avoid witch hunts and overly zealous displays of government authority, but he also muted his civil libertarian impulses. He assured the president he could handle the tasks ahead, and he modified his position to allow for flexibility in protecting speech during times of national crisis. Biddle even went so far as to tell the president that prosecuting a few select offenders under the Smith Act might have a "salutary effect" on other groups contemplating subversive actions.

The man who became known for his willingness to go after subversives in the 1940s hailed from a prominent family of proud civil libertarians. As a direct descendant of Edmund Randolph, a Founding Father and first attorney general of the United States, as well as two advocates who argued in favor of Copperhead Clement Vallandigham during the Civil War, Francis Biddle came to power naturally. He had known Franklin Roosevelt when the two young men attended school at Groton. Later, Biddle graduated from Harvard Law School and served as a clerk to US Supreme Court Justice Oliver Wendell Holmes Jr. He steadily built a career as a lawyer and judge before President

Attorney General Francis Biddle, pictured here, overruled the Board of Immigration Appeals in an effort to deport labor leader Harry Bridges. He also led the Roosevelt administration's efforts to implement the Smith Act on the eve of America's entry into World War II. Courtesy of the Library of Congress.

Roosevelt appointed him to the US Circuit Court of Appeals, a position he held for only a year before he resigned to become the US solicitor general and eventually the acting attorney general.[182]

Roosevelt persuaded his loyal cabinet officer to modify his stance on free speech—rewarding Biddle with a permanent appointment—but the president could not directly influence the Supreme Court. Roosevelt's instincts about the court's unwillingness to order Harry Bridges's deportation were correct. Bridges availed himself of the US judicial system and due process of law. He appealed the attorney general's order, losing in both the district court and the US Court of Appeals before petitioning the US Supreme Court. In *Bridges v. Wixon,* decided in June 1945, the high court ruled 5 to 3 that Bridges

could not be deported because the government had not met its burden of proof. Being sympathetic to Communist ideals, five justices decided, is not tantamount to "affiliation," as required by the statute. Justice William O. Douglas wrote the majority opinion. "Since Harry Bridges has been ordered deported on a misconstruction of the term 'affiliation' as used in the statute and by reason of an unfair hearing on the question of his membership in the Communist party," Douglas concluded, "his detention under the warrant is unlawful."[183]

Wartime Threats

The administration may have lost its fight against Harry Bridges, but FDR's men remained committed to using the Smith Act as the basis for government action against other unpopular individuals and groups. On June 27, 1941, the Federal Bureau of Investigation (FBI) raided the Minneapolis and St. Paul offices of the Socialist Workers Party (SWP), followers of the Communist Leon Trotsky, who believed that a worldwide proletarian revolution was needed to ensure fair treatment for workers. The Trotskyists controlled Local 544 of the Teamsters Union. Three weeks after the initial raid, FBI agents arrested twenty-nine SWP members, fifteen of whom belonged to the Teamsters Local 544. Members were accused of plotting to overthrow the US government. A federal grand jury issued indictments, and eighteen defendants were convicted. Sentencing occurred on December 8, 1941, the day after the Japanese attacked Pearl Harbor.[184]

Civil libertarians expressed concern that Smith Act prosecutions created a chilling effect on free speech. If the "clear and present danger" test were applied to the actions of the defendants, the convictions could not be upheld. The newly malleable Francis Biddle agreed with this analysis, but he argued that Congress deliberately chose to modify the judicial standard when it enacted the Smith Act. After a nation is at war, or close to it, the normal standards of free expression must be altered to allow for a flexible response. The immediacy of the threat is a crucial factor in peacetime, but less immediate threats can be recognized when national security is at risk. The trial court agreed with this view.

Despite his willingness to restrict seditious speech, the trial judge decided that five defendants should be acquitted owing to a lack of

sufficient evidence. The jury determined that the remaining twenty-three defendants were not guilty of violating an 1861 conspiracy statute. The eighteen defendants convicted of violating the Smith Act received relatively light sentences ranging from twelve to sixteen months. On appeal, the Eighth Circuit upheld the convictions of the eighteen Smith Act defendants, deciding that the "clear and present danger" test did not apply because, as Biddle had argued, Congress specifically had chosen to outlaw speech that presented a less immediate threat.[185]

After the US government entered the Second World War, government lawyers stepped up their Smith Act prosecutions. At the president's behest, the Justice Department targeted fascists and isolationists for special attention. In March 1942, the target was George W. Christians, an odd man by all accounts. Founder of the Crusader White Shirts, a fascist organization that issued histrionic pronouncements against the US government, Christians was a difficult man to take seriously. One Roosevelt confidant labeled the man a "harmless lunatic." Lunatic or not, his public statements and threats came under increased government scrutiny. Christians was nothing if not provocative. He outlined plans for implementing a coup d'état. "The first objective should be to take control of the local government in the following manner: March in military formation to and surround the government buildings. Then, by sheer numbers and a patriotic appeal, force the officials to accept and act under the direction of an economic adviser appointed by the President of the CFEL [Crusaders for Economic Liberty]." Learning that President Roosevelt intended to visit Chattanooga, Tennessee, Christians revealed a plan to disrupt the city's utilities, warning "Lots of things can happen in the dark!" The veiled threat might have been dismissed as jejune and easily ignored in peacetime, but with the war effort fully underway, loose talk brought action.[186]

On March 27, 1942, Christians and a co-conspirator were arrested for violating the Smith Act by "communicating to soldiers statements designed to impair their morale." Never one to waste an opportunity to publicize his cause, Christians remarked, "I consider myself a political prisoner rather than a criminal and should get better treatment."

What he got instead was a conviction for violating the act, and a five-year prison sentence.[187]

George W. Christians struck some Americans as an odd, silly man, but William Dudley Pelley, another prominent public figure with a penchant for promoting strange causes, appeared to be more dangerous than Christians. Pelley was a self-educated spiritualist, writer, and fascist sympathizer who spent his early years engaged in multiple ventures. He worked in a toilet paper factory, covered the crime beat for the *Boston Globe,* and published more than one hundred articles and short stories in national magazines. He eventually landed in Hollywood writing screenplays before his life unraveled and he suffered a nervous breakdown.

After he experienced a near-death experience in 1927, Pelley found his calling as a spiritualist. Moving to Asheville, North Carolina, he churned out pamphlets on all manner of subjects, most of them involving wacky theories about heaven and hell. He claimed that his "mental radio" kept him in tune with voices from other dimensions, leaving some souls in this world convinced he was not altogether connected to the current dimension.

On January 31, 1933, the day after Adolf Hitler became chancellor of Germany, Pelley founded an organization known as the Silver Legion of America. Swearing his allegiance to the "constitutional government set up by the forefathers," Pelley and his "Silver Shirts," an Americanized version of Nazi SS officers, traveled the country to spread their peculiar gospel of hate, blaming a global Jewish cabal for society's ills. By 1934, he listed fifteen thousand members of his group.

Pelley denounced Franklin Roosevelt as a "Dutch Jew" at the helm of the "Great Kosher Administration," but he stopped short of uttering specific threats. He also urged his followers to obey the law regardless of how loathsome it might be. Perhaps it was asking too much to recruit Nazi sympathizers with vitriolic appeals about Jewish conspiracies and the wayward nature of American policy and expect everyone to behave in a lawful manner. Predictably, some Silver Shirts ignored the admonitions to observe legal niceties. On their own initiative, they engaged in violence without direct sanction from "Chief Pelley." Thus, Silver Shirts in Salt Lake City, Utah, beat a suspected

Communist half to death in 1933. Some chapters trained a paramilitary force to prepare for an armed confrontation with their enemies.

Always a fellow whose reach exceeded his grasp, Pelley announced his candidacy for the presidency of the United States in 1935. Under the banner "For Christ and Constitution," the chief embarked on his quixotic quest by issuing a series of provocative statements. He publicly announced that "the time has come for an American Hitler." Presumably, he would assume the mantle of the führer of the United States. His platform included a pledge to push through a constitutional amendment disenfranchising Jews.

Although Pelley believed that an American Hitler was the antidote for what ailed the nation, a majority of voters disagreed. Pelley's name appeared on only one state's ballot in 1936—Washington—and he received only 1,598 of more than 700,000 votes cast. Disappointed in his failed presidential bid, the candidate could only chalk up his loss to a Jewish conspiracy that undoubtedly sabotaged the voting machines. No other explanation made sense to a man predisposed to see conspiracies lurking around every corner.

When an isolationist movement swept the United States on the eve of World War II, Pelley latched onto the issue. His support did not enhance the likelihood of success for groups such as America First, an organization of patriots who believed the country should not become embroiled in another bloody, costly European adventure. After the United States entered the war, Pelley argued that Roosevelt knew of the impending Japanese attack on Pearl Harbor and deliberately did nothing to prevent it. He also charged that the US Pacific fleet had been almost completely destroyed on December 7, 1941. Following the attack, the Roosevelt administration minimized the losses to forestall panic. Pelley's charges about the condition of the Pacific fleet cut to the quick because they were more or less true.[188]

Because he feared the power of demagogues to rouse the rabble, President Roosevelt took a close personal interest in Pelley's case. On several occasions, the president had expressed disdain for the spiritualist owing to public statements Pelley had made against Roosevelt throughout the years. Now, with the advent of the Second World War, it was time to show the impudent Nazi a thing or two about the use

of authoritarian power. The government indicted Pelley under the Espionage Act of 1917 for making "false statements with intent to interfere with the operation or success of the military or naval forces of the United States or to promote the success of its enemies." The jury convicted him on eleven counts, and Judge Robert Baltzell sentenced Pelley to fifteen years in prison.

The fascist wannabe sought redemption through democratic institutions, appealing his conviction to the Seventh Circuit Court of Appeals. Alas, the court upheld the conviction. The US Supreme Court declined to hear the case. Pelley served ten years in prison before being paroled in 1952 on the condition that he refrain from participating in future "political activities." He continued to espouse his odd beliefs, but William Dudley Pelley's hour upon the national stage had come and gone.[189]

The American Hitler was already serving time when he was charged with a Smith Act violation in July 1942—along with twenty-five other defendants. It was a terrible time for the United States and her allies. Germany and the fascist tide seemed to be on the rise and about to engulf all of Europe. Anyone who uttered or circulated "anti-American" messages was suspect. The defendants in the 1942 cases were a diverse group of fringe figures who expressed public support for Germany—fascists, anti-Semites, Socialists, isolationists, and nativists. Aside from Pelley, some of the more colorful indicted characters included Lawrence Dennis, an ideological philosopher who made a name for himself in the 1890s as the "Mulatto Boy Evangelist" and later authored a tract titled *The Coming American Fascism* arguing that capitalism was doomed. Elizabeth Dilling was a former leader of the Mother's Crusade to keep the United States out of World War II and was leader of the Patriotic Research Bureau, a group dedicated to keeping tabs on Communists in the United States. Robert Noble and Ellis O. Jones were directors of the antiwar group Friends of Progress, which staged a mock impeachment of Franklin Roosevelt and argued that a new world order must accommodate a victorious Nazi Germany. The defendants appeared to have little in common other than their anti-Roosevelt, pro-German proclivities, but prosecutors nonetheless alleged that a conspiracy existed. Interestingly, the indictments did

not include Ku Klux Klan members or the well-known administration critics Reverend Gerald L. K. Smith, a fundamentalist preacher who reveled in anti-Semitic prophesies, and Father Charles Coughlin, a Roman Catholic priest who used popular radio addresses to offer support for Adolf Hitler and Benito Mussolini.[190]

The arrests of 1942 became the Great Sedition Trial of 1944, a politically motivated series of prosecutions based on scant evidence. Prosecutors pursued offenders who could not call on widespread public support. The goal was to demonstrate that the defendants' public statements and writings were so similar to Nazi propaganda that the men and women charged with sedition were part of an international conspiracy against the interests of the United States.

After multiple delays, the defendants were tried in proceedings that stretched on for more than seven months in 1944, from April until November. The cases were weak to begin with, and the interminable proceedings did nothing to strengthen the government's hand. Prosecutors could not demonstrate beyond a reasonable doubt that espousing a message of support for America's enemies or castigating Jews amounted to a direct threat to the national interest. In November, the court declared a mistrial after the trial judge unexpectedly died of a heart attack. Government authorities debated whether to retry the defendants, but the Allied victory at the end of the war obviated the need to make an example of the defendants.[191]

Dennis v. United States

The end of the Second World War momentarily stemmed the tide of Smith Act prosecutions, but the statute was not dead. Congress amended the law in the 1940s and 1950s, modifying various provisions but leaving it in effect. The beauty of the Smith Act was its versatility. It could be employed against the left as well as the right, and it was useful in wartime or in times of peace. Cases required only a creative prosecutor and at least one unpopular defendant.

If right-wing fanatics were the targets of choice during World War II, leftists became the undesirables *du jour* a decade later. Pursuing fascists was so 1940s, but a new scapegoat had taken their place: Communists. They seemed to be everywhere and behind every status

quo–threatening development—in labor disputes; in the nascent civil rights movement; in liberal movements on behalf of the poor and aged; in art, music, and literature; in the promiscuity rampant among people of color, unmarried young people, and homosexuals. Even the teaching of evolution in the schools, according to reactionary forces, smacked of a Communist conspiracy.

During the 1950s, the US Supreme Court reviewed Smith Act prosecutions of Communists in two high-profile cases. In *Dennis v. United States*, eleven Communist defendants convicted under the statute appealed to the US Supreme Court. The original indictment charged the defendants with "wilfully and knowingly conspiring (1) to organize as the Communist Party of the United States of America a society, group and assembly of persons who teach and advocate the overthrow and destruction of the Government of the United States by force and violence, and (2) knowingly and wilfully to advocate and teach the duty and necessity of overthrowing and destroying the Government of the United States by force and violence."[192]

The defendants were affiliated with the Communist party of the United States (CPUSA) at a time when the United States was suffering through what historians have labeled a "little red scare." Opinions on the CPUSA varied. Some observers feared that party members were agents of the Soviet Union, dangerous spies who were searching for secrets to pass along to America's foremost enemy in the world. Even if individual members were not willing agent provocateurs, they were hopelessly misguided young people who, as "malleable objects," had fallen under the spell of Communist organizers from abroad.

A more benign view portrayed CPUSA members as radical social revolutionaries who embraced Socialist or Communist doctrines during the Second World War because they saw the Soviet Union as staunch anti-Nazis. According to this perspective, CPUSA adherents were not enemies of the United States. They were socially conscious, principled citizens who sought a method for improving conditions for impoverished peoples around the world. Communism was the means to an end. As a forceful alternative to right-wing authoritarian governments, the ideology was hardly perfect, but it was preferable to fascist movements spreading in countries decimated in World War II.

The latter view of CPUSA supporters required a nuanced under-standing that few Americans shared. Anyone who feared an alien philosophy infecting the citizenry as though it were a worldwide bio-logical contagion with no antidote in sight could not afford to carry on without some sort of inoculation. The anti-Communist movement that arose in the postwar years to combat the spread of the Communist disease was just what the doctor ordered. These civil servants, with the motto "better dead than red" top of mind, would arrest the infection, whatever the cost to the body politic. For some anti-Communists, the CPUSA was a front for agents engaged in active espionage against the United States. For others, the party represented a free-spirited phi-losophy that would lead to "race-mixing" and encourage "Godless atheism" along with other strange ideas that threatened traditional American values. Business leaders feared that Communists encouraged the growing popularity of labor unions, which seemed to jeopardize the capitalist, entrepreneurial principles that had become a part of the national fabric.[193]

The Republican Party took control of both houses of Congress during the 1946 midterm elections for the first time since 1932. Now gripping the reins of power, Republicans, especially those on the far right, declared themselves fiercely anti-Communist. Powerful interest groups such as the American Legion, the US Chamber of Commerce, and the National Association of Manufacturers joined them as allies. After years of left-leaning policies propagated under Franklin Roosevelt and Harry Truman, the United States moved decidedly to the right.[194]

During the late 1940s, a series of international crises illustrated the threat that Communism posed across the globe. At the Yalta Conference only a few months before he died in office, an ailing, seemingly befuddled President Roosevelt appeared all-too-willing to surrender American rights to Poland, dooming that country to Soviet domination for years to come. A year later, Soviet dictator Joseph Stalin predicted that the Communist and capitalist worlds inevitably would clash, with the former emerging triumphant. Former British Prime Minister Winston Churchill appeared to agree with Stalin about the inevitably of conflict, but not the identity of the victor, when he proclaimed in a 1946 speech that an Iron Curtain

had descended over parts of Europe. The Cold War had begun. The Soviets menaced the free world in Iran, Turkey, and Greece. The Truman administration announced that the United States would assist nations opposing authoritarian governments and launched the Marshall Plan to rebuild war-torn Europe. In 1948 and 1949, Americans were forced to rescue an isolated Berlin, Germany, by air-lifting in supplies. The Soviets exploded an atomic bomb in 1949. In 1950, China fell to the Communists. Americans who believed that the red menace was on the rise could cite ample evidence to buttress their claims.[195]

It is little wonder that openly-avowed supporters of the CPUSA would find themselves dragged into court given developments around the world. Even if the eleven defendants had not posed a "clear and present danger" in their actions, as those terms had been interpreted in prior cases, their support for an ideology dedicated to world domination suggested that danger existed. A war was on, but it was a different kind of war—a war for hearts and minds.

The sensational CPUSA trials lasted almost a year, from November 1948 until October 1949. The prosecution's case was flimsy, based on the defendants' beliefs rather than any overt acts they committed. During the course of the proceedings, Communist party members espoused their philosophy at every opportunity. CPUSA General Secretary Eugene Dennis represented himself without a lawyer so that he could utter speeches to the jury without filtering his message through an attorney.[196]

Communists also targeted government officials in a sustained harassment campaign designed to convince the government to abandon its case. The trial judge, Harold Medina, a former Columbia University law professor who had only recently joined the bench when the case commenced, was a prominent target. After newspapers reported the apparent suicide of US Secretary of Defense James V. Forrestal in May 1949, the judge received messages urging him to jump from a window in a tall building, exactly as Forrestal had done. Medina was unnerved by the harassment, but he insisted, "I will not be intimidated." He stayed through to the bitter end until the Communists were convicted in due course.[197]

The defendants appealed to the US Court of Appeals for the Second Circuit. Judge Learned Hand wrote an opinion rejecting the petitioners' claim that the Smith Act violated their First Amendment free speech rights. The US Supreme Court agreed to hear the case.[198]

The Justices were troubled by the free speech implications of *Dennis,* but a 6 to 2 majority upheld the convictions. Writing for the majority, Chief Justice Vinson quoted Judge Hand's opinion: "In each case we must ask whether the gravity of the 'evil,' discounted by its improbability, justifies such invasion of free speech as necessary to avoid the danger." Although an imminent threat was not present, in time the defendants would engage in overt acts because their ideology called for action. "Their conspiracy to organize the Communist Party and to teach and advocate the overthrow of the Government of the United States by force and violence created a 'clear and present danger' of an attempt to overthrow the Government by force and violence," the chief justice concluded. "They were properly and constitutionally convicted for violation of the Smith Act." Six justices believed that the "evil" of Communism had to be suppressed even if free speech suffered.[199]

In an eloquent dissent, Justice Hugo Black could find no clear and present danger. Being a Communist does not present an imminent danger of lawless action. He presciently lamented, "There is hope, however, that in calmer times, when present pressures, passions and fears subside, this or some later Court will restore the First Amendment liberties to the high preferred place where they belong in a free society." The cure, he believed, was worse than the disease.[200]

Justice Douglas agreed. In a separate dissent, he wrote, "If this were a case where those who claimed protection under the First Amendment were teaching the techniques of sabotage, the assassination of the President, the filching of documents from public files, the planting of bombs, the art of street warfare, and the like, I would have no doubts. The freedom to speak is not absolute; the teaching of methods of terror and other seditious conduct should be beyond the pale along with obscenity and immorality." Yet the *Dennis* defendants were only preaching unpopular, perhaps offensive ideas. They were not urging listeners to engage immediately in unlawful activities.[201]

Robert G. Thompson, formerly a decorated army officer turned Communist, and Benjamin J. Davis Jr., a black lawyer and New York City councilman expelled for his Communist ties, were two of the many defendants in the Smith Act trials of Communist party leaders. Thompson and Davis are shown in 1949 leaving the federal courthouse in New York City surrounded by supporters. Courtesy of the Library of Congress and the *World Telegram & Sun*, C.M. Stieglitz, photographer.

Yates v. United States

Justice Black's "Calmer times" occurred six years later in *Yates v. United States*, a 1957 case decided in conjunction with *Richmond v. United States* and *Schneiderman v. United States*. Although judges and justices typically claim to base their decisions on the law without considering evidence outside of the case, external events cannot help playing a role in decision-making. By 1957, Communism was far less menacing than it had seemed less than a decade earlier. Stalin died in 1953. The Korean conflict ended that same year. Red-baiting US Senator Joseph McCarthy, a strident demagogue who reveled in the attention he received from capriciously spreading rumor and innuendo

that smeared his enemies as Communists, had been exposed as a fraud. In addition, personnel changes on the US Supreme Court ensured that the judiciary was less reactionary than it had been in the late 1940s and early 1950s.[202]

In *Yates*, fourteen Communist party members were convicted under the Smith Act. This time, the high court narrowly construed the statute, requiring "concrete speech urging action and specific intent," not merely abstract words advocating the desirability of overthrowing the government. Announced on the same day as *Watkins v. United States*, which limited congressional authority to investigate individuals' private affairs with unfettered discretion, the *Yates* case was denounced by some law-and-order advocates as a victory for Communists and subversives. Anti-Communists vehemently lambasted the court for its "Red Monday" decisions, which they believed were detrimental to national security. Supporters hailed the opinions as a victory for civil liberties and an end to the Communist hysteria so prevalent in the 1940s and 1950s. Journalist I. F. Stone remarked that Monday, June 17, 1957—the day the court announced its decisions in *Yates* and *Watkins*—"will go down in the history books as the day on which the Supreme Court irreparably crippled the witch hunt."[203]

Justice John Marshall Harlan II wrote the majority opinion. He claimed to be interpreting the Smith Act, but his verbal maneuvering to distinguish *Yates* from *Dennis* impressed some observers as a semantics shell game. Harlan argued that advocating unlawful conduct, as the *Yates* defendants had done, was not punishable unless the advocacy set forth specific, concrete action. Unlike Justice Holmes and others who followed the "clear and present danger" test, Harlan was less concerned about the immediacy of danger than he was about the specificity of danger. *Dennis* had assumed that Communists by virtue of their affiliation with the party advocated the violent overthrow of the US government, but *Yates* rejected the assumption.[204]

For all intents and purposes, the *Yates* decision destroyed the Smith Act as a means of prosecuting undesirable persons who express distasteful opinions. Harlan's requirement that prosecutors prove specific, concrete acts in furtherance of a conspiracy imposed an insurmountable evidentiary obstacle for a majority of prosecutors. In most

instances involving the CPUSA, party members preached a Marxist-Leninist doctrine that Communism eventually will destroy capitalism, and they often expressed a fervent desire that the day would arrive sooner rather than later, but they seldom articulated a plan of action to hasten the Communist revolution. The statute remains on the books as of this writing, but it no longer serves as a useful tool for political oppression.[205]

Chapter 5

INTERNMENT OF JAPANESE-AMERICANS DURING WORLD WAR II

The very fact that no sabotage has taken place to date is a disturbing and confirming indication that such action will be taken.

—GENERAL JOHN L. DEWITT,
FINAL REPORT: JAPANESE EVACUATION FROM THE WEST COAST, FEBRUARY 14, 1942[206]

On December 7, 1941, Japan launched a surprise attack on the US naval base at Pearl Harbor on the Hawaiian island of Oahu, decimating the American Pacific fleet. The following day, President Franklin D. Roosevelt asked a joint session of Congress for a formal declaration of war. "Yesterday, December 7, 1941—a date which will live in infamy—the United States of America was suddenly and deliberately attacked by naval and air forces of the Empire of Japan," he thundered. "The United States was at peace with that nation, and, at the solicitation of Japan, was still in conversation with its government and its emperor looking toward the maintenance of peace in the Pacific." In a speech lasting slightly more than seven minutes, the president outlined his case for war, concluding with a stark request: "I ask that the Congress declare that since the unprovoked and dastardly attack by Japan on Sunday, December 7, 1941, a state of war has existed between the United States and the Japanese Empire." Thirty-three minutes after the speech ended, an outraged Congress provided the president with the support he needed. The US Senate voted unanimously in favor of war while the House of Representatives voted 388

to 1. Montana Republican Jeannette Rankin cast the negative vote, as she had done against a declaration of war in 1917. "As a woman, I can't go to war and I refuse to send anyone else," she said.[207]

Following the attack, military officers worried that the Japanese might invade the West Coast of the United States. To prepare for that possibility, the president signed proclamations directing the Federal Bureau of Investigation to arrest aliens deemed to be "dangerous to public peace or safety." Some two thousand names of Issei, or first-generation Japanese immigrants to the United States, appeared on a list compiled by the Justice Department as potentially subversive. The FBI arrested these suspicious individuals. Afterward, the Bureau conducted warrantless searches of Japanese households without probable cause, but their searches uncovered precious few clues about plans for sabotage or fifth-column support for the empire of Japan. The US navy beached boats owned by Japanese Americans to prevent them from aiding the enemy. In the meantime, the Treasury Department froze the assets of Japanese nationals and suspended their licenses to sell produce.[208]

For all the frenetic activity among government agents, the American public remained surprisingly calm in the weeks following Pearl Harbor. In the absence of mass hysteria, the president's military advisors were divided on whether the Japanese population on the West Coast posed a serious threat. A report prepared by Republican businessman Curtis B. Munson during the fall of 1941 on the "Japanese Situation in Hawaii" concluded that the overwhelming majority of Japanese living in Hawaii and the West Coast were loyal to the United States. Navy Secretary Frank Knox toured Hawaii shortly after the attack and formed a different opinion. On December 15, after delivering a report to the president, Knox informed the press he had "recommended to the President and Secretary of War" that the government "take all the aliens out of Hawaii and send them off to another island." Although some administration officials and military planners agreed with Knox's assessment and mulled over the desirability and logistics of detaining persons of Japanese ancestry, initially no groundswell appeared to propel the government into taking swift or decisive action. Even FBI Director J. Edgar Hoover, not a man noted for his concern

over civil liberties, refused to support the navy secretary's findings. As December 1941 wound to a close, the American military struggled to cope with devastating losses, but no one within the administration acted to detain Japanese living in the United States.[209]

The Internment Decision

Roosevelt's men scrambled to shore up homeland defenses and place the nation on a wartime footing, clearly their top priorities in the dark days of December 1941. Plans also circulated for long-term changes. One proposal, contained in a memorandum titled "Program for West Coast Japanese," called for Nisei, or "American-born Japanese," to assume control of Issei property under the supervision of a custodian. The thinking was that persons born in the United States would be more likely to be loyal to the land of their birth. They could be counted on, under proper direction and surveillance, to police elders who had not been born in the country and who might be more sympathetic to the Japanese empire. Named for Curtis B. Munson and Lieutenant Commander Kenneth Ringle, the plan briefly attracted attention at the highest levels of government. President Roosevelt initially seemed receptive, although he quickly lost interest. Compared with what came later, the Munson-Ringle plan was relatively benign, for it did not require the removal of any citizens from their homes or their internment behind barricades. Nonetheless, it was a revolutionary idea in one sense. The scheme assumed that private property owned by persons of a particular racial lineage could be placed under government control in a time of war without normal due process considerations.[210]

American policy toward Japanese living in the country changed quickly in the new year. Historians continue to debate the factors that shaped the administration's stance. One school of thought suggests that civic organizations such as the Los Angeles Chamber of Commerce and the American Legion publicly raised the alarm, stoking the fires of racial prejudice against persons of Japanese descent. Other scholars contend that military planners reached their own conclusions independently, based on wartime exigencies without considering outside pressures.

Whatever the impetus, a group of military officers called for plans to counter an expected uprising among West Coast Japanese sympathetic to America's enemies. Leading the charge was a career army officer, General John L. DeWitt. Sixty-one years old that December day when the surprise attack occurred, the general assumed the daunting task of establishing a Western defense should the enemy storm the beaches at Santa Barbara. He initially balked at the thought of interning most or all of the one hundred seventeen thousand Japanese living on the West Coast. The logistics involved in such an operation would consume valuable resources that might be put to better use preparing for other wartime contingencies. Dismissing wholesale evacuations as "damned nonsense," he preferred a system of registration and "pass-permits" for alien control.[211]

As December gave way to January, paranoia set in. DeWitt nervously awaited an imminent invasion that never occurred. He remembered standing in San Francisco when the air raid sirens sounded the alarm following the attack on Pearl Harbor. He was disgusted at how ill prepared the city defenders were after a report indicated that thirty-five Japanese airplanes had been spotted over the city. When San Francisco was not bombed or invaded, DeWitt intimated that perhaps a few well-placed bombs would have been exactly what the United States government needed to destroy civilian complacency.[212]

The general came to believe that the nonsense he had dismissed two months earlier wasn't so "damned" after all. Perhaps he changed his thinking because civilian authorities had dragged their feet in investigating Japanese residents. Attorney General Francis Biddle had authorized a series of "spot" raids, but he had not allowed Justice Department officials or FBI agents to engage in a massive campaign of warrantless searches. Perhaps DeWitt was reacting to the rising hue and cry from civilian groups, including the Los Angeles Chamber of Commerce, which issued the first major call for the removal of Japanese-Americans from the City of Angels. Perhaps DeWitt was tapping into a long-standing antipathy toward "Orientals" in general, and Japanese in particular, that extended back to the nineteenth century when immigrants came from Asia to the United States seeking improved living conditions and found themselves relegated to second-class citizenship.

However his thinking evolved, General DeWitt became an enthusiastic proponent of Japanese internment.[213]

The next order of business was to convince President Roosevelt. He had been consumed with strategic planning at the highest levels in the weeks since Congress had declared war. After initially suggesting he would refrain from acting against Japanese nationals, Roosevelt turned his attention elsewhere. In the meantime, his wife, Eleanor, expressed concern that people of Asian descent were victims of discrimination, and the president took note. He could be sentimental on occasion. He also could be ruthless, for Franklin Delano Roosevelt was first and foremost a political creature. A man does not win election to the highest office in the land four times without possessing a high degree of political savvy.

When he considered the matter again toward the end of January 1942, the president was confronted with conflicting reports. Yes, his wife and the Munson-Ringle plan counseled moderation, but their voices soon were drowned in a cacophony of hysteria. The State of California's Joint Immigration Committee issued a scathing report about the behavior of "treacherous Japs" who served as fifth columns; that is, they were undermining the nation from within by providing useful intelligence to agents of the Japanese military as part of a dastardly plan to invade the West Coast. Newspapermen, always anxious to report dramatic stories, peppered their columns with unconfirmed reports of Japanese espionage. The Japanese undoubtedly existed as "enemy agents," Damon Runyon reported from the pages of the Hearst newspapers.[214]

Mail arrived at the White House imploring the president to deal with the "Jap menace" before it was too late. "Kindly give some thought to ridding our beloved Country of these Japs who hold no love or loyalty to our God, our ideals or our traditions, or our Government," read one typical plea. Other citizens implied that treachery was already afoot in the land, even if the writer could offer no more proof than General DeWitt's general belief that the lack of credible information was all the more compelling because of the paucity of data.[215]

Politicians recognized a groundswell when they saw one—or at least the opportunity to create popular support for mass hysteria, which

would become a self-fulfilling prophesy. Conservative Congressman Leland Ford from Los Angeles dispatched a telegram to Secretary of State Cordell Hull complaining of the Japanese and "the treacherous way in which they do things." Later, he wrote to Secretary of War Henry L. Stimson, Attorney General Biddle, and Secretary of the Navy Knox arguing in favor of evacuation and internment of Japanese. In subsequent testimony before Congress, Congressman Ford presented the ideal trial-by-ordeal scenario. Loyal Japanese could prove their loyalty by submitting to evacuation and internment without objection. Any person of Japanese ancestry who refused to comply with an order of the US government to abandon their homes and property and live behind bars voluntarily was, by definition, suspect and unpatriotic. The term "Catch-22" had not yet been coined, but it certainly applied to Ford's tortured logic.[216]

A report issued late in January 1942 provided additional support for exercising a heavy hand against the Japanese. Chaired by US Supreme Court Justice Owen Roberts, the Commission on Pearl Harbor was charged with the duty "to ascertain and report the facts relating to the attack made by Japanese armed forces upon the Territory of Hawaii on December 7, 1941." Roosevelt had established the committee on December 18 to examine the causes of the surprise attack and provide recommendations on shoring up defenses. Justice Roberts met twice with the president—on January 18 and 24—before releasing the report to the public. Although no record of their conversations exists, Roberts later spoke of Japanese disloyalty and the need to handle the "menace" using a military solution because the FBI had not effectively addressed the problem. Presumably, Roberts told Roosevelt something similar, even if he couched it in politically palatable terms for the president.

Then as now, official Washington was intent on assigning blame for the failure to be prepared in the event of an attack. The Roberts Commission explained in its report, "The purposes of the required inquiry and report are to provide bases for sound decisions whether any derelictions of duty or errors of judgment on the part of United States Army or Navy personnel contributed to such successes as were achieved by the enemy on the occasion mentioned, and, if so, what

these derelictions or errors were, and who were responsible therefor." Justice Roberts and the four committee members from the US military found that Admiral Husband E. Kimmel and General Walter C. Short were guilty of "dereliction of duty" for failing to take reports of a possible attack seriously. The Roberts Commission, as it came to be known, did not excoriate the Japanese living in Hawaii, but commission members asserted that "spies" had contributed to the success of the Pearl Harbor attack. "There were, prior to December 7, 1941, Japanese spies on the island of Oahu," the report concluded. "Some were Japanese consular agents and others were persons having no open relations with the Japanese foreign service. These spies collected and, through various channels transmitted, information to the Japanese Empire respecting the military and naval establishments and dispositions on the island."[217]

The language of the report was more measured and nuanced than Justice Roberts's private remarks, but newspapers seldom publicized the finer points. Gone were the distinctions between "Japanese consular agents and other persons having no open relations with the Japanese foreign service" and Issei and Nisei residents. As far as many newspaper reporters and readers could see, possibly subversive activity by Japanese persons could occur whether a formal connection existed with agents of the Japanese government. Declaring that "I hate the Japanese, and that goes for all of them," columnist Henry M. McLemore wrote a vituperative column in the *San Francisco Examiner* on January 29, 1942. "I am for the immediate removal of every Japanese on the West coast to a point deep in the interior. I don't mean a nice part of the interior either. Herd 'em up, pack 'em off and give 'em the inside room in the badlands. Let 'em be pinched, hurt, hungry and dead up against it." Lest anyone doubt his racist intentions, McLemore explained that "If making one million innocent Japanese uncomfortable would prevent one scheming Japanese from costing the life of one American boy, then let the million innocents suffer." Reactionary columnist Westbrook Pegler echoed the sentiment when he wrote, "The Japanese in California should be under armed guard to the last man and woman right now and to hell with habeas corpus until the danger is over."[218]

On and on it went, with citizens, reporters, and prominent elected officials piling on, adding to the hysteria of early 1942. Even Liberal Democrat Culbert Olson, governor of California, jumped on the bandwagon. "Since the publication of the Roberts Report," he told General DeWitt, loyal California citizens "feel that they are living in the midst of enemies. They don't trust the Japanese, none of them."[219]

It would have taken a man of forceful resolve, unflinching character, and an unwavering commitment to constitutional protections to resist the onslaught of negative public opinion against Japanese-Americans. Since John L. DeWitt possessed none of these qualities in abundance, he soon adjusted his thinking. The more he thought about it, the more the general officer became convinced that Japanese living inside the United States were up to no good. The man who had fretted over the practical difficulties of rounding up tens of thousands of potentially disloyal persons became convinced that internment was the preferred course of action. In a February 1942 recommendation dripping with racism and twisted logic, DeWitt observed:

> The Japanese race is an enemy race and while many second and third generation Japanese born on United State soil, possessed of United States citizenship, have become "Americanized," the racial strains are undiluted. To conclude otherwise is to expect that children born of white parents on Japanese soil sever all racial affinity and become loyal Japanese subjects, ready to fight and, if necessary, to die for Japan in a war against the nation of their parents. That Japan is allied with Germany and Italy in this struggle is not ground for assuming that any Japanese, barred from assimilation by convention as he is, though born and raised in the United States, will not turn against this nation when the final test of loyalty comes. It, therefore, follows that along the vital Pacific Coast over 112,000 potential enemies, of Japanese extraction, are at large today. There are indications that these were organized and ready for concerted action at a favorable opportunity.[220]

The good general saved the most convoluted reasoning for last. "The very fact that no sabotage has taken place to date is a disturbing

and confirming indication that such action will be taken," he argued. The lack of evidence, in his view, was more worrisome than credible, actionable intelligence. The comment might serve as a motto for all paranoids who fear a lurking, heretofore unknown subversive threat.[221]

A series of meetings among government officials in January and February 1942 led to President Roosevelt's decision to intern Japanese-Americans. As usual, Attorney General Francis Biddle recommended caution, but he faced an uphill battle. Secretary of War Stimson was particularly insistent that a Japanese invasion of the West Coast was a distinct possibility. As Japanese military forces marched through the Pacific arena mostly unopposed, Stimson was convinced it was only a matter of time before the enemy turned its attention back to the United States. If the US government did not take immediate steps to neutralize Japanese fifth columns, the battle for California, Oregon, and Washington might be over before it started. On February 11, 1942, he sent a memorandum asking whether "the President was willing to authorize us to move Japanese citizens as well as aliens from restricted areas?" Unable to schedule a meeting in person, Stimson spoke to the president on the telephone. Acknowledging "there will probably be some repercussions but it has got to be dictated by military necessity," FDR instructed his war secretary to do whatever he thought was best. Stimson thought evacuation and internment were best.[222]

Through all the fits and starts, the vacillation and second-guessing, the administration had reached a decision. Military necessity supposedly required that tens of thousands of persons of Japanese ancestry, many of whom were children, must be rounded up and herded into camps to ensure the safety and security of the US homeland. If their constitutional rights were violated as a direct consequence of this action, so be it. Security trumps liberty in times of crisis.[223]

Executive Action and Its Consequences

On February 19, 1942, the president issued Executive Order 9066 identifying "exclusion zones" and "military areas" "from which any or all persons may be excluded." Although the executive order did not specifically mention a particular nationality, it became the basis for a subsequent decision to exclude persons of Japanese ancestry from

the West Coast, essentially all of California and much of Oregon, Washington, and Arizona. Roosevelt eventually issued Presidential Proclamations 2525, 2526, and 2527 designating Japanese, German, and Italian nationals as enemy aliens.[224]

Historians are divided on the reasons why the president ultimately signed the executive order. Perhaps Americans' deep, long-simmering antipathy toward Asians was a factor. The administration might have feared an imminent attack on the mainland, and the possibility that some Japanese living in the country would provide intelligence to the assailants. Given the increasing popularity of relocating the Japanese, Roosevelt may have allowed political calculations to take precedence over constitutional rights. As is often the case when a traumatic event occurs, Americans reacted viscerally. They sought a clear explanation and a convenient scapegoat for what happened. Only distance and hindsight allow for a dispassionate assessment of what happened, and why.[225]

The executive order did not specify how persons would be excluded from military zones. It was possible for Japanese-Americans to move voluntarily, and some affluent persons did exactly that. In many instances, however, the people affected by the order did not possess the financial means to relocate without assistance, assuming they agreed to comply in the first place. Moreover, officials in neighboring states issued statements that Japanese-Americans were not welcome there. With few resources devoted to relocating and few places to go even if they decided to move, Japanese-Americans were placed in an untenable position.[226]

It was clear the army would have to intervene. Voluntary exclusion simply was not effective. On March 26, 1942, General DeWitt revoked travel permits for Japanese-Americans living in exclusion zones and ordered the populace to wait for removal by the army. DeWitt and his men divided the excluded areas into military districts. Persons of Japanese descent living in the districts received instructions through a series of civilian exclusion orders telling them when and where to report for registration. After registration rolls were compiled, army officers ordered affected persons to prepare for evacuation day. Families could bring personal effects such as toiletries, cups and bowls, and extra

In this April 1942 photograph, Japanese-Americans line up in San Francisco, California, to register with the US government four months after the attack on Pearl Harbor. Courtesy of the Library of Congress.

clothing, but they had to leave behind pets, furniture, automobiles, and real property. They were told to sell their property, hand it over to whites, or abandon it. Later, the US government allowed Japanese families to store packaged household goods in government warehouses with no promise of safe return at war's end.[227]

The task of registering Japanese-Americans and arranging their evacuation was only part of the government's problem. Faced with the logistical challenge of what to do with evacuees, the military resolved to construct a series of internment facilities. Even today, the designation of the camps stirs controversy because of their euphemistic names. Several types existed. The first, known as "Civilian Assembly Centers," were temporary camps, often located at a horse track, where the Nisei were housed immediately after they were removed from their homes.

Eventually, displaced persons were shuffled into "relocation centers," a convenient euphemism for internment camps. If evacuees submitted to the assignment without complaint, they remained in a specific relocation center for months or even years. Government agents sent disruptive Japanese-Americans to US Department of Justice detention camps, Citizen Isolation Centers, federal prisons, or US army facilities.[228]

Long-term plans were needed to police the camps. On March 18, 1942, the president signed Executive Order 9102 creating the War Relocation Authority (WRA), a civilian agency tasked with operating the camps. Milton S. Eisenhower, General Dwight D. Eisenhower's younger brother, served as the first WRA director. The agency operated from March 1942 until June 30, 1946.[229]

Eisenhower did not remain long at the WRA. In June, after only ninety days on the job, he resigned. Philosophically opposed to the relocation decision, he had argued that women and children should not be subject to military evacuation. He lost that battle. After the Japanese began arriving at the hastily constructed camps, Eisenhower desperately sought for a productive way to use their time. He believed that Japanese-American citizens who had been studying at American universities should be allowed to continue their studies. He also thought that able-bodied men and women could be employed on nearby farms that lacked a ready source of labor owing to the absence of men who were fighting or otherwise assisting in the war effort. Concerned at the loss of valuable property, Eisenhower lobbied Federal Reserve Banks to protect Japanese homes and businesses left behind. He also appealed to governors and elected officials in states and locales far removed from the exclusion zones to allow Japanese-Americans to resettle there to avoid incarceration. In light of the animus that many whites felt toward Japanese persons, Eisenhower faced insurmountable obstacles. He reluctantly resigned when he realized he would not be able to administer the WRA as he saw fit.[230]

The WRA eventually operated ten Relocation Centers, eighteen Civilian Assembly Centers, eight Justice Department detention centers, three Citizen Isolation Centers, three federal prisons, and eighteen US army facilities for Japanese-American detainees. Manzanar

This photograph shows the Manzanar War Relocation Center located near the ironically-named Independence, California, in wintertime. Courtesy of the Library of Congress.

Relocation Center in California was the most infamous of the WRA relocation camps. By the end of the war, approximately thirty-one thousand suspected enemy aliens and their families had been interned. Approximately one hundred twenty thousand persons were held in the camps at one time or another.[231]

Eisenhower's successor, Dillon S. Myer, was an expert in agriculture, having served in the Agricultural Adjustment Administration and the US Department of Agriculture before being tapped to head up the WRA. Stepping into his new role in June 1942, he served for four years until the agency was dissolved. Myer came to see the internment as a mistake, but he had a job to do. Administering the camps as best he could, he recognized the need to resettle Japanese prisoners after the war. To that end, he authorized a program for Nisei to work outside the camps provided they were not employed in or near the exclusion zones. If persons living near the camps could see the Japanese laboring mightily, later they might accept such workers into society and smooth the postwar transition.[232]

After learning of the resettlement program, the US House of Representatives Un-American Activities Committee (known as the Dies Committee, named after its chairman, Congressman Martin Dies Jr. of Texas) called Myer to testify during the summer of 1943. Rumors had circulated that the WRA was "coddling" Japanese prisoners and the camps had become hotbeds of anti-American activity. Legislation was advancing in the US Senate to abolish the WRA and transfer its duties to the War Department. Myer skillfully rebutted each charge leveled by the Dies Committee. With the help of administration supporters, the bill to undermine the WRA died in the Senate. Unfortunately for Japanese-Americans, the high-profile charges, although unfounded, continued to outrage a public already predisposed to view Asians as somehow less than patriotic.[233]

War Relocation Authority (WRA) Director Dillon S. Myer accompanied First Lady Eleanor Roosevelt on a tour of the Gila River War Relocation Center near Phoenix, Arizona, on April 23, 1943. Courtesy of the National Archives & Records Administration.

Court Cases

Because so many Japanese forced to move from their homes were US citizens and presumably entitled to due process of law, it was inevitable that the courts would become involved. The first major case to reach the US Supreme Court on appeal involved Gordon Kiyoshi Hirabayashi, a twenty-three-year-old graduate of the University of Washington. When General DeWitt issued a curfew for enemy aliens on March 24, 1942, young Hirabayashi was inclined to obey. In the aftermath of DeWitt's order, authorities issued Civilian Exclusion Order No. 57, dated May 10, 1942, directing that after noon on May 16, 1942, all persons of Japanese ancestry, both alien and non-alien, would be excluded from a specified portion of Military Area No. 1 in Seattle, including Hirabayashi's residence. A designated member of each family affected was directed to report on May 11 or May 12 to a designated Civil Control Station in Seattle.

Hirabayashi deliberately failed to appear, as ordered, on May 11 or 12. Instead, he surrendered to the FBI on May 16 and acknowledged his failure to comply with the curfew. He also announced he would not comply with the upcoming removal order. As expected, officials jailed Hirabayashi while he awaited trial.

After five months, he was tried for violating the curfew and refusing to obey the removal order. As a defense, Hirabayashi contended he was an American citizen who had never professed or displayed allegiance to the Empire of Japan. He also argued that the curfew was an unconstitutional delegation of congressional authority. The jury deliberated for ten minutes before delivering a guilty verdict on both counts, and the judge sentenced Hirabayashi to prison for three months on each count, with the sentences to run concurrently. Afterward, the defendant appealed to the Ninth Circuit Court of Appeals. When the court declined to hear the case, he petitioned the US Supreme Court.[234]

After granting *certiorari*, the high court heard oral arguments on May 10 and 11, 1943, almost a year to the day after Hirabayashi was required to appear before the Seattle Civil Control Station. In his majority opinion, Chief Justice Harlan Fiske Stone wrote, "We are immediately concerned with the question whether it is within the

constitutional power of the national government, through the joint action of Congress and the Executive, to impose this restriction as an emergency war measure." A majority of the justices believed that the law was constitutional.

"Distinctions between citizens solely because of their ancestry are by their very nature odious to a free people whose institutions are founded upon the doctrine of equality," the chief justice acknowledged. "For that reason, legislative classification or discrimination based on race alone has often been held to be a denial of equal protection." Yet war changes everything, including constitutional protections. "We may assume that these considerations would be controlling here were it not for the fact that the danger of espionage and sabotage, in time of war and of threatened invasion, calls upon the military authorities to scrutinize every relevant fact bearing on the loyalty of populations in the danger areas," Stone observed.[235]

The chief justice had reiterated a point that recurs throughout American history. Due process of law is an important component of the US legal system, but it is not sacrosanct. In times of war, distinctions that otherwise would be "odious" can be made in the interests of national security. "We cannot say that these facts and circumstances, considered in the particular war setting, could afford no ground for differentiating citizens of Japanese ancestry from other groups in the United States," the chief justice explained. "The fact alone that attack on our shores was threatened by Japan rather than another enemy power set these citizens apart from others who have no particular associations with Japan." In short, denying persons of Japanese descent their civil liberties was justified by exigencies of war.[236]

Justice William O. Douglas, a well-known civil libertarian, might have been expected to issue a dissent, but he, too, recognized the extraordinary circumstances that required speedy action on the part of military officials. "It is true that we might now say that there was ample time to handle the problem on the individual rather than the group basis. But military decisions must be made without the benefit of hindsight. The orders must be judged as of the date when the decision to issue them was made," Douglas offered in a separate concurrence. "To say that the military in such cases should take the time to

weed out the loyal from the others would be to assume that the nation could afford to have them take the time to do it. But as the opinion of the Court makes clear, speed and dispatch may be of the essence. Certainly we cannot say that those charged with the defense of the nation should have procrastinated until investigations and hearings were completed. At that time further delay might indeed have seemed to be wholly incompatible with military responsibilities."[237]

Justice Wiley B. Rutledge also filed a concurrence—he argued that the question of whether a military officer can exercise discretion is subject to judicial review—but it was Justice Frank Murphy's concurring opinion that invited speculation.[238] Murphy originally intended to issue a dissenting opinion, but Justice Felix Frankfurter persuaded him to present a united front to improve the legitimacy of the majority opinion. In deference to Frankfurter's entreaties, Murphy called his opinion a "concurrence," but it employed the powerful, uncompromising language of a dissent.[239]

War, he contended, does not change the applicability of the US Constitution. Murphy was disturbed because the government could round up "suspects" whose only "crime" was their lineage. "Distinctions based on color and ancestry are utterly inconsistent with our traditions and ideals," he insisted. "They are at variance with the principles for which we are now waging war." In an eloquent passage that would resonate with critics of the administration's decision in the years to come, Murphy equated the American relocation effort with actions undertaken by the totalitarian regimes of Europe:

> Today is the first time, so far as I am aware, that we have sustained a substantial restriction of the personal liberty of citizens of the United States based upon the accident of race or ancestry. Under the curfew order here challenged no less than 70,000 American citizens have been placed under a special ban and deprived of their liberty because of their particular racial inheritance. In this sense it bears a melancholy resemblance to the treatment accorded to members of the Jewish race in Germany and in other parts of Europe. The result is the creation in this country of two classes of citizens for the purposes

of a critical and perilous hour—to sanction discrimination between groups of United States citizens on the basis of ancestry. In my opinion this goes to the very brink of constitutional power.[240]

For all the moral force he brought to the case, Gordon Hirabayashi could not overcome the Justices' fears, shared by many white Americans, that an enemy within lurked somewhere among all those strange-looking peoples huddled together along the West Coast. Even Justice Murphy's impassioned defense of civil liberties could not overcome a plea of wartime necessity.[241]

Hirabayashi v. United States and its companion case, *Yasui v. United States,* involved challenges to the curfew imposed on Japanese living in the exclusion zones. Another landmark decision, *Korematsu v. United States,* challenged the entire relocation procedure. *Korematsu* subsequently became one of the most infamous Supreme Court cases in American history, earning a special brand of opprobrium reserved for the court's most misguided opinions, including *Dred Scott v. Sandford* and *Plessy v. Ferguson.*[242]

The facts were similar to the *Hirabayashi* case except that the defendant in the latter case, Fred Toyosaburo Korematsu, did not turn himself in for prosecution as an act of civil disobedience. At the time he was arrested, Korematsu was a twenty-three-year-old Japanese-American living in California. He was walking down the street with his girlfriend in San Leandro, California, on May 30, 1942, well past the time when he should have reported for evacuation from the area pursuant to Civilian Exclusion Order No. 34. Korematsu had taken great pains to escape prosecution. He had submitted to plastic surgery in hopes of disguising his Asian features. When police officers stopped him for questioning that day, he claimed that his name was Clyde Sarah and he was a citizen of Spanish-Hawaiian origin. The attempted subterfuge did not fool his interlocutors. Korematsu reluctantly confessed he was Japanese. He claimed that his family was confined in the Tanforan Assembly Center in San Bruno, twelve miles south of San Francisco. Korematsu hoped to remain free so he could work and save enough money to move to the Midwest with his girlfriend.[243]

With his plot foiled, Korematsu was arrested, tried, and convicted of violating the law. He appealed the conviction to the US Supreme Court. On December 18, 1944, the US Supreme Court upheld Korematsu's conviction by a six-to-three vote. Writing for the court majority, Justice Hugo Black explained that wartime activities sometimes require extreme actions to protect national security. "Korematsu was not excluded from the Military Area because of hostility to him or his race," Black wrote in an opinion that has been lambasted for its duplicity. "He was excluded because we are at war with the Japanese Empire, because the properly constituted military authorities feared an invasion of our West Coast and felt constrained to take proper security measures, because they decided that the military urgency of the situation demanded that all citizens of Japanese ancestry be segregated from the West Coast temporarily, and, finally, because Congress, reposing its confidence in this time of war in our military leaders—as inevitably it must—determined that they should have the power to do just this." Justice Frankfurter concurred in the court's judgment.[244]

Unlike the *Hirabayashi* case, the high court could not present a united front in *Korematsu*. Three justices—Owen Roberts, Frank Murphy, and Robert Jackson—dissented. Each man objected to the idea that the US government could round up persons and involuntarily incarcerate them in an internment camp based on their race. Roberts argued this was not a case of keeping people off the streets, as in *Hirabayashi*, but "it is the case of convicting a citizen as a punishment for not submitting to imprisonment in a concentration camp, based on his ancestry, and solely because of his ancestry, without evidence or inquiry concerning his loyalty and good disposition towards the United States." Accordingly, "I think the indisputable facts exhibit a clear violation of Constitutional rights."[245]

Justice Robert H. Jackson, soon to take a leave of absence from the court to serve as US chief of counsel for the prosecution of Nazi war criminals at the Nuremberg Trials in Germany, observed that "Korematsu was born on our soil, of parents born in Japan. The Constitution makes him a citizen of the United States by nativity, and a citizen of California by residence. No claim is made that he is not loyal to this country. There is no suggestion that, apart from the matter

involved here, he is not law-abiding and well disposed. Korematsu, however, has been convicted of an act not commonly a crime. It consists merely of being present in the state whereof he is a citizen, near the place where he was born, and where all his life he has lived." His only crime was being the child of Japanese parents. "Now, if any fundamental assumption underlies our system, it is that guilt is personal and not inheritable. Even if all of one's antecedents had been convicted of treason, the Constitution forbids its penalties to be visited upon him, for it provides that no attainder of treason shall work corruption of blood, or forfeiture except during the life of the person attainted. But here is an attempt to make an otherwise innocent act a crime merely because this prisoner is the son of parents as to whom he had no choice, and belongs to a race from which there is no way to resign." He concluded by arguing that the prisoner should be discharged.[246]

Justice Murphy penned another eloquent opinion questioning the necessity of the government's action against the Japanese. This time, it was written as a dissent. "This exclusion of 'all persons of Japanese ancestry, both alien and non-alien,' from the Pacific Coast area on a plea of military necessity in the absence of martial law ought not to be approved. Such exclusion goes over 'the very brink of constitutional power,' and falls into the ugly abyss of racism," he began. In a stirring passage, he exposed the administration's actions as a constitutionally impermissible abuse of power:

> The judicial test of whether the Government, on a plea of military necessity, can validly deprive an individual of any of his constitutional rights is whether the deprivation is reasonably related to a public danger that is so "immediate, imminent, and impending" as not to admit of delay and not to permit the intervention of ordinary constitutional processes to alleviate the danger. Civilian Exclusion Order No. 34, banishing from a prescribed area of the Pacific Coast "all persons of Japanese ancestry, both alien and non-alien," clearly does not meet that test. Being an obvious racial discrimination, the order deprives all those within its scope of the equal protection of the laws as guaranteed by the Fifth Amendment. It further deprives

these individuals of their constitutional rights to live and work where they will, to establish a home where they choose and to move about freely. In excommunicating them without benefit of hearings, this order also deprives them of all their constitutional rights to procedural due process.[247]

In time, the dissenters' views would be heralded for their strong support of civil liberties, but *Korematsu v. United States* was decided in 1944, when war raged between the United States and Japan. A majority of the Justices on the US Supreme Court, reflecting the views of many white Americans, could not set aside its wartime fears to understand the importance of constitutional protections in wartime as well as in times of peace.[248]

The Aftermath

In the decades since the internment, public opinion has evolved. Many Americans who have studied the case have denounced the circumstances as based in large measure on racial prejudice. Justice William O. Douglas, reflecting on the cases toward the end of his life, admitted that he regretted his decision in *Hirabayashi* and *Korematsu,* lamenting they were "ever on my conscience." Earl Warren served as attorney general of California in 1942 and publicly announced his support for the evacuation. He later acknowledged his error, observing that the internment of persons absent legal due process is "not in keeping with our American concept of freedom and the rights of citizens."[249]

The US Supreme Court changed course in a series of opinions. In *Ex parte Endo,* a case decided the same day as *Korematsu,* the high court held that the US government could not detain a citizen who was "concededly loyal" to the United States. *Endo* was difficult to reconcile with *Korematsu* since the court had ruled against Fred Korematsu's petition. Some commentators have suggested that because *Korematsu* involved relocation and *Endo* concerned detainment, the cases were logically consistent. Another interpretation raises a perverse scenario. Had Fred Korematsu submitted to illegal incarceration instead of attempting to avoid evacuation through subterfuge, he might have won his case.[250]

The decision about how to handle the Japanese living on the West Coast highlighted the inconsistencies and contradictions in American law and policy. With *Endo,* however, the US government moved away from the harsh racism inherent in the wartime executive orders. In *Oyama v. California,* a 1948 case, the justices struck down a portion of California's notorious Alien Land Act, which held that Asian immigrants who were "ineligible" for citizenship could not own agricultural property.[251] In *Takahashi v. Fish and Game Commission,* a case decided less than five months after *Oyama,* the court struck down a California law that restricted "alien Japanese" from obtaining a fishing license. Also in 1948, Congress enacted the Evacuation Claims Act authorizing internees who could document the loss of their property to obtain compensation from the US government. Unfortunately, the claims process was inefficient and difficult to navigate. A decade later, only twenty-six thousand of the approximately one hundred twenty thousand persons of Japanese ancestry interned during the war had received compensation. The average amount was $1,400 per person, a sum substantially lower than the value of the property confiscated or sold at a fire sale.[252]

In *Duncan v. Kahanamoku,* a military police officer, Duke Paoa Kahinu Mokoe Hulikohola Kahanamoku, arrested Lloyd C. Duncan, a civilian working with the US navy, for public intoxication. Because Hawaii was not yet an American state, the islands were governed under martial law. Duncan was tried and convicted by a military tribunal. He appealed to the US Supreme Court, which reaffirmed a Civil War-era case, *Ex Parte Milligan,* holding that a military tribunal cannot hear cases involving civilians when civilian courts are operating. Although the 1946 case did not directly concern the Japanese internment, it typically serves as a contemporaneous court opinion on the proper limits of military power over civilians.[253]

Throughout the years, other branches of the federal government also confronted the mistakes made in the frenzied days following the Pearl Harbor attack. On February 19, 1976, President Gerald R. Ford issued Proclamation 4417 to acknowledge, "We now know what we should have known then—not only was that evacuation wrong, but Japanese-Americans were and are loyal Americans." The president

noted that the celebrations marking the nation's bicentennial anniversary were appropriate to commemorate proud events in American history, but an "honest reckoning . . . must include a recognition of our national mistakes as well as our national achievements." The proclamation observed:

> February 19th is the anniversary of a sad day in American history. It was on that date in 1942, in the midst of the response to the hostilities that began on December 7, 1941, that Executive Order 9066 was issued, subsequently enforced by the criminal penalties of a statute enacted March 21, 1942, resulting in the uprooting of loyal Americans. Over one hundred thousand persons of Japanese ancestry were removed from their homes, detained in special camps, and eventually relocated.[254]

At the conclusion, President Ford proclaimed "that all authority conferred by Executive Order 9066 terminated upon the issuance of Proclamation 2714, which formally proclaimed the cessation of hostilities of World War II on December 31, 1946. I call upon the American people to affirm with me this American Promise—that we have learned from the tragedy of that long-ago experience forever to treasure liberty and justice for each individual American, and resolve that this kind of action shall never again be repeated."[255]

A presidential proclamation was a welcome acknowledgment of past injustices, but some observers believed that additional action was necessary. In 1980, the US Congress created the Commission on Wartime Relocation and Internment (CWRIC) to review the issue. On February 24, 1983, the CWRIC published a report, *Personal Justice Denied*, characterizing the internments as "unjust and motivated by racism rather than real military necessity." Members of the commission recommended reparations for victims of the program.[256]

Also in 1983, the US District Court for the Northern District of California vacated Fred Korematsu's conviction. Appearing before the court, sixty-four-year-old Korematsu uttered a simple, eloquent plea. "I would like to see the government admit that they were wrong and do something about it so this will never happen again to any American

citizen of any race, creed, or color," he said. In 1987, the Ninth Circuit Court of Appeals vacated Gordon Hirabayashi's conviction.[257]

Korematsu's wish came true when President Ronald Reagan signed the Civil Liberties Act of 1988 providing $20,000 for each surviving internee, a total of $1.2 billion dollars. The act also contained a formal

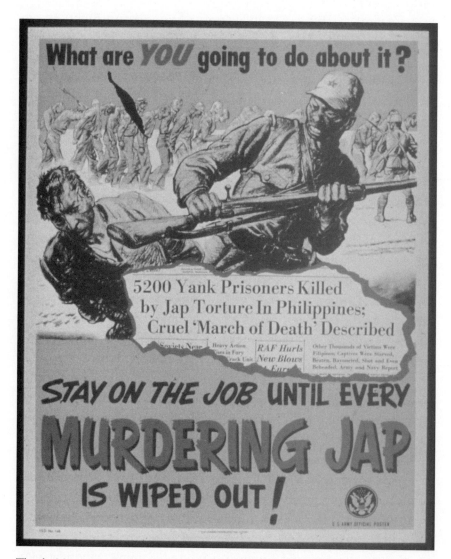

The decision to "relocate" Japanese-Americans to detention camps was possible because many Americans objectified the "murdering Jap," as this 1944 US army poster illustrates. Courtesy of the Library of Congress.

apology from the US government to Japanese-Americans. Questions about who should receive reparations and how much they should receive remained contentious. The Civil Liberties Act Amendments, enacted on September 27, 1992, appropriated $400 million in additional funding. On December 7, 1991, President George H. W. Bush issued another apology, this time on the fiftieth anniversary of the Pearl Harbor bombing. "The internment of Americans of Japanese ancestry was a great injustice, and it will never be repeated," he said.[258]

The injustice stemmed from a fear of alien persons who reputedly were hostile to the nation's values. Although some Americans had nursed an antipathy toward Asians in the prewar years, wartime propaganda contributed to the stereotype of the "murdering Jap" that somehow was not fully human. Citizens responded viscerally by objectifying persons of Japanese ancestry as the "other." Psychologically, it is easier to deny the "other" legal rights designed to protect individuals from arbitrary government action. As happens time and again, when citizens and their leaders set aside the rule of law in the interests of expediency, the reaction to subversion can be more damaging to American values than the original act. This is a lesson that Americans have never quite learned, and yet can never quite forget.[259]

Chapter 6

THE INTERNAL SECURITY ACT OF 1950 (THE MCCARRAN ACT)

To permit freedom of expression is primarily for the benefit of the majority, because it protects criticism, and criticism leads to progress.

—HARRY S. TRUMAN,

VETO MESSAGE FOR HR 9490, THE INTERNAL SECURITY BILL, SEPTEMBER 22, 1950[260]

The Internal Security Act of 1950, also known as the Subversive Activities Control Act of 1950 or, in shorthand, the McCarran Act—named for the sponsor, Senator Pat McCarran of Nevada—was among the many measures debated during a troubling era. Similar to the time when a red scare infected the country following World War I, the early 1950s was a period of enormous social unrest. In 1949, the Soviets acquired the atomic bomb and mainland China fell to the Communists. In February 1950, a senator from Wisconsin, Joseph R. McCarthy, charged that Communists had infiltrated the US State Department, among other institutions in American life. On June 26, 1950, North Korea fired on South Korean positions south of the thirty-eighth parallel, and the two sides suddenly found themselves engulfed in a ground war involving tank and infantry forces. The McCarran Act was a reaction to the hysteria of the time.[261]

Americans of the era consumed a steady diet of newspaper accounts, articles, books, television programs, and movies about the Communist menace. Descriptions almost always depicted the ideology as a disease. Persons who succumbed to the illness were transformed

into malcontents whose sole purpose was to disrupt the political world and tear apart the social fabric. To make matters worse, rooting out Communists was exceedingly difficult, for they were "Masters of Deceit," as FBI Director J. Edgar Hoover characterized them. They were expert manipulators who wore a false front—a mask of normalcy that disguised the depravity lurking beneath the surface of the public façade.

Dime-store psychoanalysts of the 1950s pontificated on the causes and effects of prolonged exposure to Communism. The conclusion was alarming: a person immersed in Communist propaganda for too long would suffer from neurosis, at best, and a litany of psychological abnormalities at worst. This disease must be contained and eradicated as soon as possible, or the consequences for Western civilization would be too catastrophic to contemplate.[262]

Elected officials and citizens alike panicked, for it seemed that everywhere the forces of oppression threatened to overtake the free world. The rapidity with which Communism enjoyed unprecedented successes convinced some observers that the triumph of this dangerous ideology was more than a mere coincidence. The Truman administration must be incompetent or complicit in all manner of nefarious activities, for nothing else explained why American foreign policy had fallen short of its goals of promoting global stability in the wake of World War II. Senator William Jenner believed he understood the problem: Secretary of Defense George Marshall was a "front man for traitors." A bevy of Republican members of Congress leveled accusations against Secretary of State Dean Acheson, with one senator going so far as to charge that the secretary was stained "with the blood of our boys in Korea." Almost every Republican member of Congress, and many Democrats, criticized the US State Department, which must be riddled with Communist agents and sympathizers.[263]

The Desire for Internal Security

With anti-Communist feeling at a fever pitch, it was inevitable that a member of Congress would seek to gain an advantage from public fear. It fell to Senator Pat McCarran of Nevada, once described as "an aging hack," to offer up a solution. McCarran had built a congressional career

as a fierce anti-Communist, a poor man's Joe McCarthy. A red-baiting demagogue with little regard for details such as factual accuracy, the senator was tailor-made for the McCarthy era. His reactionary politics, nurtured over a decade and a half in Washington, finally fit with the tenor of the times. In the aftermath of McCarthy's inflammatory comments, McCarran pushed legislation through Congress to combat the subversives he knew to be prevalent in the US government.[264]

Two Republican congressmen, Karl Mundt of South Dakota and Richard Nixon of California, had sponsored a bill to track subversives as far back as 1947, but the measure had languished in Congress for years. A second bill, known as Mundt-Ferguson, also failed to muster enough votes. With American soldiers fighting Communists in Asia, Nevada's senior senator recognized an opportunity to revive the earlier bills by retrofitting them to suit the era of the Korean War, and he took it. Pat McCarran was never accused of being a deep thinker, but he knew a legislative opening when he saw one. Almost any red-baiting member of Congress who played on the fears of the populace would enjoy enormous success in the early 1950s, as McCarthy had so vividly illustrated.[265]

Pat McCarran, a US senator from Nevada and a self-professed anti-Communist, sponsored the Internal Security Act of 1950. Courtesy of the Library of Congress.

McCarran's bill only reinforced a movement sweeping the nation. Numerous cities and several states were debating and enacting bills requiring public employees to swear a loyalty oath as a condition for employment. Public libraries instituted policies requiring that any book that "promoted Communism" must be pulled from the shelves immediately. Everyone, it seemed, was vigilant lest the "enemy within" undermine the American way of life.

With fears of a red menace echoing across the nation, McCarran's bill sailed through Congress with few dissenting voices raised in protest, passing the House of Representatives on August 29, 1950, by a vote of 354 to 20. In the US Senate, the measure garnered 51 votes (with seven nays) on September 20.[266]

The statute, officially known as the Internal Security Act of 1950, created a new five-member Subversive Activities Control Board (SACB) "to determine whether any organization is a *Communist-action organization* within the meaning of paragraph (3) of section 3 of this title, or a *Communist-front organization* within the meaning of paragraph (4) of section 3 of this title." The law also imposed registration and record-keeping requirements on "Communist-action organizations" and, in some instances, set forth registration requirements for the individual members of "Communist-action organizations." Communist-action organizations were compelled to provide the names of officers and members as well as a list of funding sources. Registered organizations could not qualify for tax exemptions. Contributions to such organizations could not be deducted from a donor's income tax return. If an organization or member failed to register with the US Attorney General, criminal sanctions would apply.

The act banned all members of registered organizations from government employment and prohibited registered organizations from engaging in government defense work. A registered organization was required to label broadcasts and publications as the product of a "Communist organization." If an insurrection occurred, the president of the United States was authorized to detain anyone he believed was involved "in all acts of espionage or sabotage." The law did not allow detainees the right of judicial review, although an administrative hearing was permissible.[267]

To ameliorate the more draconian sections of the law, the authors provided for immunity from criminal prosecution if a person had not engaged in subversive conduct. Organizational membership alone was insufficient. Section 4(f) provided "(1) that neither the holding of office nor membership in any Communist organization shall constitute a violation of Section 4(a) or 4(c) of the Act or of any other criminal statute; and (2) that the fact of the registration of any person as an officer or member of a Communist organization shall not be received as evidence against that person in a prosecution for violations of Sections 4(a) or 4(c) of the Act or of any other criminal statute." Despite this belated attempt to distinguish between a person's status as a member of an organization and his or her conduct, the statute was designed to stigmatize, if not quite punish, a person's membership in an unapproved organization. Civil libertarians feared it was a distinction without a difference.[268]

On its face, the act violated an individual's Fifth Amendment right against self-incrimination because it required a person to label himself a subversive on penalty of law. Anyone who voluntarily wore the "Communist" label would face legally-sanctioned discrimination. One commentator called the statute "clearly one of the most massive onslaughts against freedom of speech and association ever launched in American history."[269]

Many elected officials understood the constitutional problems with the law, but they were wary of speaking out on fear of being branded Communist sympathizers. McCarthy and McCarran were powerful showmen playing to a largely appreciative audience. Political courage is always a rare commodity, but it seemed virtually non-existent during the early 1950s.

President Harry Truman was the exception that proved the rule. Realizing the threat to freedom of speech and association, he expressed disgust for the McCarran anti-Communism bill. His political advisers cautioned him to downplay his objections and allow the measure to pass, but the president would not heed their advice. Exhibiting a bit of the political courage in short supply, he vetoed the bill on September 22, 1950.[270]

In Truman's veto message, he observed that the McCarran Act "would make a mockery of our Bill of Rights would actually weaken

our internal security measures." Citing an example from American history, Truman pronounced the bill "the greatest danger to freedom of speech, press, and assembly since the Alien and Sedition Laws of 1798." In a stirring passage near the end of his message, he observed, "We can and we will prevent espionage, sabotage, or other actions endangering our national security. But we would betray our finest traditions if we attempted, as this bill would attempt, to curb the simple expression of opinion. This we should never do, no matter how distasteful the opinion may be to the vast majority of our people. The course proposed by this bill would delight the communists, for it would make a mockery of the Bill of Rights and of our claims to stand for freedom in the world."[271]

The Internal Security Act of 1950 passed over President Truman's veto. Courtesy of the Library of Congress.

Had the president vetoed the bill before the Soviets acquired a nuclear weapon, China fell to Communist forces, or war erupted on the Korean peninsula, he might have stayed the measure successfully. Too much had happened by 1950, and Truman's popularity was too low. With Republican Members of Congress denouncing the Truman administration almost daily and McCarthy constantly on the prowl for Communists burrowing into the internal structure of the country, few Americans possessed a level-headed perspective. To the president's chagrin, the US House of Representatives overrode the veto by a 286-48 vote that same day with virtually no debate. The Senate ferociously debated the bill, but in the end, 57 senators agreed to override the veto and 10 voted to sustain it. In both houses, the votes were far beyond the constitutionally required two-thirds majority. Even members of Truman's own party abandoned him in the face of a rumored Communist onslaught.[272]

Court Cases

With statutory authority in place, the SACB went to work. Throughout the 1950s, the Board interrogated hundreds of witnesses as it tracked the activities of Communist organizations and Communist fronts. Along with Joe McCarthy and the House Un-American Activities Committee (HUAC), the SACB—and much of official Washington, for that matter—launched a series of investigations of subversive individuals and organizations during the height of the Cold War. The fruits of such arduous labors remain highly contentious. Whether the country was safer because government officials rooted out would-be subversives or worse off owing to a wholesale violation of civil liberties depends on one's perspective. In a later age, after Communism has fallen out of favor throughout most of the world, the frenetic search for Communists and other undesirables appears quaint and more than a little baffling.[273]

Not surprisingly, the Communist party of the United States (CPUSA) challenged the McCarran Act in court. On November 22, 1950, the attorney general of the United States petitioned the SACB to issue an order requiring the party to register under the terms of the statute. The CPUSA filed suit in the US District Court for the

District of Columbia seeking an injunction to prevent the SACB from issuing such an order. The district court refused to grant a preliminary injunction, but it stayed the proceedings pending appeal. On appeal, the US Supreme Court declined to extend the stay.[274]

With the way clear to issue an order requiring the CPUSA to register, the SACB held hearings on the matter for over a year in 1952 and 1953. The attorney general's office presented twenty-two witnesses while the Communist party provided three witnesses. The hearings included more than five hundred exhibits. At the end of the presentations, the SACB determined the CPUSA was a "Communist-action organization," as defined in the law. Accordingly, the Board ordered the party to register.[275]

Not satisfied with the outcome, the CPUSA challenged the hearing process in court, this time filing a motion to present additional evidence showing that three of the attorney general's witnesses had perjured themselves before the board. The court refused to allow additional evidence to be presented. Afterward, the CPUSA petitioned the US Supreme Court, which agreed to hear the case.[276]

Justice Felix Frankfurter wrote the opinion for the high court in a 1956 case, *Communist Party of the United States v. Subversive Activities Control Board*. The court refused to address the constitutional questions because the matter could be resolved without considering such issues. Frankfurter, a well-known judicial restraintist, believed that unelected federal judges must not announce new constitutional doctrines or broadly interpret statutes unless no other means of deciding a case are possible. Fundamental changes in law or policy must be left to the elected branches of government. In this instance, the court did not need to consider the constitutional claims to dispose of the case. Because the attorney general had not denied the perjury allegations, which was a matter crucial to the outcome of the case, the evidence was tainted. The justices remanded the case to the SACB to reconsider the matter absent the tainted testimony.[277]

On remand, the Board disallowed the testimony of the three witnesses in question, but the outcome did not change. The CPUSA was ordered to register as a Communist-action organization pursuant to the legislation. Once again, the party appealed, the appellate

court upheld the Board's decision, and the CPUSA petitioned the US Supreme Court. The high court agreed to consider the matter a second time.[278]

More than a decade after the attorney general asked the SACB to issue an order to the CPUSA under the McCarran Act, the Supreme Court announced a decision in *Communist Party v. Subversive Activities Control Board* (1961). The appeal presented several constitutional arguments. First, the petitioners charged the McCarran Act was in essence an unconstitutional bill of attainder, which punishes individuals without affording the defendants a trial beforehand. The appeal also argued the legislation violated the First Amendment's guarantee of free speech and association. As a third point, the appellants believed the law violated the Fifth Amendment's requirement that a person cannot be compelled to incriminate himself. Finally, the appeal argued that the appellants' right to due process of law had been violated.[279]

Justice Frankfurter again wrote for the majority. This time, he addressed the constitutionality of the statute's registration requirements. According to Frankfurter, the law was constitutionally permissible because it did not target organizations, only the conduct of individuals and organizations. "The Act is not a bill of attainder," he determined. "It attaches not to specified organizations, but to described activities in which an organization may or may not engage."[280]

In an especially audacious passage, the justice conceded the statute may have inhibited free speech, but the threat posed by the specter of international Communism justified the intrusion. "On the basis of its detailed investigations, Congress has found that there exists a world Communist movement, foreign controlled, whose purpose it is by whatever means necessary to establish Communist totalitarian dictatorship in the countries throughout the world, and which has already succeeded in supplanting governments in other countries. Congress has found that, in furthering these purposes, the foreign government controlling the world Communist movement establishes in various countries action organizations which, dominated from abroad, endeavor to bring about the overthrow of existing governments, by force if need be, and to establish totalitarian dictatorships subservient to that foreign government," he wrote. "And Congress has

found that these action organizations employ methods of infiltration and secretive and coercive tactics; that, by operating in concealment and through Communist front organizations, they are able to obtain the support of persons who would not extend such support knowing of their true nature; that a Communist network exists in the United States, and that the agents of Communism have devised methods of sabotage and espionage carried out in successful evasion of existing law. The purpose of the Subversive Activities Control Act is said to be to prevent the worldwide Communist conspiracy from accomplishing its purpose in this country." Frankfurter refused to decide whether such purposes were exaggerated or repugnant to constitutional protections. "It is not for the courts to reexamine the validity of these legislative findings and reject them."[281]

The court rejected the claim that the appellants had been denied their Fifth Amendment right against self–incrimination because such a contention was premature. "The privilege against self-incrimination is one which normally must be claimed by the individual who seeks to avail himself of its protection," Frankfurter explained. "We cannot know now that the Party's officers will ever claim the privilege. There is no indication that, in the past, its high-ranking officials have sought to conceal their identity, and no reason to believe that, in the future, they will decline to file a registration statement whose whole effect, in this regard, is further to evidence a fact which, traditionally, has been one of public notice."[282]

Frankfurter moved to the last crucial issue. "It is next asserted that the Act offends the Due Process Clause of the Fifth Amendment by predetermining legislatively facts upon which the application of the registration," he wrote. Yet the SACB found credible evidence to support Congress's conclusion that the CPUSA was controlled by the Soviet Union. "None of the operative facts were 'predetermined,' except in the sense in which any statute, as construed, designates the nature of the facts pertinent to issues which may be litigated under it."[283] In affirming the lower court decision, Frankfurter concluded that "we must decline, of course, to enter into discussion of the wisdom of this legislation. The Constitution does not prohibit the requirement that the Communist Party

register with the Attorney General as a Communist action organization pursuant to Section 7."[284]

Chief Justice Earl Warren filed a dissent, as did Justices Hugo Black, William O. Douglas, and William Brennan. Justice Black was especially eloquent in stating his objections to the statute. "I do not believe that it can be too often repeated that the freedoms of speech, press, petition and assembly guaranteed by the First Amendment must be accorded to the ideas we hate or sooner or later they will be denied to the ideas we cherish," he wrote. "The first banning of an association because it advocates hated ideas—whether that association be called a political party or not—marks a fateful moment in the history of a free country. That moment seems to have arrived for this country."[285]

Following its loss in the Supreme Court, the CPUSA remained as defiant as ever, refusing to register under the McCarran Act despite the legal requirement to do so. The party's determination to resist and the SACB's refusal to yield all but guaranteed further legal proceedings. By the time yet another case inevitably wound up in the high court, a new day had dawned. It was 1965 and the McCarthy era had given way to the era of civil rights and Vietnam.[286]

In *Albertson v. Subversive Activities Control Board*, Justice William Brennan wrote the majority opinion. "Petitioners address several constitutional challenges to the validity of the orders," he remarked at the outset, "but we consider only the contention that the orders violate their Fifth Amendment privilege against self-incrimination."[287] After determining the case was ripe for adjudication, Brennan agreed with a central argument the CPUSA had advanced since passage of the McCarran Act, namely that registration under the act's provisions carried an untenable risk of criminal prosecution. "The risks of incrimination which the petitioners take in registering are obvious," Brennan observed. "Form IS–52a requires an admission of membership in the Communist Party. Such an admission of membership may be used to prosecute the registrant under the membership clause of the Smith Act, 18 U.S.C. 2385 (1964 ed.), or under 4 (a) of the Subversive Activities Control Act, 64 Stat. 991, 50 U.S.C. 783 (a) (1964 ed.), to mention only two federal criminal statutes."[288]

A fundamental proposition in criminal law is that conduct, not status, is punishable. The McCarran Act, among other Cold War-era laws enacted in the heat of the moment, appeared to violate this well-established principle. The US Supreme Court of the McCarthy era would not recognize that branding a group with a particular label vitiated long-established constitutional precepts because, in the convoluted reasoning of that time, the threat posed by the Communist ideology was too great to allow policy-makers to honor all aspects of the Bill of Rights. By the mid-1960s, however, the court was no longer as concerned about a Communist victory as it was about the erosion of Bill of Rights protections. On other occasions—especially after the end of the Warren Court in 1969—the court would back away from a strong commitment to civil liberties, but in 1965, when it decided the *Albertson* case, the court had come to see what the McCarran Act critics had known all along: Punishing persons who join groups that espouse unpopular ideas not only imperils the rights of free speech and association of group members, but it threatens the rights of all Americans.[289]

Selective Enforcement and the Paul Robeson Episode

After the Supreme Court struck down portions of the McCarran Act as unconstitutional, Congress repealed the registration requirements in 1968. As of this writing, most of the law has been overturned, yet a few sections remain intact. Current federal law in 50 U.S.C. § 797 (Section 21 of the Internal Security Act of 1950), for example, still governs security on military bases and other sensitive installations. In all other respects, the act essentially died in 1973 when Congress refused to appropriate sufficient funds for enforcement.[290]

In its heyday, the McCarran Act served as a complement to the House Un-American Activities Committee (HUAC) investigations during the 1950s as well as the FBI's COINTELPRO efforts in the 1950s and 1960s, both of which are discussed in this book. Yet the act could not be characterized as especially effective. For all the brouhaha surrounding its enactment as well as the tortuous path to the US Supreme Court in the CPUSA cases, the McCarran Act was only selectively enforced even before Congress withheld funding in 1973.

Arguably the most infamous case of enforcement involved actor-singer Paul Robeson, who found his passport cancelled owing to his support for Communist principles.[291]

As the years passed and fears over an imminent triumph of Communist ideology dissipated, Americans looked back with astonishment at the absurdity of the general reaction. Elected officials and concerned citizens questioned whether the cure had been worse than the disease. In combating potential subversives, officials may have harmed American values and rights worse than their enemies ever could. As an example, in 1961, a left-wing group called the Delaware Valley Committee for Democratic Rights published a poster criticizing the law and calling on President Kennedy to delay prosecutions. The poster employed the expected language of histrionic outrage, but it also asked the reader to put himself in the place of someone facing possible prosecution under the McCarran Act, which it labeled "today's McCarthyism." It was not necessary to be a Communist party member to face prosecution under such a broad statute. "Maybe your activities in your union are considered 'radical'? Have you been too 'impetuous' in your work for integration? Have you been contemptuous of fallout shelters? Do you reject rubber-stamp thinking? Do you belong to an organization that works for change?"[292]

The reference to integration was especially telling, for enforcers of the McCarran Act equated political dissent with disloyalty to the United States and a possible Communist affiliation. Anyone who dared to question the status quo was attacked as a Communist or Communist sympathizer, including civil rights activists of the 1950s and 1960s. Men and women demonstrating for black political rights could not possibly be patriotic Americans seeking equal justice under law regardless of their skin color. They must be Communist agents hellbent on destroying the American way of life. Although the CPUSA had reached out to blacks on numerous occasions stretching back to the infamous Scottsboro Boys trials where eleven young Negroes were falsely charged with raping two white women in Alabama in 1931, the party enjoyed only modest success. Most Black Americans were not Communists. They did not seek to destroy the American dream; they sought to live it.[293]

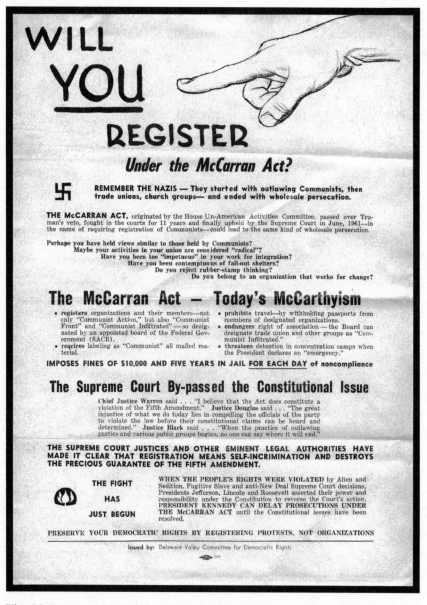

This 1961 poster criticized the McCarran Act as leading to "wholesale persecution" of suspected Communists. Moreover, the law "destroys the precious guarantee of the Fifth Amendment" because it requires registrants to incriminate themselves. Courtesy of the Delaware Valley Committee for Democratic Rights.

Few Black Americans of the era were as confrontational or controversial as Paul Robeson. A multi-talented singer, actor, and activist, he was a living, breathing reminder that the central tenets of segregation and racial discrimination—that blacks were inferior beings unworthy of equal treatment in society—amounted to a colossal lie. He also refused to adopt the traditional attitude of the subservient Negro who exhibited extreme deference to whites. Everything about him was oversized—he stood six feet, three inches tall and weighed 219 pounds during his salad days as a football player, first at Rutgers University and later in the National Football League. He became the valedictorian at Rutgers University, graduated from Columbia Law School, and spoke multiple languages. It was little wonder he refused to bow to any man. Paul Robeson knew he was the equal of anyone and, it might be argued, better than most.

As a young man, Robeson was not especially interested in politics. As he came of age, he bristled at the racial discrimination he saw around him, even when he lived in northern states. By the 1930s, he had become increasingly politicized. During the late 1930s and early 1940s, he voiced support for labor unions and praised the Soviet Union for its willingness to treat its citizens without regard to race. As early as 1941, the FBI began keeping tabs on this strange cultural figure that would not conform to the Jim Crow regime.

Even as the anti-Communist hysteria reached a fever pitch during the late 1940s and early 1950s, Robeson refused to moderate his political pronouncements. He visited the Soviet Union several times and made speeches critical of the United States. In a meeting with President Truman in 1946, Robeson urged the administration to take vigorous action against Negro lynching before black citizens took matters into their own hands. Perceiving the comment to be an insolent threat, Truman promptly adjourned the meeting. It seemed that no matter when and where Robeson opened his mouth, he assailed the American experience and offended the powers that be.[294]

In 1950, as the Cold War deepened and Congress enacted the McCarran Act over President Truman's veto, Robeson spoke at a civil rights rally in Madison Square Garden. Aside from criticizing the president's decision to deploy ground troops in Korea, he urged blacks

to ignore the international conflict and focus on securing civil rights at home. In response to the speech as well as Robeson's continued agitation on multiple fronts, the State Department cancelled his passport. When he protested, he received predictably vague answers about the department's reasoning. It was "contrary to the best interests of the United States" for the artist to travel internationally, he was told. Another stated reason was because his well-known complaints about the treatment afforded blacks in the United States "should not be aired in foreign countries."[295]

Robeson's supporters expressed astonishment at the passport cancellation. In one sage's estimation, Robeson was "the only living American against whom an order has been issued directing immigration authorities not to permit him to leave the continental confines of the United States." Robeson commented that it was "rather absurd" that he was not "allowed to travel because of my friendship—open, spoken friendship—for the Soviet people and the peoples of all the world." It was big talk, but Robeson did more than talk. He challenged the action in court.[296]

He faced a hostile judiciary. In 1951, a US district court refused to overturn the State Department's decision. Robeson lost again on appeal. In a short *per curiam* opinion, the United States Court of Appeals, District of Columbia Circuit, concluded that Robeson had not filed a passport renewal application and, therefore, the case was not ripe. The court acknowledged that the State Department's actions "are characterized as depriving appellant of his right to travel abroad, and as arbitrary, discriminatory and violative of due process of law." Yet "the steps said to have been taken to prevent appellant's departure are incident to invalidation of his passport. Nowhere among the allegations of his travel plans or desires or business activities dependent upon his travel is there a suggestion of plans, desires or activities which would take appellant to any place outside the United States where under existing law and regulations a passport might not be required." In the court's view, "A fair reading of the complaint discloses no case, independent of the consequence of invalidation of the passport, of alleged infringement of rights by restraint upon appellant's freedom of movement beyond the United States."[297]

The federal government revoked actor Paul Robeson's passport under the McCarran Act supposedly owing to Robeson's Communist ties. Courtesy of the Library of Congress.

The situation grew worse. Robeson soon found himself blacklisted from Hollywood and hauled before HUAC to defend his views. Suffering from health problems, including a bout of depression, Robeson appeared before the congressional committee under subpoena on July 23, 1956. In keeping with his character, the man would not be humbled. "I will continue to speak out. My struggle for a passport is a struggle for freedom—freedom to travel, freedom to earn a livelihood, freedom to speak, freedom to express myself artistically and culturally," he told his interlocutors.[298]

He was so famous for his talents and his outspoken, critical views that Robeson became a lightning rod in the culture wars of his day. Because of the entertainer's well-known willingness to criticize the regime, any "uppity Negro" in the United States could be denounced for "being Paul Robeson." Even his mere presence at an event was controversial. When Robeson appeared at a concert or took part in a demonstration, the event was characterized as a Communist demonstration simply because he was there. The FBI constantly monitored his movements and associations. As

J. Edgar Hoover remarked, whenever anyone such as Robeson spoke of "equal rights" and "self-determination"—terms that Robeson frequently used—that person was parroting the Communist party's "chief slogans for Negroes" and therefore evincing "obedience to Soviet foreign policy." A Washington state legislator—the notoriously rabid anti-Communist Albert F. Canwell, chair of his state's Joint Legislative Fact-Finding Committee on Un-American Activities, a state-level interim committee modeled on HUAC—did not mince words. "If someone insists there is discrimination against Negroes in this country," Canwell charged, "there is every reason to believe that person is a Communist." In short, a black man who objected to being treated as a second-class citizen was obviously a Communist precisely because he exercised his supposedly American right to free speech.[299]

In time, the excesses of the era passed and the McCarran Act no longer served as an effective means of chasing down subversives. Paul Robeson eventually received a new passport, and traveled outside of the United States in 1956 for the first time in six years. He also enjoyed a brief resurgence in his career until declining health forced him to retire in the 1960s. With the benefit of hindsight, historians regard the statute and those groups and persons who were prosecuted under it as monuments to the hysteria that occasionally consumes Americans in times of crisis and uncertainty.[300]

Chapter 7

THE HOUSE UN-AMERICAN ACTIVITIES COMMITTEE (HUAC)

Until the day I die, I shall wonder how Whittaker Chambers got into my house to use my typewriter.

—ALGER HISS, DECEMBER 15, 1948,

EXPLAINING HOW A TYPEWRITER BELONGING TO HIS WIFE COULD HAVE BEEN USED TO PRODUCE INCRIMINATING DOCUMENTS[301]

The House Un-American Activities Committee (HUAC) was an investigative committee of the US House of Representatives created in the 1930s to determine whether subversive forces threatened the welfare of the American republic. In 1945, the House voted to make HUAC a standing committee. Afterward, it reached the height of its infamy searching for evidence of Communist subversion in the aftermath of World War II.[302]

When HUAC was created, the use of a congressional committee to investigate activities related to the health and welfare of the regime was nothing new. As early as 1792, the US House of Representatives established a committee to explore the circumstances surrounding a calamitous campaign against American Indians. As the decades passed, Congress created select committees to examine all manner of suspicious activities or suspected malfeasance. Armed with subpoena power and a broad grant of authority, investigative committees became important vehicles for ferreting out crucial information that might otherwise remain obscure. In the hands of overzealous investigators or opportunistic members of Congress, however, congressional committees sometimes abridged constitutional protections and exercised a chilling effect on citizens who sought only to speak the truth to power.[303]

In the early years of the republic, congressional committees appeared to have few limitations on their authority until the US Supreme Court considered the matter in *Kilbourn v. Thompson*. In that 1880 case, a gentleman named Hallet Kilbourn was served with a subpoena *duces tecum* ordering him to appear, along with a series of documents, before a House committee investigating the bankruptcy of Jay Cooke & Company, an influential investment firm that filed for bankruptcy protection during the Panic of 1873. Kilbourn complied with the subpoena and appeared before the committee, but he refused to answer some questions and failed to produce the required documents. Held in contempt of the House, Kilbourn was placed into custody until he agreed to testify and tender the necessary documents. The much-aggrieved witness eventually filed suit for false imprisonment. The US Supreme Court subsequently reviewed the case and held that Congress possesses the power to punish contempt, but the crucial issue here concerned the authority of a congressional committee to exercise what appeared to be judicial authority. In the court's view, Kilbourn had been improperly summoned before the committee and imprisoned for contempt. A congressional committee must not be convened for investigative purposes unless the committee acts in accordance with a reasonably well-defined legislative goal.[304]

The Supreme Court provided additional guidance on congressional committees in *McGrain v. Daugherty*. In that 1927 case, the court ruled that while a Senate committee is presumed to have a legislative purpose and can compel witnesses to appear, a witness can refuse to answer questions that are not pertinent to the investigation. As a consequence of *Kilbourn* and *McGrain*, congressional committees were vested with broad discretion to investigate critical issues, but their authority was not absolute. Witnesses were afforded basic due process rights, although this critical finding was not always honored in the years to come.[305]

Origins of the Dies Committee

HUAC is remembered today as a mechanism for attacking leftist organizations, and it has been criticized for its willingness to brand unpopular ideas and persons as "un-American." Yet HUAC was not

the first congressional committee to explore "un-American" activities. A predecessor committee delved into right-wing organizations in the 1930s.[306]

As fascist movements swept through Europe during the Mussolini and Hitler regimes, numerous rightist groups sprang up in the United States. In response, anti-fascist organizations formed to counterbalance the rampant anti-Semitism promoted by the Nazis and fascists. Congress eventually recognized the need to investigate the proliferation of these and other anti-American organizations. In 1934, Congressman Samuel Dickstein of New York introduced HR 198, a resolution to investigate fascist groups. Passed by the House of Representatives in March 1934, the resolution created the Special Committee on Un-American Activities Authorized to Investigate Nazi Propaganda and Certain Other Propaganda Activities. The committee, sometimes called the McCormack-Dickstein Committee after Chairman John W. McCormack, a Massachusetts Democrat, and Congressman Dickstein, conducted hearings for "information on how foreign subversive propaganda entered the US and the organizations that were spreading it." The committee served from 1934 until 1937. In the 1990s, investigators found records in the Soviet archives indicating that Dickstein was a paid Soviet agent during the 1930s.[307]

Its successor became far better-known than the anti-fascist version. In the beginning, however, Dickstein proposed creating a new committee to take up where the prior committee had left off. When the new committee formed in May 1938, the chairman, Congressman Martin Dies Jr. of Texas, set out to investigate the German-American Bund, a pro-Nazi group that had attracted twenty-five thousand members by 1938. A year later, more than thirty thousand enthusiasts flocked to Madison Square Garden to hear Bund leaders spew out anti-Semitic invectives and express their undying admiration for all things German, including Adolf Hitler. In his quest to determine whether the Bund represented an active threat to the United States government, Dies followed the tradition that McCormack and Dickstein had established with the original organization. For his encore performance, Dies looked to the earlier Fish Committee, named for the rabid

anti-Communist Congressman Hamilton Fish III of New York, who investigated the Communist threat as early as 1930.[308]

Dies was a vehement critic of President Franklin D. Roosevelt and the New Deal, convinced that Roosevelt was a traitor to his class and the administration was riddled with Communists. "If Democratic government assumes the responsibility for abolishing all poverty and unemployment," he said, "it is simply preparing the way for dictatorship. . . ." The Dies Committee, as it was called during the Texas Democrat's tenure, soon expanded its investigation beyond the New Deal to examine a multitude of leftist organizations.[309]

A decade before Joseph McCarthy searched for Communists lurking beneath every nook and cranny of government, Martin Dies demonstrated his skill as a master of the unsubstantiated charge. He hurled epithets that would have made McCarthy proud. Dies branded the American Civil Liberties Union a "Communist-controlled organization." No one, even the most seemingly innocuous of groups, was above reproach. His committee cast aspersions on the Boy Scouts and the Camp Fire Girls. A witness testifying before the committee ruminated on Shirley Temple's liberal leanings. Even among paranoids hungry for conspiracy theories, the committee's fantastic, unbelievable reports were met with skepticism. When asked to comment on Dies's charges that members of his cabinet were under the direction of Soviet dictator Joseph Stalin, President Roosevelt replied, "Ho-hum." It was all so silly that a serious answer seemed unnecessary.[310]

The Federal Bureau of Investigation took the charges seriously, but an investigation revealed nothing to substantiate the allegations. Satisfied that the matter was concluded, Attorney General Francis Biddle dismissed the committee's assertions as "clearly unfounded," a comment that unleashed Dies's wrath. Using the demagogue's tried-and-true method of questioning the patriotism of critics, Dies alleged that Biddle himself was committed to employing subversives. The committee chairman, in a pique of self-righteousness, proclaimed his indefatigability. No matter how many obstacles the forces of Communism tossed in his path, he would not be dissuaded from his task. He vowed never to relax his vigilance lest the enemies of the American way of

Martin Dies Jr. of Texas was the first chairman of the House Un-American Activities Committee. Courtesy of the Library of Congress.

life triumphed and sent the citizenry cascading down the road to perdition.[311]

Martin Dies's red-baiting created sensationalistic headlines, but as World War II came to America's shores and the United States forged an uneasy alliance with the Soviets to battle the Nazi menace in Europe, the committee lost favor. Dies chose not to seek reelection in 1944, and he quickly disappeared from the scene. His zeal for fighting Communists waned when the news stories dried up, but he left a powerful legacy. His pioneering efforts to besmirch disfavored persons and organizations eventually would pay handsome dividends for opportunistic politicians, but the timing was not right until after the Allies emerged victorious from the war.[312]

In January 1945, as the war in Europe drew to a close and the nation was poised on the cusp of a new era, Mississippi Congressman

John E. Rankin proposed the creation of a new committee to investigate un-American activities, but with one crucial change. This time, it should exist as a standing committee. Because the Dies Committee had been created as a special or temporary committee, the House had to reauthorize the work each year. A standing committee would be permanent until the House took specific steps to disband the group. Rankin's proposal was a bold and ultimately successful attempt to ensure that the new committee would be a permanent, potentially powerful fixture in Washington. Not surprisingly, the new anti-Communist champion assumed the chairmanship. Within a few years, the new iteration of the House Un-American Activities Committee would become a well-known feature of the postwar landscape.[313]

Rankin hatched big plans for his new committee. In keeping with a long line of legislators from his state, the audacious Mississippi congressman was a well-known hater who reserved special vituperation for Communists, Jews, blacks, and intellectuals, not necessarily in that order. In a congressional career that spanned more than three decades, Rankin demonstrated a willingness and aptitude for offending almost everyone who did not share his retrograde views. In one astonishing exchange on the floor of the House of Representatives in 1947, Rankin used the word *nigger*. Adam Clayton Powell Jr., a congressman from New York whose district included the legendary black enclave Harlem, objected. Rankin waved him away. "It is not a disgrace to be a real Negro," he told the black legislator. "If I were a Negro, I would be as black as the ace of Spades. I could then go out with Negroes and have a real good time."[314]

With these sensibilities, Rankin appeared to be well-positioned to carry on Martin Dies's tradition of accusing innocents of objectionable activities with little or no regard for factual accuracy. He certainly thirsted for a chance to wear a demagogue's mantle. Yet Rankin never settled on a suitable agenda or a coordinated plan of attack. By 1947, he was out as the committee chair, replaced by New Jersey Republican J. Parnell Thomas.[315]

Although Thomas was not a southerner, he shared his predecessor's prejudices about blacks, Jews, and undesirables as well as a mistrust of the New Deal and any proposal or policy that smacked

of liberal proclivities. Unlike Rankin, Thomas brought organizational skills and a well-developed plan of action to the table. Where the Mississippi chairman had thrashed about in chaos and disorder, Thomas set out with a purpose: to uncover Communist sympathizers in the labor movement, in the nation's educational institutions, and in Hollywood. He knew how he would achieve his goals, too. Thomas resolved to compile massive dossiers on persons suspected of undermining American values, and he would institute a propaganda campaign aimed at combating the insidious material circulated by Communist agents who planned to denigrate the United States of America.[316]

The committee set off on its ambitious task beginning in 1947. By the end of the following year, Thomas and his investigators had gathered information on more than twenty-five thousand individuals and seventeen hundred organizations. The committee proved adept at organizing and indexing the material. Raw data that could not be accessed easily would possess only limited value. If HUAC intended to publicize the hidden Communist menace, the committee's files needed to be organized efficiently so that the data could be used in the most effective manner possible.

Thomas understood the value of holding public hearings. Aside from displaying the committee's work and unmasking Communists in public, a hearing allowed committee members to garner presumably favorable public attention. Thomas and his gang used their time in the spotlight to good effect.[317]

The hearings commenced on a dramatic note. After a reformed Communist named Louis Budenz identified a "shadowy figure" as the "real head of Communism in America," HUAC focused on the figure, Gerhart Eisler, a German Communist who had moved to the United States in 1933 ostensibly to escape fascism. Eisler refused to appear before the committee unless he could make a three-minute opening statement. Thomas agreed to the stipulation but only after the witness was sworn in and questioned. The timing of the statement became a sticking point. Incensed, Eisler argued with Thomas. Both men ended the exchange with shouting. The chairman soldiered on, peppering his hostile witness with questions about whether Eisler had ever joined the Communist party and, if so, whether he had provided information to

the party. Eisler would not provide a straight answer. Cited for contempt, he was dispatched to Ellis Island where he had previously been held on charges of passport fraud.[318]

A young congressman from California, Richard M. Nixon, used the incident as the subject of his maiden speech in the House of Representatives. Elected the previous November, Nixon was anxious to make a name for himself. He had finagled his way onto HUAC, a prestigious assignment for a freshman congressman, and he was determined to use his high-profile membership to good effect, advancing a cause near and dear to his heart, namely the promotion of Richard M. Nixon. As far as the new legislator was concerned, America's top Communist needed something other than a contempt citation from a single committee. On February 18, 1947, the congressman made his move. Rising on the floor to demand that the full House find Eisler guilty of contempt of Congress, Nixon was at his best. He outlined Eisler's subversive activities, describing the man as a "seasoned agent of the Communist International" and "an arrogant, defiant enemy of our government." Nixon bemoaned the Immigration Service's failure to keep tabs on a man who clearly meant to harm American interests. As for persons who believed that HUAC was on a witch hunt, Nixon could not agree. He lamented the "tendency in some quarters to treat this case as one of a political prisoner, a harmless refugee whom this committee is persecuting because of his political belief." For anyone on the right of the political spectrum, it was an impressive performance and marked Nixon as an up-and-comer.

The motion holding Eisler in contempt passed, and the recalcitrant witness soon faced a year in prison. Following his release on bail, Eisler jumped bail to stow away on a departing ship. He later made his way to East Germany and a hero's welcome. For all the subsequent charges lodged against HUAC as an instrument of state-sanctioned repression, the committee's credibility enjoyed a tremendous boost when it became clear that Eisler was a Communist. A witch-hunt is difficult to condemn if it dredges up a few witches along the way.[319]

HUAC's Eisler investigation was successful, but the committee attracted international attention while holding hearings on possible Communist infiltration in Hollywood, the home of the celebrated

motion picture industry. A HUAC subcommittee announced that "scores of screen writers who are Communists have infiltrated into the various studios and it has been through this medium that most of the Communist propaganda has been injected into the movies." During an initial week of hearings, the committee heard from "friendly" Hollywood actors, directors, producers, and writers, some of whom expressed their suspicions that Communism was rife in the motion picture industry.

Eventually, between two hundred fifty and three hundred artists suspected of leftist leanings found themselves blacklisted in Hollywood. A few left the country to live overseas, or they used aliases to continue working. The Hollywood Ten was the most infamous group of black-listed producers, writers, and directors, and their plight became a cause célèbre. The ten were Alvah Bessie, Herbert Biberman, Lester Cole, Edward Dmytryk, Ring Lardner Jr., John Howard Lawson, Albert Maltz, Samuel Ornitz, Robert Adrian Scott, and Dalton Trumbo. The German writer Bertolt Brecht was originally included in the group, but he left the country before he could be questioned. The others appeared before the committee and earned contempt citations for refusing to answer questions. They received prison sentences of one year and were ordered to pay a $1,000 fine.[320]

While he was in prison, Dmytryk agreed to cooperate and name names, but his nine colleagues refused to cooperate as a matter of principle. As a consequence, they saw their careers destroyed when they were blacklisted in Hollywood. Trumbo and Lardner eventually rebounded after the hysteria died in the 1960s, but they were the rare exceptions. Most Hollywood artists smeared by the HUAC campaign did not represent a genuine threat to the American republic, but they were unfortunate victims of the fear sweeping through the country.[321]

Elizabeth Bentley: The Blond Spy Queen

Arguably HUAC reached the apex of its power and influence in the late 1940s investigating the Alger Hiss-Whittaker Chambers case. It began with Elizabeth Bentley, an American who had spied on behalf of the Soviet Union in New York. In July 1948, HUAC called her to testify, and Bentley identified several Soviet spies in the United States,

including Whittaker Chambers, a *Time* magazine editor. It was dramatic, headline-grabbing testimony.

Bentley, described as the "blond spy queen" by one source and the "red spy queen" by another, admitted she had fallen in with the wrong crowd. She started life with great promise, graduating from Vassar College in 1930 with a degree in English, Italian, and French. After briefly flirting with fascism while studying in Italy, she became horrified at the ideology. Returning to the United States, she studied for a master's degree at Columbia University and attended meetings of the American League Against War and Fascism, later known as the American League for Peace and Democracy, an organization created by the Communist party of the United States (CPUSA) in 1933. Bentley told HUAC in 1948, "I was quite infuriated with what I had learned about fascism in Italy, and the only people who would listen to me were the people in the American League Against War and Fascism, and, as I said, I gradually got into that, and gradually there I met Communists, both in Columbia and downtown, and gradually my ideas began to change. I suppose, in a way, I was a very confused liberal, and, unfortunately, we confused liberals have a tendency to look for guidance some place and a tendency to admire efficient people who know where they are going and seem to be doing a good job in the right direction."[322]

Falling in with the wrong people was one thing, but Bentley became immersed in the CPUSA's activities. In 1938, she met Jacob Golos, a Russian émigré who served as a Communist agent in the United States. The two became lovers, and Bentley became a courier between Golos and other Communist operatives in the United States. She confessed to passing him plans on airplane production such as the types of new designs, places where the planes were being shipped, and other sensitive military information. Bentley was involved with a network of agents who worked for Nathan Gregory Silvermaster, an economist with the US War Production Board (WPB). The Silvermaster Group was responsible for transmitting numerous classified files to the Soviet Union. Bentley was a crucial conduit for passing along information.[323]

After Golos died suddenly of a heart attack toward the end of 1943, Bentley took over some of his functions. She gradually became

disillusioned with Communism and the Soviet Union, which treated "human beings as if they were little more than pawns on a chessboard," and she decided to reveal what she knew to the FBI. As she told HUAC:

> I actually stopped paying dues to the party in July of 1944, but it took me about a year to more or less get it out of my system and get to the point where I could get in the frame of mind of going to the authorities about it. As to why: Having worked with Mr. Golos, whom I took to be a great idealist, a man who was working for what I considered to be the betterment of the world, I had been terrifically shielded from the realities behind this thing, and when he died I was thrown in direct contact with Russians who had just come over from Russia—at least as I understand it.[324]

She appeared at the New Haven branch of the FBI and told her story. Although they harbored deep suspicions about the accuracy of her information, bureau agents were delighted to have a window into Communist party activities. They interrogated Bentley repeatedly. During the lengthy interviews, she provided information on 150 alleged Soviet agents. Because many of the names she supplied were already under surveillance, the FBI began to accept her reports as truthful. FBI Director J. Edgar Hoover was convinced of her veracity after the Venona Project, a classified counter-intelligence program designed to decrypt Soviet intelligence, uncovered cables referring to Bentley's code name and her contacts, which she had already disclosed to the bureau.

The agents encouraged her to continue her duties with the CPUSA and provide information on her activities. The effort to transform Bentley into a double agent might have paid enormous dividends— and Hoover ordered that the strictest security measures possible be put into place—but the secret leaked. The director informed the British Secret Intelligence Service (SIS or MI6) of the operation, but unbeknownst to anyone at the time, Kim Philby, a spy working in British intelligence, passed along the details to the Soviet Union. In response,

the Soviets deactivated their agents and shut down their espionage operations before Bentley could gather additional information.[325]

Although she could not assist the bureau as a double agent, Bentley proved her value by implicating several top government officials. Harry Dexter White, assistant secretary of the treasury to Henry Morgenthau Jr. during the Roosevelt administration, was probably the highest-ranking official she named. A renowned economist who helped to design the International Monetary Fund (IMF) and the World Bank, White adamantly denied the allegations. He asked to appear before HUAC to clear his name. Already troubled with coronary artery disease, White suffered a series of heart attacks immediately following his testimony. He died three days later.[326]

Perhaps the most poignant case to arise from Bentley's allegations involved William Remington, a government economist employed at numerous agencies, including the Tennessee Valley Authority, the War Production Board, and the US Department of Commerce. Bentley claimed that Remington, a "clean-cut American lad," had met with her on several occasions over a two-year period beginning in March 1942. When questioned about this association, Remington claimed he had met with Bentley, but he never provided her with "one single scrap of confidential information." He thought she was a reporter researching a story. To almost everyone who heard the story, it did not make sense. Nonetheless, by the time these allegations came to light, Remington, who had supported leftist causes as early as his student days at Dartmouth, had become a staunch anti-Communist. The FBI investigated his actions, but the bureau found little of interest.[327]

By all accounts, Remington was a supremely gifted young man. Bentley called him the "infant prodigy." A boyhood friend remembered Remington warmly, saying "never a brighter light appeared on the horizon." *The New York Herald-Tribune* once remarked that he was "brilliant of mind, handsome in appearance, engaging in manner." After earning his undergraduate degree at Dartmouth University and a master's degree at Columbia University, he entered government service. His career path seemed to be limitless until Bentley named him during a grand jury appearance. Subpoenaed to testify, he acquitted himself well.

Yet matters only grew worse for Remington. Elizabeth Bentley appeared on a radio show and mentioned the man's name. In a fit of pique, he filed suit for libel and won. Unfortunately for Remington, HUAC investigators discovered that he had joined the Communist party as a college student. Remington had previously testified that while he embraced some liberal causes as a young man, he had never officially joined the Communist party. The federal government tried him for perjury, and he was found guilty. Although his conviction was overturned, he was again convicted at a second trial. Sentenced to three years in prison, Remington was murdered by two inmates who were upset by news of his Communist affiliation.[328]

The Hiss-Chambers Case

Another man soon found his fate intertwined with the spy queen. When Elizabeth Bentley mentioned his name, Whittaker Chambers was already well-known to the FBI. If anything, her testimony corroborated much of what Chambers had already told the bureau. Agents had listened to many fantastic tales from Chambers, and they were not sure whether to believe him. Pudgy, short, and fidgety, he did not come off as a credible witness. The man had a troubled, and troubling, past, too. He was known to enjoy more than a taste of alcohol, and he had indulged in numerous sexual affairs with both men and women. No one quite knew what to do with this strange fellow and his testimony. After Bentley provided details that were strikingly similar to what Chambers said, FBI agents paid additional attention to their informant. Perhaps he was not a crackpot after all.

Chambers joined the Communist party as a young man in 1924 after reading Vladimir Lenin's work. He eventually moved inside the Communist Underground, becoming a courier for stolen documents traveling between New York and Washington. By 1938, he had become disillusioned with the party in the wake of Joseph Stalin's purges. He came to believe that Communists were dangerous and might try to exterminate him and his family. By this time, Chambers was married with children, and he later said he feared for their lives.

Chambers took his story to Assistant Secretary of State Adolf Berle, a member of President Franklin Roosevelt's Brain Trust, in the

fall of 1939. Berle thought that the tale was vague and uncorroborated, but he brought it to the president's attention, nonetheless. Nazi Germany had just invaded Poland, and World War II was at hand. Roosevelt had more important matters to consider than a possibly fabricated cloak-and-dagger story. He dismissed it. In March 1940, Berle contacted the FBI. The bureau talked with Chambers in 1942 and 1945, but the Soviets were American allies at the time, and the investigation, such as it was, went nowhere.

Chambers joined the staff of *Time* magazine in 1939, and steadily rose through the ranks to become one of the publication's most popular writers. His past associations seemed to be dead and buried until Elizabeth Bentley testified before HUAC on July 31, 1948. Four days later, Chambers appeared as well. As he had done with Secretary

Whittaker Chambers, a former Soviet spy who became a central figure at the Alger Hiss perjury trial, is pictured here in 1948. Courtesy of the Library of Congress.

Berle in 1939 and with the FBI several times during the early 1940s, Chambers "named names." One of the alleged spies he identified, Alger Hiss, was a State Department official who had been instrumental in several post-World War II conferences during the Roosevelt years. Chambers claimed he had met with Hiss repeatedly when both men had worked for the Communist party.[329]

In many ways, Hiss was the "golden boy" of the Roosevelt administration. A handsome, bright, Harvard-educated lawyer, he was one of the new generation of leaders that hoped to guide public policy in the postwar United States. His career was impressive. After graduating from law school, Hiss clerked for legendary Associate Supreme Court Justice Oliver Wendell Holmes Jr. He subsequently practiced law in a prestigious firm before holding a number of important, high-ranking posts in American government. As an employee of the US State Department, Hiss played a critical role in several meetings scheduled to plan world affairs after the eventual defeat of the Axis powers. He served as executive secretary at the Dumbarton Oaks Conference that mapped out plans for creating the United Nations (UN). Later, he was secretary-general at the United Nations Conference on International Organization in San Francisco, the meeting that established the UN. Most famously, Hiss accompanied the top echelon of American political leaders, including President Franklin Roosevelt, to the Yalta Conference in February 1945 where the three major victorious nations from World War II—the United States, Great Britain, and the Soviet Union—discussed postwar affairs. At the time Chambers fingered him before HUAC, Hiss was serving as president of the Carnegie Endowment for International Peace. It would have been difficult to find someone who symbolized the Eastern Establishment elite more than Alger Hiss.[330]

For all his polish and poise later in life, Hiss was in some ways a self-made man. He had been reared in a Baltimore neighborhood once described as a place of "shabby gentility." His father committed suicide when Hiss was a toddler. Later, Hiss's sister also committed suicide and a brother died of Bright's disease, a kidney ailment. He was not blessed with an abundance of wealth, but the young Hiss had resolved to make something of his life and bathe the family name in glory. He

was a gifted student with a penchant for working hard and impressing his elders. Almost everyone who encountered him came away with a feeling that here was a young fellow who was going places.[331]

If Hiss hoped to continue on his meteoric rise in government service, he needed to confront the allegations immediately. Many witnesses who appeared before HUAC refused to answer questions, citing their Fifth Amendment right not to incriminate themselves. Hiding behind such legalisms struck committee members as curious because the three-year statute of limitations on espionage had expired in most instances. Only a guilty person would refuse to answer questions. Hiss understood the risks to his reputation. As a result, he declined to take refuge behind his constitutional rights. When his name appeared in screaming headlines following Chambers's testimony, Hiss sent a telegram to HUAC lead investigator Robert Stripling offering to appear and answer any questions the committee cared to ask. It was a bold gamble, but Hiss was confident he would emerge triumphant.[332]

Accompanied by his attorney, William Marbury, he appeared before HUAC for the first time on August 5, 1948. Tall, thin, handsome, and impeccably dressed, Alger Hiss carried himself with an air of confidence bordering on arrogance. He presented a marked contrast to the frumpy, disheveled Whittaker Chambers. Richard Nixon noted the man's obvious charms, but found Hiss's manner "coldly courteous and, at times, almost condescending." Both Nixon and Hiss had started out in life from similar circumstances, but their paths had diverged since that time. Nixon had developed an almost pathological loathing for the sort of Eastern, Ivy League-educated career government official that Hiss embodied.

The patrician witness began his testimony by reading an opening statement denying his involvement with the Communist party. He also said he had never seen or heard of Whittaker Chambers before this episode. He handled himself so well that some committee members waffled, apparently fearful of confronting a powerful witness who could boast of important friends, including former Secretary of State Dean Acheson, State Department official and future perennial presidential candidate Adlai Stevenson, Associate

Elizabeth Bentley appears at a meeting of the House Un-American Activities Committee (HUAC) flanked by guards. Attorney William Marbury and his client, Alger Hiss, are pictured at the right. The photograph dates from August 5, 1948, when Hiss first appeared before the committee. Courtesy of the Library of Congress.

Supreme Court Justice Felix Frankfurter, and a score of other Establishment figures.[333]

Hiss might have escaped further scrutiny but for Richard Nixon. The young congressman would not let the matter drop. Cajoling his fellow committee members to persevere lest they commit political suicide, Nixon insisted that Hiss knew Chambers and had perjured himself during his testimony. He also argued against turning the matter over to the Justice Department, which would be a sign the committee was too weak to investigate the salient issues. Relying on his considerable powers of persuasion, Nixon lobbied his colleagues, with investigator Robert Stripling vigorously offering his support. The committee agreed to delve deeper into the matter. The full committee established

a subcommittee to question Whittaker Chambers in executive session to determine whether he or Hiss was lying.[334]

And so began the strange, yet strangely compelling, odyssey of Whittaker Chambers, Alger Hiss, and HUAC. Nixon established his reputation at this juncture, taking a lead role in questioning Chambers and running down documents and witnesses. He and Stripling became a precision team, discussing the facts, comparing notes, and methodically preparing the case against Alger Hiss. The timing was no accident. With the 1948 election only a few months away, the Republicans hoped to sweep the Democrats out of office in both Congress and the presidency. HUAC became a tool in the political wars as Republican committee members sought to highlight the pattern of Communist influences in the New Deal. If enough of the American people believed that Truman and Roosevelt had been influenced by Communism, they might reward the Republican Party with a sweeping electoral victory and approve of the dismantling of the far-reaching New Deal social programs put into place fifteen years earlier. The committee had a great deal riding on its investigations, not simply the question of whether Alger Hiss had lied under oath.[335]

When the committee reconvened a week-and-a-half after Hiss's original appearance, it was a different scenario. Nixon peppered Hiss with questions and asked whether he knew Chambers. Under the relentless interrogation, Hiss began to equivocate. In a dramatic moment, he finally relented, acknowledging that he may have met Chambers under a different name: George Crosley. In a face-to-face meeting with Chambers, Hiss identified the man as Crosley. While still denying he was involved in espionage, Hiss had provided Nixon and HUAC with a crucial bit of information. Hiss and Chambers knew each other.[336]

While this crack in the story damaged Alger Hiss's credibility, it was not tantamount to a proverbial smoking gun. That bit of damning evidence came later when Hiss's attorney, William Marbury, asked Chambers if he had any documents in his possession to corroborate his charges. Apparently, no one had thought to ask this question previously. Chambers said he did.[337]

By this time, President Truman and the Democrats had won a surprising victory in the 1948 elections. Rather than face the prospect

of solidifying political control in Washington, the Republicans faced a newly energized president who was intent on using his political capital to the fullest advantage. Among other things, Truman described HUAC as "obsolete" and "unnecessary." He told his attorney general to prepare a resolution asking the Democratic Congress to disband the committee. The plan might have succeeded if Whittaker Chambers had not stolen the spotlight from Truman by announcing that he possessed documents to prove his charges.[338]

HUAC members, most especially Nixon, were stunned at the revelation. In all the many hours Nixon had spoken with Chambers, the man had never mentioned the existence of the documents. Furious and feeling betrayed, Nixon initially decided to abandon the chase. It was only because Robert Stripling badgered him to confront Chambers a final time that Nixon learned Chambers had handed over some documents to the Justice Department but held back additional evidence. Before going on a vacation cruise with his wife, Nixon ordered a subpoena delivered on Chambers to produce the second set of documents.[339]

It was the stuff of great spy drama. When two HUAC investigators arrived at Chambers's farm, he led them into a pumpkin patch and reached into a hollowed-out pumpkin. Pulling his hand free, he produced rolls of microfilm containing State Department documents dating from the mid-1930s. Some files contained Alger Hiss's handwriting.

The headlines exploded with the news. Contacted on board the cruise ship, Nixon agreed to return immediately, leaving his wife, Pat, to complete the cruise alone. A Coast Guard PBY Catalina flying boat retrieved the congressman, who was suddenly in high demand, and whisked him away to Washington. The event may have been fortuitous or staged, but in any case, it was terrific publicity for the young legislator.[340]

A struggle ensued among HUAC, the Justice Department, and the FBI for control of the so-called Pumpkin Papers. The material presented a problem for Nixon and his committee. The papers still did not definitively show that Alger Hiss was involved in espionage, but it clearly indicated Whittaker Chambers's guilt. Worried that the

Congressman Richard Nixon of California, a House Un-American Activities Committee (HUAC) member, made a name for himself by investigating the Alger Hiss case in 1948. Here Nixon (right) poses with HUAC chief investigator Robert Stripling in an iconic photograph showing the two men examining microfilm that reputedly contained State Department files. Whittaker Chambers stored the microfilm inside a hollowed-out pumpkin. Courtesy of the Library of Congress.

Justice Department might indict his star witness for perjury or even espionage, Nixon decided to use the best weapon available to him—publicity. He called a hasty press conference on December 5, 1948, to provide the public with a glimpse of the microfilm. Nixon and Stripling also posed for an iconic photograph showing them examining the film with a magnifying glass, hardly the most effective tool for reading microfilm.[341]

Nixon ultimately turned over the microfilm to the FBI to avoid facing a contempt charge. By then, however, the news was out that HUAC had pinned its man. The FBI had located a typewriter belonging to Priscilla Hiss, Alger's wife. Chambers claimed that a Communist photographer from Baltimore had microfilmed some documents while Priscilla Hiss had typed others on her typewriter. After the documents had been copied, Hiss returned the originals to the State Department and Chambers passed the copies along to a Soviet intelligence agent. Chambers kept a separate set of copies inside the pumpkin on his farm.[342]

The case was passed to a grand jury to determine whether Hiss had perjured himself in his earlier testimony. Pressed to explain how his wife's typewriter could be linked to the documents on the microfilm if he had never been associated with Chambers, Hiss could think of no logical explanation. "Until the day I die," he sputtered, "I shall wonder how Whittaker Chambers got into my house to use my typewriter." The comment produced laughter in the grand jury room, but it did not help Hiss's cause. His protests appeared so feeble and self-serving that the grand jury lost no time in indicting Hiss on perjury charges. The statute of limitations prevented prosecutors from pursuing an espionage case.[343]

After one trial ended with a hung jury, Hiss stood trial a second time and was convicted on two counts of perjury. An appeals court upheld the verdict, and the US Supreme Court declined to grant *certiorari*. Sentenced to a term of five years in prison, Hiss served three years and eight months. To the end of his long life, he argued he was innocent, the victim of right-wing hysteria.[344]

Reactions to the verdict varied according to one's politics. Right-wingers were elated. A major threat had been uncovered, and it was

clear to Americans of a conservative bent that the Roosevelt and Truman administrations could not be trusted to safeguard national security. Liberals were aghast at what they viewed as a travesty of justice, the "tragedy" of a man with a good name who had been unfairly impugned. Dean Acheson, the former secretary of state who had been something of a mentor to Hiss, remarked at a press conference, "I do not intend to turn my back on Alger Hiss." Not everyone in his party shared the man's sentiments. Alger Hiss had become a political pariah, and it was not wise to express public support for a convicted perjurer and Communist.[345]

As for the man who made it happen, Richard Nixon was no longer merely a freshman congressman. He was a shrewd political figure on the rise. He also had demonstrated that chasing Communists was politically beneficial to an ambitious public figure. It was a lesson well-learned. Two weeks after the Hiss verdict hit the newspapers, Senator Joseph R. McCarthy, a Wisconsin Republican searching for a way to make his mark, set off on his own witch hunt—an endeavor made possible by the HUAC trailblazers.[346]

Assessing HUAC

HUAC indefatigably investigated Communist subversion in the 1940s and 1950s. Its glory years continued, to some extent, with Senator McCarthy's witch hunt. After McCarthy was discredited and condemned, HUAC entered a period of slow decline. A backlash occurred against government abuses during the 1960s as many citizens objected vehemently to the use of congressional resources to blacklist "undesirable" liberals in Hollywood. In particular, anti-Vietnam protesters targeted HUAC as an instrument of oppression and a means for witch-hunting. In 1969, to forestall additional criticism, the committee changed its name to the Internal Security Committee and limped along for another six years. In 1975, Congress abolished the committee altogether.[347]

It has become fashionable to regard HUAC's activities as an overblown Communist witch-hunt. With the benefit of hindsight, historians several generations removed from the battlefront have criticized the committee's activities as detrimental to the health and welfare of a

nation founded on principles of freedom of speech and thought. It is true that committee members frequently pursued their inquiries with a zeal that crossed the boundary between good public service and an abuse of power, caring more for sensational headlines than for distinguishing between bad actors posing a threat to American interests and good people who indulged a youthful infatuation with leftist political causes.[348]

Despite the well-documented misdeeds perpetrated by HUAC investigators, the committee did uncover evidence of Communist plots on American soil in an era when the Communist threat appeared to be genuine and growing. Gerhart Eisler, Jacob Golos, and Elizabeth Bentley, among many others, cannot be dismissed as idealistic young people who naively embraced the central tenets of Marxist ideology without fully appreciating the totalitarian impulses of a Communist regime in practice. They were seasoned operatives knowingly involved in espionage against their host country. A government is obliged to protect its citizens from security threats, and HUAC performed a public service in fulfilling that obligation.

In the final analysis, even Alger Hiss apparently betrayed his country. For decades, until his death in 1996, he proclaimed his innocence. The case divided Americans for generations. Eastern elites insisted that a fine, upstanding statesman had been unfairly smeared by reactionary Neanderthals who cared more about advancing their own careers than they did about finding the truth. Persons on the right of the political spectrum viewed the affair through a different prism. They saw Hiss and his defenders as smug, condescending liberals who dismissed charges against Communist agents as inconvenient details that interfered with their presumed right to assume positions of power and prestige.[349]

Scholars of the Cold War incessantly debated the evidence for and against Hiss, arguing that the answer could probably be found in Soviet files. Yet the debate continued after the Soviet Union dissolved in 1991 and the archives surfaced. Although the files do not definitively resolve the matter, the weight of the evidence suggests that Hiss probably was a Soviet agent. Whether his contributions amounted to much is difficult to assess, but political conservatives point to the case

as illustrative of the dangerous path followed by American liberals who turned a blind eye to the dangers of Communism in the modern world.[350]

Assessing HUAC's place in history is complicated by the committee's mixed record. In ferreting out potential threats, the committee acted on the maxim that the ends justify the means. International Communism represented such an enormous threat that normal civil liberties protections had to be set aside in the interests of national security. If a few innocent people—or perhaps numerous innocent people—were damaged during the investigations, it was a small price to pay in defense of the United States.

The "national security" excuse is cited in virtually every instance in which a powerful government seeks to justify otherwise unjustifiable actions. Yet if the Bill of Rights is ignored in instances where such protections matter the most, why have a bill of rights in the first place? In times of peace and prosperity, when national interests do not appear to be under assault, civil liberties are not tested. It is when a crisis occurs and Americans believe they face an existential threat that legal protections from a potentially abusive government become crucial. If those are the times where a government sets aside constraints on its behavior in the name of expediency, perhaps the Bill of Rights should be jettisoned once and for all. If citizen rights matter only when they are not tested, perhaps it is time to recognize them for what they are: a convenient, but outdated, ruse. Such cynicism is one legacy of the rise and fall of HUAC.[351]

Chapter 8

THE FBI AND COINTELPRO

Never once did I hear anybody, including myself, raise the question: "Is this course of action which we have agreed upon lawful? Is it legal? Is it ethical or moral?"

—WILLIAM C. SULLIVAN,

FORMER *FBI* ASSOCIATE DIRECTOR, IN TESTIMONY
BEFORE THE UNITED STATES SENATE SELECT COMMITTEE
TO STUDY GOVERNMENTAL OPERATIONS WITH RESPECT TO
INTELLIGENCE ACTIVITIES, NOVEMBER 1, 1975[352]

The Federal Bureau of Investigation (FBI) is a legendary law enforcement agency housed within the US Department of Justice (DOJ). During decades of operations, the bureau has earned a reputation as an elite entity, its leaders and agents viewed as among the most professional police officials in American history. A predecessor agency, the Bureau of Investigation (BOI), dates from 1908. In those early days of the twentieth century, Americans were alarmed at a perceived rise in crime. News stories appeared about the proliferation of anarchists and radical Socialists intent on harming American interests and endangering lives. Citizens demanded that their government keep them safe. A new, well-funded, professional, aggressive federal agency seemed to fit the bill.

For most of American history, law enforcement had been the province of local officials. In some cities and towns, constables on patrol worked part-time, juggling multiple duties. Investigative and forensic techniques such as fingerprinting were in their infancy. Few local policemen were conversant with the latest advances, and law enforcement training and procedures were not uniform or consistent. By almost any standard, municipal police departments, in places where they existed at all, were unprofessional enterprises. A major impetus

for creating the BOI was to modernize law enforcement by relying on the latest scientific data to prevent criminal activity, whenever possible, and to punish perpetrators after the fact, as necessary. If crime was an undeniable feature of modern life, a cutting-edge law enforcement agency would address any threat.

United States Attorney General Charles Joseph Bonaparte created the Bureau of Investigation on July 26, 1908, and tapped a longtime DOJ employee, Stanley W. Finch, to serve as the first agency chief. Bonaparte acted on orders from President Theodore Roosevelt, who was attuned to public opinion on crime and knew that government must respond. Finch stayed at the helm for four years. After he departed, the agency shuffled through a series of directors before finding J. Edgar Hoover, a young lawyer who had gained a reputation as a diligent law enforcement enthusiast.[353]

Hoover was well-suited to his new position. Although not yet thirty years old when he stepped into his post, he proved to be indefatigable, a workaholic's workaholic. He never married or raised a family. Hoover's life was devoted to his career, and he was meticulous in compiling data on crime and suspicious persons. Early in his career, he had headed the DOJ Alien Enemy Bureau, an agency tasked with arresting suspicious foreigners under the Espionage Act of 1917. The experience colored his perspective for the rest of his life. Foreigners and suspicious organizations could not be trusted. They must be monitored constantly lest they threaten the republic. In 1924, when he became the head of the BOI, Hoover resolved to carve out a niche that would change the nature of law enforcement. In that regard, he succeeded beyond anyone's expectations. Hoover held his position as the agency head from the time of his appointment until his death almost forty-eight years later. The BOI officially became known as the FBI in 1935.

Hoover's legacy was mixed. On one hand, he brought a level of professionalism and organizational genius to the position. He understood the importance of maintaining records on all manner of subversive activity, and his comprehensive files on enemies of the state as well as on the peccadilloes of politicians and public figures became the stuff of legend. At the time of his death at age seventy-seven in 1972, Hoover was a divisive, controversial figure—romanticized by some as

J. Edgar Hoover served as FBI director from 1924 until his death in 1972. He is pictured here in 1961. Courtesy of the Library of Congress.

a "G-man" extraordinaire and reviled by others as a power-hungry, megalomaniacal bureaucrat. Many presidents of the United States were said to detest Hoover, but they dared not fire him lest he leak damaging information on innumerable Washington power brokers— and perhaps on the chief executive who removed him from power.[354]

The Counterintelligence Program

Late in Hoover's tenure, information about the bureau's counterintelligence program, code named COINTELPRO (short for COunter INTELligence PROgram), garnered public attention. The "dirty tricks" practiced by the agency against suspects who may or may not have engaged in criminal activity tarnished the agency's reputation in the eyes of many citizens. As the facts became known, an incensed public learned that COINTELPRO originated in 1956 in response to

Hoover's concerns about the supposedly nefarious activities of subversive groups. The goal was to disrupt the operations of individuals and organizations that Hoover and his men disliked by destroying their members' reputations, which could be accomplished through planting public stories, true or untrue, about a target's conduct based on data gathered through surveillance. A tried-and-true tactic was to send anonymous letters to group members threatening to expose a compromising secret or publish a salacious photograph if the subject did not comply with the agency's wishes. Agents also sought to create discord among members of supposedly subversive groups by infiltrating the organization with an informant who deliberately encouraged members to quarrel. FBI agents or local law enforcement personnel, at the bureau's behest, conducted surveillance by unlawfully breaking into people's homes to plant electronic listening devices or gather up letters and other records to use toward discrediting the target.

Hoover assigned long-time FBI agent William C. Sullivan to head up COINTELPRO operations. Born in 1912, Sullivan joined the bureau during World War II and progressively gained new power and responsibilities as he advanced through the ranks. At one point, he was Hoover's heir apparent. The men eventually had a falling out, and Sullivan retired in 1971, less than a year before Hoover died.

When he headed up COINTELPRO, Sullivan's rupture with his powerful benefactor had not yet occurred. He was a loyal agent. Reflecting on those activities years later, Sullivan defended the work. "The counterintelligence techniques we brought to our fight against the Klan has been thoroughly damned by the press and the public, but our successful use of these techniques is what finally broke them up. As far as I'm concerned, we might as well not engage in intelligence unless we also engage in counterintelligence. One is the right arm, the other the left. They work together." Yet Sullivan came to see the dangers in allowing a federal agency with almost unfettered discretion to act without proper oversight or accountability. In 1975, he told a Senate committee investigating the program, "Never once did I hear anybody, including myself, raise the question: 'Is this course of action which we have agreed upon lawful? Is it legal? Is it ethical or moral?'"

Sullivan's soul-searching musings were far in the future when he stepped into his role as the COINTELPRO chief. It was little wonder the FBI relied on counterintelligence, a program in which a government prevents spies from uncovering secrets by proactively attacking suspects so they cannot learn those secrets or by planting inaccurate data so enemies discover false information. Hoover had been a proponent of counterintelligence since his early days in the bureau. He was especially fixated on developing programs to use against suspected Communists. The director believed that Communist conspiracies lurked around every corner. If occasionally he was correct, such corroboration only served to increase his fear that for every conspiracy he uncovered, many more existed. Critics charged that Hoover was so devoted to rooting out Communists from positions of influence that he failed to prosecute cases involving a multitude of other threats to American interests.

He was a paranoid, suspicious man, this J. Edgar Hoover who built an empire at the FBI. In some ways, the bureau became his own private fiefdom, and he ran the place as though his every whim was law. Always careful to court powerful patrons in Congress and the White House, Hoover believed he could act with little oversight as long as he produced results and issued periodic warnings about hidden threats to American citizens and institutions. His targets sometimes represented genuinely dangerous persons and organizations, but sometimes they were not criminal organizations. Persons and entities that ran afoul of Hoover's own sense of righteousness and morality became candidates for law enforcement scrutiny that might last for years or even decades. He evinced an almost pathological aversion to individuals he deemed to be "deviant," especially persons of color and anyone outside the mainstream of white, conservative, Middle America.

When the modern civil rights movement emerged, Hoover instructed his agents to investigate movement leaders on suspicion of Communism—Martin Luther King Jr. was a favorite target—without affording the same high level of scrutiny to white racists who sometimes attacked those same black leaders under FBI surveillance. Hoover's antipathy for subversive organizations and his racially biased views blinded him to the realities of changing times. He could not

or would not differentiate between groups voicing loyal opposition to government policy and groups dedicated to harming the citizenry through violence. Only after incidents against civil rights groups escalated to a point where the perpetrators could no longer be ignored did the bureau investigate and prosecute the offenders.

COINTELPRO was a prime example of Hoover's (and the FBI's) apparent inability to distinguish between persons petitioning their government for a redress of grievances and malcontents who genuinely endangered the polity. The program monitored groups thought to pose a security risk to the US government, including the Ku Klux Klan, the Nation of Islam, the Black Panther Party, nonviolent civil rights groups, and leftist organizations such as Weatherman. As they undertook their COINTELPRO duties, FBI agents generally circumvented constitutional requirements and other legal niceties. Among other techniques, agents relied on electronic surveillance without a warrant or judicial oversight. Aside from violating the Fourth Amendment to the US Constitution, which requires law enforcement officials to procure a warrant from an appropriate magistrate prior to invading a citizen's privacy—with some exceptions, such as exigent circumstances—the bureau browbeat suspects into changing their behavior even if the behavior was not illegal.[355]

The Civil Rights Movement and
Black Nationalist Hate Groups

Part of what made COINTELPRO especially controversial was the FBI's choice of targets. Had the bureau focused on groups the public perceived to be dangerous, the backlash might have been less severe. Revelations of illegal activity by FBI agents would be controversial no matter what circumstances were involved, but the benign nature of some COINTELPRO targets only heightened widespread public criticism.

Two targets, in particular, demonstrated the FBI's lack of public accountability and the dearth of political or legal controls over the agency's activities. The first group of targets involved black activists. Although the COINTELPRO operation against black organizations officially dates from 1967, the bureau's interest in Negro agitators

commenced much earlier. Because FBI leaders and agents were conservative white males who possessed little or no understanding of the systematic racial discrimination and the innumerable series of humiliations that Negroes in America had suffered for generations, they could not fathom why a loyal American, whatever his race, would rail against the status quo. When a man such as Martin Luther King Jr. stood at a podium and delivered an impassioned speech assailing American policy or took to the streets to lead a nonviolent protest, the bureau viewed his actions as wicked. Surely he must be under the influence of nefarious forces—Communists, anarchists, or the bestial urges that compelled black brutes to cause trouble.[356]

Dr. King first attracted the FBI's attention in February 1956. At the time, the twenty-seven-year-old minister had become a leader in the Montgomery, Alabama, bus boycott protesting the arrest of Rosa Parks, a black woman who refused to surrender her seat to a white patron on a public bus. Although Dr. King's public statements about his adherence to nonviolent civil disobedience and his apparent willingness to follow his own advice suggested he did not pose a threat to the peace, the FBI became convinced he was a radical Negro who was up to no good. King's public persona suggested he was a man of peace, but the agency had little doubt that a dangerous subversive lurked beneath a thin facade.[357]

The bureau believed that several of Dr. King's aides and advisers, notably Stanley Levison, Jack O'Dell, and Bayard Rustin, were dangerous extremists devoted to undermining American values. Levison was a white New York lawyer who had served as a financier for the Communist party of the United States. Jack O'Dell was a young black man, another close King associate who had flirted with Communism during the 1950s. Bayard Rustin merited special attention from the FBI, for he was the incarnation of virtually everything J. Edgar Hoover despised: he was black, homosexual, and a Socialist, and had participated in a laundry list of social causes. Hoover eventually persuaded Attorney General Robert F. Kennedy to authorize a wiretap on Dr. King's phones. Because the civil rights leader traveled so frequently, the bureau expanded its surveillance on King, following him around the country and assiduously recording his movements and activities.[358]

Following Dr. King's celebrated "I Have a Dream Speech" at the Lincoln Memorial during the March on Washington on August 28, 1963, the FBI became more convinced than ever that the man represented a genuine threat. Recognizing the charismatic leader's oratorical ability, the agency feared he might stir the masses to participate in God-knows-what manner of mischief. Sullivan, the bureau's point man on COINTELPRO, penned a memorandum a day after the speech, concluding, "Personally, I believe in the light of King's powerful demagogic speech yesterday he stands head and shoulders over all other Negro leaders put together when it comes to influencing great masses of Negroes. We must mark him now, if we have not done so before, as the most dangerous Negro of the future in this Nation from the standpoint of communism, the Negro and national security." Hoover and his men would monitor Dr. King for the rest of the man's life although they could not, it seems, simultaneously protect him from assassination.[359]

Other black activists received similar treatment, perhaps none more so than Malcolm X. Born as Malcolm Little, he discarded his surname, a vestige of slavery, after he converted to Islam while serving time in prison. Malcolm joined Elijah Muhammad's Nation of Islam (NOI) and quickly rose through the ranks. His mesmerizing speaking skills, his personal charisma, and his imposing physique made Malcolm X a popular and effective recruiter for the NOI. His rising stature also captured the FBI's attention.[360]

Unlike Martin Luther King Jr., who continually spoke of nonviolent protest and Christian brotherhood, Malcolm X uttered incendiary rhetoric that frightened many white listeners. He acquired a reputation as a black racist who supported armed confrontation with white "devils." Much of Malcolm's language could be interpreted as vitriolic and confrontational, but such a construction fails to appreciate his evolving character. After he broke from the NOI and returned from a visit to Mecca, Malcolm's speeches evolved. He remained passionately committed to uplifting blacks in America and around the world, but he also extended an olive branch to any person or group that assisted his efforts. His two new organizations—Muslim Mosque, Inc. (MMI) and the Organization of

Afro-American Unity (OAAU)—were outlets for Malcolm's changing message.[361]

The FBI realized that an opportunity existed to "widen the rift" between Elijah Muhammad and his former protégé. Using information gleaned from wiretaps, the FBI created an anonymous news story regarding a "war within the ranks of the Muslims' empire" and fed the text to the *Chicago Defender,* the largest Negro newspaper in the United States. Among other things, the story provided convincing details about episodes where Muhammad and Malcolm X had disagreed. The story described the NOI's belief that Malcolm was fanatical and a "true revolutionary" who was difficult to control. From Malcolm's perspective, Elijah Muhammad had been corrupted by his vast wealth and the adulation of his admirers. It must have pleased bureau personnel to know that the ruse worked exactly as planned. Wiretaps inside the NOI indicated that Muhammad and his men believed that the story originated from leaks that Malcolm X generated.[362]

On February 21, 1965, as he was preparing to speak to an audience about the OAAU in the Audubon Ballroom in Manhattan, Malcolm X was shot to death by three men with ties to the NOI. Questions persist about who ordered the assassination, and why. Among the various conspiracy theories espoused throughout the years, one version places the FBI at the center of the plot. Even if the bureau did not take an active part in the murder, efforts to exploit the gulf between Malcolm X and the NOI certainly contributed to the poisoned atmosphere that encouraged his enemies to shoot the thirty-nine-year-old activist.[363]

Martin Luther King Jr. and Malcolm X in many ways represented twin pillars in the civil rights movement of the early-to-mid 1960s. King sought to work within the existing political system to promote change through nonviolent civil disobedience while Malcolm X believed that the system was corrupt and in need of wholesale reform. As the nature of the civil rights movement changed with each passing year, a new group of activists supplanted the old masters. By 1967, with Malcolm dead and King struggling to maintain his relevance, new faces appeared. The younger generation assailed King and Malcolm, especially the former. The Congress of Racial Equality (CORE), the Student Nonviolent Coordinating Committee (SNCC), the Republic

Martin Luther King Jr., and Malcolm X, pictured here on March 26, 1964, were among the many COINTELPRO targets. Courtesy of the Library of Congress.

of New Africa, the League of Revolutionary Black Workers, and the Black Panther Party were among the more militant organizations that threatened the fabric of America society, at least from the FBI perspective. These groups, in some ways inspired by Malcolm X, charged that nonviolent resistance was too slow and passive. If change did not occur immediately, other means of change must be found. For the more radical groups, violent revolution was a legitimate alternative to nonviolent protest.[364]

Watching these developments with increasing alarm, the FBI placed each group under surveillance. On August 25, 1967, a directive from FBI headquarters characterized members of these "Black Nationalist Hate Groups" as "pernicious," "duplicitous," and "devious." To ensure that public sympathy and favorable coverage would not be afforded to such miscreants, COINTELPRO operations would be expanded to publicize the immoral conduct of group members and highlight their criminal records. The campaign included anonymous mailings to law enforcement officers, newspaper editors, and prominent elected officials outlining the shortcomings of group

leaders. When the bureau did not have credible data on the subject's criminal background or history of immoral personal conduct, agents simply fabricated it. The goal was to destroy the target's credibility— to borrow a phrase associated with Malcolm X—by any means necessary. The operation against "Black Nationalist Hate Groups" would remain in effect until the FBI formally shut down COINTELPRO in 1971.[365]

COINTELPRO—New Left

Hoover's men reputedly believed that participants in the anti–Vietnam War movement represented a threat to American security. Although this assessment of the FBI's motivations for targeting the so-called New Left is at least partially accurate—Hoover argued that Communists had infiltrated almost every American organization—it fails to capture another aspect of the FBI's war against antiwar demonstrators. One FBI memorandum drafted during the 1960s perhaps best expressed the agents' assorted motivations. The document, dating from June 1968, drips with disdain for the culture of young people with their "nonconformity in dress and speech, neglect of personal cleanliness, use of obscenities, publicized sexual promiscuity, shaggy hair, and wearing of sandals, beads, and unusual jewelry."[366]

Disgust at young people's manner of dress, speech, and lifestyle choices might have triggered FBI scrutiny, but the involvement of these counterculture hippies in efforts to influence American war policy guaranteed that the bureau would tag them for additional scrutiny. As early as 1965, the year the United States committed the first ground troops into combat operations in Vietnam, the FBI targeted antiwar protesters inside the Socialist Workers Party (SWP). Agents dispatched an anonymous "Open Letter to Trotskyites" to generate discord among SWP members. "You're a Trotskyite," the letter began. "You've struggled through the years attempting to influence others with your particular line of revolutionary socialism. You've seen your Party's membership cut time and time again by a seemingly endless series of splits, to the point where, historically, the SWP has become known as the 'party of splits.'" After outlining an array of disagreements and purges among party members, the letter concluded, "Your

humiliation in the public and radical press is now complete as you sadly observe your FORMER party press on."[367]

The bureau took further notice of the antiwar movement when the Students for a Democratic Society (SDS) announced plans for an April 1965 March on Washington to protest US military involvement in Vietnam. The SDS was a faction with the so-called Revolutionary Youth Movement that sought to undermine capitalism through a working class revolution. SDS members agreed on the ends (forcing the US government to end the war in Vietnam), but the means were a source of contention. In later years, SDS members would split into factions, some of which employed violence to achieve their ends. The Weather Underground Organization (WUO) became the most infamous splinter group to spring from the SDS. In 1965, however, the WUO had not been formed, and the SDS enjoyed a measure of legitimacy as a voice for young people affiliated with the League for Industrial Democracy, a socialist organization.

More than twenty thousand people turned out for the march, a number that exceeded the group's expectations. For reasons that were not clear, the SDS never followed up on the momentum. Pulling back from the antiwar movement, the group focused on other issues, ceding the field to other youth groups.[368]

With the absence of the SDS, other antiwar activists filled the void. Spontaneous antiwar protests sprang up on college campuses throughout the country, notably at the University of Michigan and the University of California at Berkeley. The SWP was involved in these early antiwar efforts, and the group's involvement attracted the FBI's attention. Through COINTELPRO, the bureau sought to disrupt the SWP's plans to schedule an antiwar conference in Washington, D.C. in November 1965 along with the Young Socialist Alliance.[369]

From the beginning, factions within the antiwar movement could not agree on strategies and tactics. Everyone inside the movement fervently desired an end to America's involvement in what activists viewed as an imperialist war, but the parties remained divided on how the conflict should end. Loudly calling for immediate withdrawal was

conceptually simple, but it ignored the realities of winding down a military operation involving hundreds of thousands of people. To remove many thousands of troops from the country overnight—assuming that American political and military leaders could be pushed to pursue such a course of action—would leave innocent South Vietnamese civilians at the mercy of their enemies who might well butcher them in retaliation for their complicity with American war planners. Yet any policy short of instant withdrawal was subject to interminable delays that probably would result in an ongoing American presence. The movement was divided.[370]

The FBI recognized the schisms within the antiwar camp and sought to exploit them as much as possible. From 1968 until 1970, the Indianapolis field office took a lead role in the war against radical groups. In one instance, the bureau created a fake newsletter called *Armageddon News* that purported to be a leftist publication. The goal was to offer so many ludicrous suggestions that college students reading the newsletter would be dissuaded from joining the antiwar movement. The publication was ham-fisted and so patently right-wing that virtually no one paid it any attention.[371]

Not every agency effort was as badly botched as the *Armageddon News*. In August 1968, the FBI distributed a leaflet from an alleged supporter of the Radical Organizing Committee (ROC), a short-lived arm of the Communist party of the United States, heaping praise on activists who had split from the Student Mobilization Committee to End the War in Vietnam (SMC). As the bureau knew, ROC had called for the SMC to exclude members of the Young Socialist Alliance (YSA), the student association of the SWP, from planning antiwar rallies and activities. When the ROC was unsuccessful in ousting the YSA, its members broke away from the SMC. The FBI exploited the rift.

A 1969 leaflet, "Notes from the Sand Castle," argued for violent demonstrations and criticized various antiwar factions. Driving a wedge between the parties and pushing them to break the law would accomplish multiple goals. If antiwar demonstrators busily squabbled among themselves, they would be in no position to march against the war. The activists who accepted an invitation for violence could expect

to be arrested and prosecuted, an area where the FBI and law enforcement could exact the strongest penalties. "Divide and conquer" was the hallmark of COINTELPRO operations; indeed, it has been the foundation of any effective counterintelligence program throughout history.[372]

Aside from highlighting divisions among the various antiwar factions, the FBI strove to ensure that leftist organizations would not join forces with black organizations. The two groups recognized commonalities of purpose. A disproportionately high number of young men who were drafted and sent to Vietnam were ethnic minorities and blacks. The citizens who were least able to enjoy their rights as American citizens were being forced to bear a large part of the burden of defending those rights. It was only natural that some antiwar groups would reach out to black groups and join forces against the war. The bureau sought to disrupt the formation of these coalitions by circulating missives denouncing the SDS as a racist organization. The agency dredged up articles and stories in which black activists criticized the Communist party and sent the text to Communist party leaders. Bureau efforts met with varying levels of success.[373]

In March 1969, SDS representatives met with members of the Black Panther Party in Austin, Texas, and the two forces enjoyed a measure of mutual admiration. The SDS even proclaimed the Black Panthers as the vanguard of the revolution, a development that deeply unsettled FBI operatives. They need not have worried. The rapprochement did not last. A faction of the SDS objected to the designation of the Black Panther Party as a vanguard of anything, and subsequent acrimony left all parties bitter and hostile. After Black Panther activists used misogynist rhetoric that alienated some SDS members as well as the burgeoning feminist movement, the New Left appeared to be in disarray, much to the delight of COINTELPRO agents. The nature and extent of the agency's activities in sowing the seeds of discord remains muddled and controversial.[374]

In this photograph, activists protesting the Vietnam War congregate on the Washington Mall after marching on the Pentagon on October 21, 1967. The following year, the FBI launched COINTELPRO-NEW LEFT, a covert "dirty tricks" operation designed to disrupt the antiwar movement. Courtesy of the National Archives & Records Administration.

Exposure and Legacy

The FBI showed few signs of winding down COINTELPRO until a breach of security occurred. A group calling itself "Citizens' Commission to Investigate the FBI" burglarized an FBI office in Media, Pennsylvania, in April 1971. Unfortunately for the bureau, the burglars escaped with hundreds of pages of confidential COINTELPRO files clearly showing the bureau's campaign against unpopular targets. Reacting to the media backlash after the group publicly released the files, Hoover officially dissolved COINTELPRO that year. Despite the public show of shutting down the counterintelligence program, the bureau continued to employ COINTELPRO tactics even after Hoover died in 1972. The program no longer existed under its original name, but its spirit endured. The FBI's Special Target Information Development program sent agents undercover to infiltrate "radical" organizations and conduct "back-bag jobs," that is, illegal searches inside the homes of suspected subversives.[375]

It was clear that the bureau would not abandon procedures that had served it so well in the past. Consequently, Congress investigated COINTELPRO and other FBI tactics employed in the 1950s and 1960s. In 1978, President Carter's attorney general, Griffin Bell, launched an investigation that resulted in criminal indictments brought against several high-ranking FBI officials. The days of the dashing law enforcement agency that brought down John Dillinger, "Ma" Barker, "Machine Gun" Kelly, and "Baby Face" Nelson during the 1930s appeared to have ended. The negative publicity of the post-Hoover era and the illegal nature of the surveillance program ensured that much of the information collected against supposedly subversive groups could not be used to prosecute suspected offenders. Moreover, some anti-government sources bitterly complained that while COINTELPRO formally had been shut down in 1971, many of the tactics continued under different names.[376]

It was an era when citizens cried out for government reform. During the early 1970s, a series of clandestine operations came to light, capturing enormous public attention. Aside from the COINTELPRO revelations in 1971, a year earlier Americans learned that the US army

had spied on civilians. Revelations about multiple abuses of power at the Central Intelligence Agency (CIA) also inflamed public opinion. Amidst all the turmoil and confusion, anti-Vietnam protests continued and the expanding Watergate break-in and conspiracy to cover up the crime filled newspapers.[377]

The US Senate Select Committee to Study Governmental Operations with Respect to Intelligence Activities, known as the Church Committee after Chairman Frank Church of Idaho, convened in 1975 to investigate the allegations. During the course of its investigations, the committee interviewed hundreds of witnesses, collected voluminous files from the nation's intelligence and law enforcement agencies, and issued fourteen reports in 1975 and 1976. The federal government's activities showed a systematic campaign of abuses, from spying on US citizens who had not been charged with any crimes, to plots designed to assassinate world leaders. "The Government has often undertaken the secret surveillance of citizens on the basis of their political beliefs, even when those beliefs posed no threat of violence or illegal acts," a committee report concluded, citing violations at numerous agencies. As for the bureau, "FBI headquarters alone has developed over 500,000 domestic intelligence files."[378]

The committee cited multiple reasons why the FBI felt compelled to pursue COINTELPRO. Aside from J. Edgar Hoover's personal obsession with espionage and his umbrage at the actions of people living in a world outside of mainstream white America, he and his agents believed that standard law enforcement practices were ineffective against a rising tide of lawlessness. The irony, of course, was that Hoover was worried about assaults on the country's legal system, but had he been willing to employ standard law enforcement methods instead of circumventing them, he might have discovered that he had the tools he needed without violating the very laws he claimed to uphold.

A major reason the FBI believed it could act with impunity was that the agency enjoyed relatively easy access to personal information through "the unrestrained collection of domestic intelligence." For decades, Hoover had been amassing an unprecedented level of political power, as well as the autonomy that comes with it. Members of

Senator Frank Church of Idaho (right), pictured here with President Jimmy Carter in 1977, chaired the US Senate Select Committee to Study Governmental Operations with Respect to Intelligence Activities that investigated the FBI's COINTELPRO operations, among other things. Courtesy of the National Archives & Records Administration.

Congress and presidents of the United States who might have curbed the director's authority worried they would appear soft on crime or that Hoover might dip into his files and retaliate.[379]

As a result of the investigations of the 1970s, Congress enacted a series of reforms designed to regulate government surveillance. The Attorney General's Guidelines limited the FBI's investigative role and provided detailed procedural rules. If the bureau were forced to seek authorization and approval before undertaking certain types of investigations, the likelihood of rogue operations being implemented absent accountability controls would diminish, or so civil libertarians believed.[380]

In another irony, it was exactly these legal niceties that lawmakers assailed in the wake of the 9/11 terrorist attacks in 2001. If only the bureau's investigative powers were expanded, apologists for an enhanced national security apparatus howled, perhaps another large

terrorist incident could be avoided. The argument persuaded members of Congress to act quickly in the days after 9/11 when Americans feared for their safety from imminent subversive threats. In the twenty-first century, the FBI came full circle, initiating counterterrorism intelligence operations under the auspices of the Joint Terrorism Task Forces (JTTF) without the safeguard put into place following publication of the Church Committee reports.[381]

As a result of dozens of American Civil Liberties Union (ACLU) Freedom of Information Act (FOIA) requests filed beginning in 2004, citizens learned that the bureau once again had used its resources to monitor unpopular individuals and advocacy groups without probable cause that criminal activity was afoot. A September 2010 DOJ report from the Office of the Inspector General also reviewed the FBI's surveillance on several advocacy groups, including Greenpeace, People for the Ethical Treatment of Animals, and Catholic Worker Organizations. The DOJ report concluded, in a wry understatement, "The factual basis for opening some of the investigations of individuals affiliated with the groups was factually weak." In all cases under review, "there was little indication of possible federal crimes as opposed to state crimes." Sometimes the bureau extended the duration of the investigations "without adequate basis," and in some cases, it "improperly retained information about the groups in its files." In an eerie development reminiscent of COINTELPRO, "the FBI classified some investigations relating to nonviolent civil disobedience under its 'Acts of Terrorism' classification."[382]

For defenders of law enforcement who argue that COINTELPRO represents the "bad old days" now banished forever, the FBI's post-9/11 activities offer a compelling counterargument. The temptation to use unrestrained power to maximum effect is simply too powerful to resist. This realization is hardly an indictment limited to the FBI, or any other law enforcement agency, for that matter. If power corrupts and absolute power corrupts absolutely, no one should be surprised when an agency allowed to exercise unfettered discretion does exactly that. The history of government responses to subversive threats repeats this lesson endlessly across the spectrum of American history.[383]

Chapter 9

THE POST-9/11 WAR ON TERROR

Whether we bring our enemies to justice, or bring justice to our enemies, justice will be done.

—GEORGE W. BUSH,

SPEECH BEFORE A JOINT SESSION
OF CONGRESS, SEPTEMBER 20, 2001[384]

The impetus for increasing government investigative authority in the United States during the twenty-first century originated with the September 11, 2001 (9/11) terrorist attacks. The episode became a pivotal point in American history that will remain enshrined in the national consciousness in the same manner that the Japanese attack on Pearl Harbor and the John F. Kennedy assassination were watershed moments. Almost three thousand individuals died that day, and much of the drama played out on live television for horrified people around the world to witness. For many Americans, the attacks came out of a clear blue sky, literally and figuratively. Yet the roots of the conflict extended back for decades along a fault line that only a few observant souls recognized before September 11, 2001.

A strange Saudi-born multi-millionaire, Osama bin Laden, was the mastermind behind the attacks. Almost no American citizens knew of this man before 9/11, but few failed to know his name following that day. The devastation catapulted bin Laden to the front ranks of wanted men considered an ongoing threat to American lives and interests. The US's reaction to the bin Laden threat also changed the nature of American surveillance and criminal law.

The Uniting and Strengthening America by Providing Appropriate Tools Required to Intercept and Obstruct Terrorism Act of 2001,

commonly referred to as the USA PATRIOT Act, became one enduring legacy of the attacks. The law was designed to improve techniques for intelligence officers and law enforcement personnel to detect terrorist plans beforehand and, if necessary, to punish perpetrators after the fact. The "enhanced surveillance procedures" in the act removed several legal requirements for gathering evidence against suspects and altered fundamental criminal procedures for determining when a search and seizure is permissible under the Fourth Amendment to the US Constitution. Congress rushed the statute through by circumventing the typical deliberation process that occurs when a bill is referred to a standing committee, which then sends the proposed measure to a subcommittee for testimony, discussion, and markup. Critics have argued that the PATRIOT Act was enacted in the heat of the moment, and that a "cooling off" period would have provided time for an improved statute. By pushing through legislation when Americans were still suffering from the shock and outrage of a major terrorist incident, Congress and President George W. Bush erred on the side of sacrificing civil liberties to the desire for a more powerful government. Supporters of the PATRIOT Act contend that an ongoing war on terror requires sophisticated surveillance techniques to be used against sophisticated terrorists if a 9/11-style attack is to be prevented in the future.

Origins of the Attacks

Osama bin Laden, the man who was hell-bent on attacking the United States as a symbol of the decadent West, was born in 1957 or 1958, although even the exact date of his birth—March 10 or July 30 in 1957, or perhaps in January of the following year—was not known. He hailed from an enormous family. His father was Mohammed bin Awad bin Laden, a billionaire construction tycoon with connections to the Saudi royal family. Osama's mother, Hamida al-Attas (called Alia Ghanem), was the influential man's tenth wife, and the child was the seventeenth of between fifty-four and fifty-seven offspring. Osama later inherited between $25 million and $30 million from his father's estate when the patriarch died in a plane crash in 1967.[385]

His formative years are as difficult to pinpoint as almost everything else about the man. All that is known for certain is that the

young man's parents divorced early and his mother married a family friend and associate named Mohammed al-Attas. The new couple produced children of their own, which meant that Osama came of age in a household with three half-brothers and a half-sister.[386]

As a child, he was introduced to Wahhabism, a type of militant, puritanical Islam. Followers of Wahhabism call for Muslims to return to the pure form of Islam by rejecting tenets added to the religion since the first generation of Islam. Muhammad ibn Abd al-Wahhab developed this concept in the eighteenth century to arrest the spread of Western civilization and culture. Unfortunately for al-Wahhab, Wahhabism eventually was associated with the Saudi version of Islam. Saudi Arabia is one of the more secularized nations of the Arab world.[387]

Aside from growing up under the influence of Wahhabism, bin Laden encountered the works of Abdullah Azzam, a charismatic Palestinian and follower of Sayyid Qutb, an Egyptian Muslim who visited the United States in the 1940s and denounced the culture of materialism, sexual promiscuity, racism, and "bad haircuts." Azzam and Qutb argued that anything non-Islamic is evil and corrupt. Their notion of an Islamic utopia was appealing for disenfranchised Muslims frustrated by oppressive political regimes. Bin Laden wholeheartedly embraced these values.[388]

He received a first-class education, this child of privilege, attending a prominent secular academy, the Al-Thager Model School. From there, he matriculated at King Addulaziz University in Jeddah, Saudi Arabia. Young Osama demonstrated a penchant for economics and business administration. He possibly earned degrees in civil engineering and public administration, although the records are not definitive. He may have he left the university without earning a degree.[389]

Bin Laden arrived in Afghanistan sometime around 1980. Everyone who saw him remembered the six-foot, five-inch zealot. He was admired as an accomplished horseman, runner, climber, and soccer player who also spent hours listening to tape recorded sermons of fiery Muslim clerics preaching militant Islamic rants. Osama bin Laden's vast personal fortune, imposing physical appearance, and intense charisma caused him to stand out from the crowd.[390]

Fundamentalist Muslims in Afghanistan spent much of the 1980s battling the Soviet Union after the Communists invaded in 1979. Bin Laden did not take up arms in the fight. With his financial resources and extensive contacts, he worked behind the scenes to assemble an intricate network of financiers funneling money into the country to support guerilla activities. The network was known as the "Golden Chain," an organization that equipped and trained the Afghan muja- hideen, or "holy warriors."[391]

Bin Laden argued that the battle was not an ideological struggle between First and Second World nations; it was a war against Islam waged by the West. Even countries skeptical of bin Laden's religious zealotry poured money into his coffers owing to the adage that the enemy of my enemy is my friend. Because bin Laden and the muja- hideen served as proxies for an anti-Soviet war, countries such as the United States and Saudi Arabia were eager to assist. He received no direct assistance from the United States, but money the US govern- ment sent through the Pakistani military intelligence service trained and equipped rebel forces, which freed up bin Laden's money to be used elsewhere.[392]

Bin Laden and his mentor, Abdullah Azzam, created an organiza- tion known as the Bureau of Services (Mektab al Khidmat, or MAK) to oppose the Soviets in Afghanistan. After the Soviet Union withdrew from Afghanistan following almost a decade of warfare, bin Laden and Azzam formalized the network to battle against the corrupting influ- ence of Western forces. The duo transformed the MAK into a base or foundation (known as al-Qaeda) for future jihad. Following this move, bin Laden pushed Azzam aside and assumed the leadership mantle for al-Qaeda, establishing an intelligence branch, a military committee, a financial committee, a political committee, and a propaganda commit- tee. An advisory committee (Shura) composed of bin Laden's closest associates solidified his power.[393]

The men eventually had a falling out over the direction the new organization should take. Azzam believed that a small group should limit its involvement and leverage its relatively scarce resources. The fiercely ambitious bin Laden sought to grow the organization into a global terrorist network capable of striking at Western powers, and

limitations be damned. The dispute ended dramatically on November 24, 1989, when a remote-controlled bomb killed Azzam and two of his sons. Bin Laden blamed the Israeli Mossad and the US Central Intelligence Agency, but some skeptics wondered whether bin Laden had engineered the explosion so that he could seize control of al-Qaeda.[394]

With his power consolidated, bin Laden assembled a team dedicated to disseminating al-Qaeda's message as widely as possible. Ayman al Zawahiri, an Egyptian surgeon who hated the West almost as much as bin Laden did, became a valued confidant. Omar Abdel-Rahman, the "Blind Sheikh," a spiritual guide for fundamentalist organizations such as the Islamic Group and the Egyptian Islamic Jihad, signed on as well. Abdel-Rahman could boast of an impressive resume, having inspired the 1981 murder of Egyptian president Anwar Sadat for appearing too accommodating to Western powers. The sheikh eventually moved to the United States to keep an eye on the greatest enemy of Islam.[395]

Bin Laden was on the move. In 1989, he settled in the Sudan to join forces with Hassan al Turabi, leader of the National Islamic Front, who had recently seized power in Khartoum. Turabi welcomed bin Laden in the fight against African separatists challenging his authority. The two men reached an accommodation: in exchange for al-Qaeda's assistance, Turabi provided bin Laden with a safe haven in the Sudan.[396]

Never satisfied to rest on his laurels, in August 1990, after Iraq invaded Kuwait, bin Laden contacted the Saudi royal family asking for permission to reinvigorate the mujahideen for a jihad to combat Iraq. The Saudis refused. To add insult to injury, the royal family joined a coalition headed by the United States and granted permission for the US military to base soldiers in Saudi Arabia during the First Gulf War. Bin Laden was incensed. He lashed out publicly against this decision. As punishment, the royals revoked his passport. Not long thereafter, bin Laden surreptitiously slipped out of the country under the pretext of attending a meeting in Pakistan. In response to his disobedience, the Saudis stripped him of his citizenship and froze his domestic assets in 1994. Osama bin Laden was a man without a country.[397]

His movement might have died there, but bin Laden would not surrender his vision. Even as he fought with the leaders of his home country, he established an increasingly complex series of businesses to support an increasingly global terrorist network. He appeared to be involved in every operational aspect: meeting with key allies, establishing terrorist training camps, and acquiring sophisticated weaponry.[398]

In those early years, bin Laden operated behind the scenes, in the shadows. Few intelligence services picked up on his whereabouts or his activities. His growing success also brought a new-found power and confidence. He was ready to ratchet up his public profile. In 1992, al-Qaeda issued a fatwa, or Islamic legal opinion, calling for jihad against the Western "occupation" of Islamic lands. As part of this undertaking, bin Laden singled out the United States, urging his followers to sever "the head of the snake." He did not possess the resources to carry out his threat. His comments would seem prophetic in the years to come, but in 1992 they were typical of the angry threats uttered by scores of angry militants around the world. Few observers who bothered to notice al-Qaeda thought anything of the warnings.[399]

Yet his power grew slowly and steadily over the years. When US troops landed in Somalia toward the end of 1992, al-Qaeda and allied terrorist organizations issued a fatwa to expel the invaders. The call to action met with incremental success. In December 1992, a bomb exploded at two hotels in Aden, Yemen, frequented by American military personnel. No Americans were killed, but al-Qaeda was advancing toward achieving its objectives. In the meantime, the group's operatives supplied armaments to Somali warlords for use against American armed forces. Somalis boasted that they shot down two US Black Hawk helicopters in a prominent debacle for the US military in October 1993.[400]

The 1990s witnessed a string of terrorist incidents directly or indirectly attributable to al-Qaeda. In November 1995, a car bomb exploded in Riyadh, Saudi Arabia, near a Saudi National Guard training facility, killing five Americans and two Indians. The four perpetrators caught and executed for the crime confessed that al-Qaeda had "inspired" the bombing. Al-Qaeda seemingly assisted in a notorious June 1996 bombing at the Khobar Towers building in Dhahran, Saudi

Arabia, killing nineteen Americans and wounding three hundred seventy-two people. The Saudi branch of Hezbollah Al-Hejaz (Party of God in the Hijaz) launched the attack. The extent of al-Qaeda's direct involvement remains unclear.[401]

Al-Qaeda's most dramatic endeavor before 9/11 occurred on February 26, 1993, when a truck bomb exploded in the parking garage of Tower One of the World Trade Center in New York City. Six people died and more than one thousand were injured. The explosion tore a hole in the building seven stories high.[402] A core group of men affiliated with al-Qaeda—Ramzi Yousef, Mahmud Abouhalima, Mohammed Salameh, Nidal Ayyad, Abdul Rahman Yasin, and Ahmad Ajaj, with financing from Yousef's uncle, Khaled Shaikh Mohammed—carried out the 1993 attack. Yousef later claimed he had hoped to kill two hundred fifty thousand people.[403]

Investigators captured Yousef and his co-conspirators using the same techniques that led to Timothy McVeigh, the lone wolf terrorist who blew up the federal building in Oklahoma City using a truck bomb in 1995. Law enforcement officers discovered a truck axle containing a Vehicle Identification Number (VIN) in the wreckage, and they traced it to a Ryder truck rental outlet in Jersey City. Records indicated that Mohammed Salameh had rented the truck and later reported it stolen.[404]

Authorities apprehended Salameh after he called the rental office to ask that his $400 deposit be returned. Ryder employees told him to appear in their office to process his claim. When Salameh arrived on March 4, 1993, agents from the Federal Bureau of Investigation (FBI) promptly arrested him. They apprehended his co-conspirators, Ayyad and Abouhalima, shortly thereafter.[405]

The three men were known to visit Brooklyn's Farouq mosque, home base for the Blind Sheikh, Omar Abdel-Rahman, the cleric who preached a vitriolic message of hatred for all things Western. During the investigation of the 1993 explosion, the FBI learned of the sheikh's plan to bomb the United Nations, the Lincoln and Holland tunnels, the George Washington Bridge, and a New York federal building housing FBI offices. Omar Abdel-Rahman was convicted of seditious conspiracy in 1995 and, a year later, sentenced to serve a life sentence

in federal prison.[406] In 1994, Abouhalima, Ajaj, Ayyad, and Salameh were convicted of conspiracy, explosive destruction of property, and interstate transportation of explosives. In November 1997, Yousef, the mastermind, and Eyad Ismoil, the truck driver, were convicted for the World Trade Center bombing.[407]

These militants who thought nothing of killing innocent men, women, and children were perplexing to Americans. Although members of the intelligence community had begun paying attention to al-Qaeda, citizens were largely unaware that radical zealots pursuing a bastardized version of Islam had declared war on Western culture. They did realize that worse was yet to come.

With almost inhuman patience, al-Qaeda leaders planned their next attack. They had learned several valuable lessons from the February 1993 bombing. First, transporting explosive devices presented a complicated logistical challenge that should be avoided. In addition, even the best-laid plans unraveled when the perpetrators tried to escape. Using suicide bombers reduced the tactical problems because escape was no longer an issue. Finally, a coordinated attack on multiple targets simultaneously would amplify the terror.[408]

The US intelligence community had been aware of Osama bin Laden, but they thought he was a low-level financier. The 1993 World Trade Center bombing served notice that this low-key shadowy figure existed as a dangerous new terrorist on the world stage. Investigators discovered his telephone number among the list of calls that Ramzi Yousef placed from New York safe houses. A CIA paper from April 2, 1993, characterized bin Laden "an independent actor sometimes works with other individuals and governments" to further "Islamic causes." The more the agency examined bin Laden, the more they learned of his nefarious activities. "Every time we turned over a rock," a CIA official later explained of that period, "there would be some sort of connection to bin Laden."[409] The CIA Counterterrorism Center (CTC) started monitoring the man's activities, a rare acknowledgment that a single individual required intense CIA scrutiny.[410]

Now that he was a subject of interest, bin Laden seemed to be everywhere. He returned to Afghanistan in May 1996 after the Taliban, a group of Islamic religious fundamentalists, rose to power

in the war-torn nation. On August 23, 1996, bin Laden, now safely ensconced with the Taliban leadership, issued "The Declaration of Jihad on the Americans Occupying the Country of the Two Sacred Places," a reference to Mecca and Medina in Saudi Arabia. The declaration formalized bin Laden's assertion that al-Qaeda was at war with the United States. To emphasize his intentions, bin Laden granted interviews with prominent media outlets, including Al Jazeera, an Arab-language news network, the Cable News Network (CNN), and ABC News.[411]

On February 22, 1998, bin Laden publicly announced the formation of the International Islamic Front for Jihad Against Jews and Crusaders. They stated its intentions clearly and unambiguously: "to kill the Americans and their allies—civilians and military—is the individual duty for every Muslim who can do it in any country in which it is possible." His methods might remain murky, but no one in the intelligence community could later claim surprise about his objectives.[412]

Bin Laden stepped up his campaign to sponsor violent attacks around the world. On August 7, 1998, a suicide bomber detonated a bomb at the American Embassy in Nairobi, Kenya, killing twelve Americans and 201 other people, mostly Kenyans who worked in the embassy offices. Four minutes later, a bomb erupted outside the American embassy in Dar es Salaam, Tanzania, killing eleven people and wounding eighty-five more. Once again, a direct link to bin Laden was difficult to establish, but US intelligence sources suspected he was involved in some manner.[413]

President Bill Clinton was also convinced that the al-Qaeda leader represented a clear and present danger. When Clinton learned that bin Laden would attend a meeting at the Zawhar Kili camp complex later in August, the president resolved to kill the elusive terrorist, if possible. On August 20, in "Operation Infinite Reach," five US navy destroyer ships stationed in the Arabian Sea launched seventy-five missiles at the target. The attack killed at least twenty-one Pakistani jihadist volunteers and wounded dozens more, but bin Laden escaped. With his uncanny ability to avoid detection or capture, he soon developed a reputation as a man marked by destiny, a jihadist warrior of the first rank.[414]

Also in August 1998, Clinton signed a Memorandum of Notification (MON), the first of several, authorizing the CIA to target bin Laden by using tribal resources in Afghanistan to capture or kill the fugitive. Despite the MON and efforts to locate the fugitive, American intelligence authorities never tracked him down. They did not possess enough credible sources of information to pinpoint his whereabouts in time to launch an assault.[415]

Emboldened by his success in eluding the Americans, bin Laden planned another audacious attack. On October 12, 2000, a US guided-missile destroyer, the USS *Cole,* stopped to refuel in Aden, Yemen. Two Arab men riding in a skiff approached the destroyer, smiling and waving at American sailors. Without warning, the small craft, loaded with explosives, ignited into a ball of flame, tearing a forty-foot gash in the side of the *Cole.* The blast killed seventeen sailors and wounded more than forty. With no way to locate a target, the United States did not respond to the attack. Al-Qaeda leaders noted with satisfaction that guerilla-style suicide bombs could work against a superior adversary.[416]

The *Cole* was a dress rehearsal of sorts, an intelligence-gathering operation. Evidence later suggested that Khalid Sheikh Mohammed had been planning a new round of attacks inside the United States at least since the 1993 World Trade Center bombing. Watching the lack of an effective response to the *Cole* assault convinced him that a suicide bombing on the US mainland could work if the plan was simple and implemented by a team of dedicated fighters willing to surrender their lives to the mission. Mohammed and Ramzi Yousef debated the possibility of blowing up commercial airliners in mid-flight. The more they mulled over the plan, the more they realized it could succeed, especially if they figured out a foolproof method of smuggling an incendiary device onto an airplane. The carnage would be horrific. Commercial airliners transport a large number of passengers and a large quantity of highly flammable jet fuel, and can be used to slaughter a multitude of innocent people quickly.[417]

Informed of the plan, bin Laden initially expressed skepticism. Sheikh Mohammed was undeterred. He repeatedly pressed for permission to move forward. Over time, the al-Qaeda leader came to appreciate the virtues of the concept, especially as the plan evolved.

Saudi-born Osama bin Laden founded the terrorist group al-Qaeda and helped to mastermind the attacks on September 11, 2001. Courtesy of the National Archives & Records Administration.

Instead of importing an explosive device, the airplanes themselves could serve as weapons. It was so simple, and so easy to carry out. In the hands of strong warriors, small, hand-held weapons could be used to overpower the pilots and crew on a commercial jetliner and take charge of the cockpit. Despite his initial reluctance, bin Laden actively participated in planning the operation, including discussions about suitable targets.

After bin Laden approved the scheme, two eager al-Qaeda members, Khalid al Mihdhar and Nawaf al Hazmi, signed on to participate, as did Walid Muhammad Salih bin Roshayed bin Attash, a Saudi-born bin Laden supporter suspected of planning the *Cole* attack. Relying on the nom de guerre "Khallad," bin Attash and co-conspirator Abu Bara al Yemeni initially decided to pilot the planes along with the other suicide bombers.[418] The four terrorists trained at al-Qaeda's Mes Aynak training camp in Afghanistan. After completing their training, they were instructed to enter the United States and complete lessons at flight training schools.[419]

To ensure success, al-Qaeda recruited another team of suicide terrorists. Members of the second team hailed from Egypt, the United Arab Emirates, Lebanon, and Yemen. The men had lived and studied together as part of a cell in Hamburg, Germany. Four men from this group—Mohamed Atta, Ramzi Binalshibh, Marwan al Shehhi, and Ziad Jarrah—served as operational leaders for the September 11, 2001, attacks.[420]

Al-Qaeda had a slew of zealots eager to die for the cause, but many young men did not understand Western ways and lacked knowledge of airplanes. Mohamed Atta, a thirty-three-year-old Egyptian-born Islamic fundamentalist from an affluent family, was a natural leader of these men. He knew a great deal of the West from his days living in Hamburg and he knew how to acquire the requisite skills to set the scheme into motion. Beginning in the spring of 2000, Atta sent an email to between fifty and sixty flight schools throughout the United States asking for advice on learning to fly commercial aircraft.[421]

The plan was for the four leaders to complete their training at US flight schools. On a prearranged day, each of the pilot-leaders would be accompanied by a team of four "muscle" hijackers who would keep

passengers and the crew under control while the new pilots seized control of commercial passenger planes and crashed the jets into symbolic targets.[422] After more than a year of operational planning, Atta selected the date for the attacks. Members of the cells purchased tickets on flights that departed at approximately the same time on the morning of September 11. The musclemen bought box-cutters to use during the cockpit seizure. Everything was in place.[423]

September 11, 2001

The narrative has become familiar to anyone who was alive at the time, and to many who read about it later in history books. On Tuesday, September 11, 2001, in a coordinated effort, nineteen al-Qaeda hijackers seized control of four commercial airliners traveling to San Francisco and Los Angeles from Boston, Newark, and Washington Dulles International Airport and used the airplanes as the weapons, killing almost three thousand people in the air and on the ground, including themselves, by crashing into buildings. It was the worst terrorist attack on American soil in the nation's history.

The attacks began before anyone in the United States understood there was a war. Mohamed Atta traveled that morning with his colleague and fellow terrorist Abdul Aziz al Omari. Their 6:00 a.m. flight from Portland, Maine, to Boston was uneventful. During his initial check-in, Atta was selected by the Computer Assisted Passenger Prescreening System (CAPPS) for additional screening. At the time, the system only required security personnel to ensure that Atta was on board his flight before his checked luggage was loaded onto the plane. Three of his fellow hijackers later were selected for additional screening in Boston, but, as with Atta, nothing alerted security personnel to the pending threat.[424]

Atta and his confederates boarded American Flight 11, as scheduled. The airplane departed at 7:59 a.m. from Boston bound for Los Angeles with Captain John Ogonowski and First Officer Thomas McGuinness at the controls of the Boeing 767. The last routine communication with ground control consisted of the flight crew's acknowledgment that they had received navigational instructions from the Federal Aviation Administration's (FAA's) air traffic control (ATC)

center in Boston. Sixteen seconds after that acknowledgment, ATC instructed the pilot to climb to thirty-five thousand feet. The pilots did not respond. Air traffic control received no further communications. Investigators believe that American Airlines Flight 11 was hijacked at 8:14 a.m., about fifteen minutes after takeoff. At 8:46:40, the airplane collided with the North Tower of the World Trade Center. Everyone on board died instantly along with an unknown number of persons inside the building.[425]

At approximately the same time Atta and his crew boarded Flight 11, Marwan al Shehhi, Fayez Banihammad, Mohand al Shehri, Ahmed al Ghamdi, and Hamza al Ghamdi boarded United Airlines Flight 175 in a separate terminal at Boston's Logan Airport. The flight was bound for Los Angeles, scheduled to depart at 8:00 a.m. with Captain Victor Saracini, assisted by First Officer Michael Horrocks, at the controls. Seven flight attendants and fifty-six passengers boarded the airplane that morning. United 175 pushed back from the gate at 7:58 a.m. and departed sixteen minutes later, at roughly the same time that hijackers seized control of American Airlines Flight 11. Around 8:46 a.m., the second group of hijackers seized United Flight 175. The denouement occurred quickly. At 8:58 a.m., United Airlines Flight 175 turned toward New York City. At 9:03:11 a.m., the airplane slammed into the South Tower, and everyone on board died instantly. An unknown number of people inside the building died at that moment.[426]

In the meantime, five men stepped onto American Airlines Flight 77 at Washington Dulles Airport. Three of the five, Hani Hanjour, Khalid al Mihdhar, and Majed Moqed, were singled out for CAPPS screening. Two brothers, Nawaf al Hazmi and Salem al Hazmi, attracted attention from a customer service representative at the check-in counter. One brother did not even carry photo identification and spoke no English. Incredibly, all five hijackers eventually boarded the airplane. Security measures presented a temporary inconvenience, but nothing more.

Flight 77 was scheduled to take off at 8:10 a.m. under the command of Captain Charles F. Burlingame and assisted by First Officer David Charlebois. Four flight attendants and fifty-eight passengers were on board. The airplane pushed back from the gate one minute

ahead of schedule and took off eleven minutes later. Sometime between 8:51 and 8:54, the hijackers seized control of the flight. The aircraft veered south, far off course. Someone turned off the flight transponder two minutes later so that air traffic controllers could not directly track the flight path.

Flight 77, traveling at approximately five hundred thirty miles per hour, crashed into the US Defense Department's headquarters building, the Pentagon, located in Arlington County, Virginia, just outside of Washington, D.C., at 9:37:46 a.m.[427] The impact killed everyone on board the plane, including the terrorists, as well as seventy civilians and fifty-five military service members inside the Pentagon. In addition, one hundred six people suffered serious injuries.[428]

United Airlines Flight 93 was the last of the four aircraft hijacked that morning, although no one knew how many planes had been targeted until later. Shortly after 7:00 a.m., Saeed al Ghamdi, Ahmed al Nami, Ahmed al Haznawi, and Ziad Jarrah checked in for the flight at Newark Airport in New Jersey. Between thirty and forty-five minutes later, they boarded the plane and sat in their assigned seats. On each of the other hijacked flights, the terrorists had operated in five-man teams, but only four men boarded Flight 93. An immigration officer at Orlando International Airport had denied Mohammed al Qahtani, a suspected team member and "muscle hijacker," entry into the United States. The lack of muscle may have facilitated a subsequent passenger revolt.[429]

The four terrorists were among a total of thirty-seven passengers on board United 93 that day. Captain Jason Dahl and First Officer Leroy Homer Jr. were the pilots. The flight, bound for San Francisco, departed at 8:42 a.m., four minutes before American Airlines Flight 11 crashed into the World Trade Center's North Tower and twenty-one minutes before United Airlines Flight 175 struck the South Tower. If everything had operated according to the plan, Flight 93 would have left around the same time as the other three flights, but it was twenty-five minutes late. The presence of a four-man team and the late timing for United Flight 93 proved to be crucial events.

The hijackers seized the cockpit controls and herded nervous passengers toward the rear of the plane. The late timing meant that news

had already trickled out about the previous hijackings. Passengers and crew began calling friends, family, and authorities on their cell phones. They learned that two airplanes had struck the Twin Towers in New York. The terrorists sported red bandanas and brandished knives. They repeatedly claimed to possess a bomb, although no one actually saw the device. At least one passenger was stabbed and two bodies were on the floor, possibly the captain and the first officer, although their identities were never verified.

By the time the terrorists seized control of United Flight 93, the terrorists could no longer convince the passengers they would not harm anyone. During the first three flights, the hijackers had success-fully calmed the passengers by promising to let them go. The men and women of Flight 93 knew the truth. This was a suicide mission. As a result, at 9:57 a.m., the passengers revolted. Realizing they had little to lose, they launched themselves at the terrorists.

Ziad Jarrah was thought to be at the controls of Flight 93. When the passenger revolt started, he rolled the airplane left and right. As the attack intensified, Jarrah pitched the nose of the plane up and down. The aircraft may have been headed for the US Capitol Building or the White House, but with a blitz attack from passengers under-way, it never reached the target. Instead, it crashed into the ground at 580 miles per hour in an empty field near Shanksville, Pennsylvania, at 10:03 a.m. The aircraft was a twenty-minute flight away from Washington, D.C.

The situation on the ground was equally dramatic. One hundred two minutes after American Flight 11 collided with the North Tower of New York's World Trade Center, the building collapsed. The explo-sion cut through floors 93 to 99. All three stairwells suffered severe damage. A fireball of jet fuel blew onto several floors, including the 77th, the 22nd, the West Street lobby, and B4, four stories below ground, as well as through at least one bank of elevators. Thick black smoke poured out of the upper floors and drifted over to the South Tower next door. Anyone inside the North Tower on floors 100 to 110 was trapped and died when the building fell.[430]

Seventeen minutes after the impact with the North Tower, United Airlines Flight 175 hit the South Tower. Although it was damaged

after the North Tower, the South Tower collapsed first, at 9:59 a.m., after burning for fifty-six minutes in a fire caused by the collision and the intensely hot burning jet fuel. Twenty-nine minutes after the South Tower fell, the North Tower fell, sending heavy debris onto the nearby 7 World Trade Center, which eventually collapsed at 5:20 p.m.[431]

Responding to multiple calls for assistance, the Fire Department of New York (FDNY) mobilized immediately after learning of the initial plane crash. By 9:00 a.m., two hundred thirty-five firefighters—twenty-one engine companies, nine ladder companies, four elite rescue teams, two elite squad companies, a hazardous materials (HazMat) team, and support staff—raced to the scene.[432] At 9:37 a.m., a call went out to send additional firefighters to the staging area. No one knew that the building was twenty-two minutes away from a collapse.[433] Given the quick response and the large number of personnel, it was little wonder that the FDNY suffered a large mortality rate on 9/11. The fire department lost three hundred forty-three people in both buildings while the Port Authority lost thirty-seven people and the New York Police Department lost twenty-three people.[434]

The Aftermath

The world was stunned by the terrorist attacks of September 11, 2001. Although terrorism was not a rarity on American soil, never before had such a dramatic series of events played out on live television. In response, citizens cried out for answers—answers about why the attacks occurred and how such acts could be prevented in the future.[435]

President George W. Bush benefited from a brief "rally 'round the flag" sentiment that swept the nation. His approval rating soared to 90 percent as the president promised to pursue the persons responsible for the devastation to the ends of the earth, if necessary. He spoke to a joint session of Congress nine days after the attacks, promising a quick, decisive response. "Tonight we are a country awakened to danger and called to defend freedom," the president said. "Our grief has turned to anger, and anger to resolution. Whether we bring our enemies to justice, or bring justice to our enemies, justice will be done." His remarks received rare bipartisan applause from the assembled members of Congress.[436]

President George W. Bush is shown with members of his national security team on September 12, 2001. From left to right: Secretary of Defense Donald Rumsfeld; Secretary of State Colin Powell; President Bush; and Vice President Dick Cheney. Courtesy of the National Archives & Records Administration.

In the months and years that followed, many events, including the administration's decision to send troops to Afghanistan and congressional passage of the USA PATRIOT Act, had a lasting, and controversial, effect on American public policy. Bush also used the 9/11 attacks as partial justification for the Iraqi invasion in 2003, although the linkage between al-Qaeda and Iraq was a point of contention.[437]

Vice President Richard "Dick" Cheney, a former secretary of defense and a well-known proponent of a highly-developed national security infrastructure, became the administration's most ardent defender of a vigorous prosecution of the War on Terror. Cheney not only urged congressional action to strengthen intelligence and law enforcement tools, but he argued in favor of using whatever means were available, including "enhanced interrogation techniques," to elicit information regarding possible terrorist attacks in the future. The vice president unapologetically contended that fighting terrorists required unconventional methods. In a world where a "low-probability,

high-impact event," such as the 9/11 attacks, could occur, Cheney warned that eternal vigilance was necessary. In November 2001, he articulated a doctrine that came to represent the Bush administration's preemptive approach to fighting anti-American terrorists. Following a CIA briefing indicating that a Pakistani scientist was assisting al-Qaeda members in acquiring a nuclear weapon, the vice president reputedly remarked, "If there's a 1 percent chance that Pakistani scientists are helping al-Qaeda build or develop a nuclear weapon, we have to treat it as a certainty in terms of our response." In short, the consequences of a major terrorist attack are so catastrophic that even if an intelligence report reveals that a highly unlikely plan exists, the United States must respond as though the plan will be carried out.

Vice President Dick Cheney, shown here in 2002, became the Bush administration's most vocal proponent of the War on Terror. Courtesy of the National Archives & Records Administration.

The Guantánamo Bay Detention Camp became a symbol of the Bush administration's determination to rely on enhanced interrogation techniques. The camp was opened on the site of the Guantánamo Bay Naval Base, a forty-five-square-mile swath of land and water situated on the southeastern portion of the island of Cuba. The United States first leased the site from Cuba in 1903 and has maintained a presence there since that time. The Cuban government has protested the US military presence, but to no avail.

When the United States opened the detention camp on part of the site, Defense Secretary Donald Rumsfeld explained the reasoning. Referring to the "detaineees" in the new prison, "These men are extremely dangerous, particularly when being moved, such as loading or unloading an aircraft, buses, ferries, movements between facilities, movements to and from showers and the like." The purpose of creating a new prison outside of the United States was to minimize the transfer of prisoners by isolating them in a facility where they could not harm their captors or threaten the local populace outside the camp. "The detention center in Guantánamo Bay has gone from nonexistent to a temporary facility," the secretary said in a press briefing on January 22, 2002. "The current facilities are just that, they're temporary. They didn't exist a few weeks ago. They will be replaced in the months ahead with a more permanent facility, as it becomes possible to determine the size and the scope of the problem."

Protestors around the world denounced the creation of the prison as an overreaction to the 9/11 attacks. The designation of detainees as "illegal enemy combatants" placed them in a kind of legal limbo where the due process of law under the US Constitution would not apply. In a 2003 report, Human Rights Watch complained, "Washington has ignored human rights standards in its own treatment of terrorism suspects. It has refused to apply the Geneva Conventions to prisoners of war from Afghanistan, and has misused the designation of 'illegal combatant' to apply to criminal suspects on US soil." Amnesty International characterized the facility as the "gulag of our times." In his opening press briefing, however, Rumsfeld insisted that "the detainees are being treated humanely. They have been, they are being treated humanely today, and they will be in the future."

Despite Rumsfeld's insistence that it was necessary to detain certain suspects at Guantánamo, detainees challenged their detention and their legal status in a series of court cases. *Hamdi v. Rumsfeld,* a 2004 US Supreme Court case, held that a US citizen detained at Guantánamo Bay had the right to due process in challenging his detention. Another 2004 case, *Rasul v. Bush,* held that US courts can exercise jurisdiction over foreign nationals held at Guantánamo even though "ultimate sovereignty" of the site rests with Cuba. *Hamdan v. Rumsfeld,* a 2006 case, involved a noncitizen held at Guantánamo Bay and was tried before a military court. Afghani forces captured Salim Ahmed Hamdan, Osama bin Laden's former chauffeur, in November 2001 and turned him over to US forces. Satisfied that Hamdan was an enemy of the United States, officials dispatched the captive to the Guantánamo Bay facility. President Bush eventually decided that Hamdan and other detainees could be tried by a military commission. In the meantime, the prisoner challenged his indefinite detention by filing a petition for a writ of habeas corpus and a writ of mandamus in federal district court. Before the district court ruled on the petition, Hamdan received a hearing from a military tribunal. The tribunal designated him an "unlawful enemy combatant." Hamdan appealed, and the US Supreme Court agreed to hear the case. By a 5-to-3 vote, with Chief Justice Roberts not participating, the high court held that the president could not authorize the use of a military commission to try a defendant absent express authorization from Congress.[438]

While these events occurred, the man who had caused so much grief was nowhere to be found. Recognizing that the American military would react despite its unwillingness to do so in the past, Osama bin Laden disappeared late in 2001. Teams of American armed forces followed a trail, sometimes only hours or minutes old, as al-Qaeda members fled through the mountains of Afghanistan. He would remain an elusive figure in hiding for almost a decade. The Bush administration left office, and a new man took up residence in the White House. The al-Qaeda mastermind seemed to be out of mind, but the US intelligence community never abandoned the quest to find the man who had struck at the heart of the American regime.[439]

Sometime in 2005, bin Laden quietly moved into a specially-constructed compound in Abbottabad, Pakistan, a city of one hundred thousand residents situated in the Hazara region of the Khyber Pakhtunkhwa Province, approximately seventy-four miles northeast of the capital city of Islamabad.

In August 2010, US intelligence officials informed President Barack Obama that the CIA believed it had found bin Laden living in the Abbottabad compound. President Obama authorized Sea, Air and Land teams, commonly called SEALs, the US navy's principal special operations force, to conduct a commando raid to capture or kill bin Laden. SEALs are part of the Naval Special Warfare Command as well as the US Special Operations Command, among the most effective elite units in the US military.[440]

Preparations and training required months, but eventually the plan, known as Operation Neptune Spear, was in place. On May 1, 2011, two modified Black Hawk and three Chinook helicopters lifted

In this iconic photograph, President Obama (second from left) and his military advisors watch a video feed of Operation Neptune Spear unfolding in real time. The raid by Navy SEALs killed Osama bin Laden. Courtesy of the White House, Peter Souza, photographer.

off from an airfield in Jalalabad, Afghanistan, crossed the border into Pakistan, and headed for Abbottabad under cover of night. After entering the main house on the compound grounds, the SEALs located bin Laden and shot him dead. The SEALs snatched his body as well as documents and equipment. The operation lasted just forty minutes. Except for the loss of a helicopter, it had been a textbook operation. The SEALs suffered no casualties.[441]

During the evening of May 2, 2011, President Obama spoke to the world on television. "Tonight, I can report to the American people and to the world that the United States has conducted an operation that killed Osama bin Laden, the leader of al-Qaeda, and a terrorist who's responsible for the murder of thousands of innocent men, women, and children." The president reminded an audience that needed no reminding why the operation had been necessary. "It was nearly ten years ago that a bright September day was darkened by the worst attack on the American people in our history. The images of 9/11 are seared into our national memory—hijacked planes cutting through a cloudless September sky; the Twin Towers collapsing to the ground; black smoke billowing up from the Pentagon; the wreckage of Flight 93 in Shanksville, Pennsylvania, where the actions of heroic citizens saved even more heartbreak and destruction."[442]

The USA PATRIOT Act

With Osama bin Laden dead and no major terrorist attacks on American soil in recent memory, Americans have focused on what was lost and gained with the enactment of the USA PATRIOT Act (USAPA). The statute is among the most enduring legacies of the post-9/11 landscape. The new law won passage forty-five days after the carnage of 9/11. Federal law enforcement officials received enhanced police powers to investigate and presumably prevent future incidents. Roving wire taps, the expansion of authority to request pen registers and trap-and-trace devices, including Internet records, the ability to request "any tangible thing," and the expansion of National Security Letter (NSL) authority (similar to subpoena authority, but not issued by a judicial officer) all represented powerful data-mining tools in the War on Terror. The new powers allowed the federal government to

cast a wide net in the hopes of collecting information to detect terrorist planning and support.[443]

Roving wiretaps allow federal officials to pursue a suspect without obtaining a search warrant each time the suspect uses a new communications device. In most criminal prosecutions, a warrant is required for each device, but the investigative process is hampered when a savvy suspect uses multiple communications tools or changes devices frequently. By allowing investigators to focus on tracking a person instead of a device, a roving wiretap simplifies the hunt for would-be terrorists.[444]

A pen register allows investigators to capture telephone numbers when a person places an outgoing call. Trap-and-trace devices capture telephone numbers for incoming calls. Although the tools are not designed to record the content of the transmissions, they can provide a snapshot into the network of people with whom a suspect is communicating. Searching Internet records with information on frequently dialed telephone numbers can yield valuable information about the identity of the people engaged in the conversations.[445]

Section 505 of the USAPA allows the FBI to serve an administrative subpoena on a communications company such as a telephone company or an Internet service provider. The company must provide noncontent information about a suspect's transactions. If the FBI authorizes it, the recipient of the NSL must not disclose the existence of the letter to anyone. The use of NSLs under the USAPA had been controversial and challenged in court in a number of cases.[446]

According to critics, increased government authority after 9/11 created a "chilling" effect on civil liberties. With enhanced surveillance techniques, the federal government is able to access more electronic information about people than it has in the past. Distrustful citizens argue they have no idea what information has been accessed, stored, and analyzed due to the confidentiality provisions that apply to most post-9/11 national security-related activities.

Apologists explain that all actions undertaken in the interests of national security are subject to review by the US Foreign Intelligence Surveillance Court (FISC). Created by the Foreign Intelligence Surveillance Act of 1978 (FISA), the FISC is charged with balancing

the competing values of individual freedom and government authority. The court oversees the federal government's covert surveillance activities of foreign entities and "subversive" individuals inside the United States while maintaining the secrecy supposedly necessary to protect national security.[447]

Aside from concerns about national security, criminal law has been affected by post-9/11 laws. Arguably the most controversial change was the PATRIOT Act's expansion of a Delayed Notice Warrant, euphemistically called a "sneak and peek" warrant, reflecting significant changes from long-held criminal procedures protecting the rights of those who have not been convicted of a crime. Such warrants allow law enforcement personnel to enter a person's premises and search for evidence without notifying the individual beforehand. The "sneak and peek" warrant authority is not confined only to terrorist or intelligence investigations. An overwhelming majority of "sneak and peek" warrants—estimated at 98 percent—are issued for nonterrorist or national security investigations. Justifying enhanced police authority owing to a need to protect the nation from 9/11-like attacks is difficult if terrorism is not the underlying concern.[448]

Critics charge that it is difficult to conceive of a rollback of government authority under the USAPA. It is also impossible to measure with any precision the impact of the changes on national security or individual liberty. Civil libertarians recommend that Congress ensure open, transparent judicial review and oversight, not simply FISC scrutiny. Appropriate public dissemination of data and information about the use of enhanced powers and their impact on national security and individual liberty should be allowed so that the public can make an informed judgment on the efficacy and desirability of extraordinary police powers.[449]

The USAPA's broad investigative reach was not controversial in the immediate wake of the 9/11 attacks as Americans desperately sought for a means of feeling safe from further attacks. In the intervening years, however, civil liberties experts questioned whether an ongoing "war on terror" justified privacy violations and whether government agents were abusing their powers. The issue became politically charged in June 2013 when a former contractor for the National

Security Agency (NSA), Edward Snowden, leaked details of an ongoing surveillance program to a British newspaper, *The Guardian.*

Snowden had been working as a contractor with access to classified information. He became disgusted, he said, when he realized that US intelligence personnel, notably Director of National Intelligence James Clapper, had lied to Congress and the American people about the nature and extent of the government's surveillance. In May 2013, Snowden flew from Hawaii, where he had been living, to Hong Kong to meet with journalists from *The Guardian.* After Snowden leaked classified NSA documents, the US Department of Justice charged him with two counts of violating the Espionage Act of 1917 and stealing government property. The State Department revoked his passport. As a man without a country, Snowden eventually landed in Russia. Lacking a Russian visa, he lived in Moscow's Sheremetyevo International Airport for thirty-nine days until authorities granted him temporary asylum for a year. During his time in the airport, Snowden applied for asylum in twenty-one countries. In 2014, the Russians issued a three-year residency permit.

Snowden was hailed as a hero for exposing a shameful legacy of NSA abuse and calling attention to the lack of transparency in government surveillance in the era of the USAPA, although his actions involved more than a single statute. As a whistleblower who dared to speak the truth to power, Snowden received accolades from civil liberties and human rights groups around the world. His detractors see him as a traitor who exposed secrets that severely undermined the safety and security of Americans living in a post-9/11 world. Many government officials, including President Obama, have called on Snowden to come back to the United States and "face the music" by standing trial.

Asked during a January 2014 interview whether he would return to the United States to be tried for his alleged crimes, Snowden explained his reluctance. "The Espionage Act was never intended— it's from 1918—was never intended to prosecute journalistic sources for informing the newspapers about information that is in the public interest. It was intended for people who were selling documents and secrets to foreign governments or bombing bridges or sabotaging communications—not people who were serving the public good." As

far as Snowden was concerned, he was not a traitor or a terrorist. He was a citizen calling attention to a serious problem with the US surveillance system. "So it's, I would say, illustrative that the President would choose to say someone should face the music when he knows the music is a show trial," Snowden concluded.[450]

The Snowden incident sparked a new round of debates regarding the need for increased transparency in fighting terrorism. If a war against terrorism is a permanent feature of life in the twenty-first century, does this reality mean that the increased governmental powers granted by the USAPA and attendant laws will permanently curtail civil liberties that have been a hallmark of American life—with some exceptions, as noted in this book—since the founding of the republic? Perhaps such questions are naive, or perhaps they are the most important queries of this, or any other, era.

Chapter 10

LESSONS LEARNED

Freedom, n. Exemption from the stress of authority in a beggarly half dozen of restraint's infinite multitude of methods. A political condition that every nation supposes itself to enjoy in virtual monopoly.

—AMBROSE BIERCE,
THE DEVIL'S DICTIONARY (1906)[451]

In 2013, when Edward Snowden, a former system administrator for the Central Intelligence Agency (CIA), leaked classified information about domestic surveillance undertaken by the National Security Agency (NSA), he reignited the twenty-first-century version of a never-ending debate about the appropriate relationship between a government and its citizens. The debate is far older than the republic. Since democratic governments were first first instituted, the question of how much freedom an individual should have versus how much authority a government should exercise has lurked, explicitly or implicitly, within every discussion. Freedom and authority are antithetical values: the presence of one lessens the other. The proper balance between the two values is a perennial political problem because no "perfect" answer exists. At some times in American history, citizens have demanded greater individual freedoms. On other occasions—especially after high-profile attacks such as Pearl Harbor and 9/11—Americans have voluntarily surrendered a measure of freedom in exchange, they hope, for heightened governmental protections.[452]

The notion that tension exists between the needs and desires of individuals and the authority a government exercises is rooted in an Anglo-American understanding of regime values. A political tradition constructed on an authoritarian foundation need not inventory

citizen opinion. By contrast, a democratic system predicated on social contract theory must account for the actions of its government. Yet a crucial dilemma exists. If a government requires the consent of the governed to legitimize its actions, the question must continually be asked whether the governed must approve of all actions the government undertakes. To offer informed consent, the citizenry must be able to observe the actions of the sovereign. Therein lies the problem. Governments protest that state secrets must be kept if citizens are to be protected, but secrecy reduces the transparency that lies at the core of consensual government.

Aside from the challenge of monitoring a government that seeks to safeguard its secrets and hence lessen its transparency, the decisions that citizens make regarding the appropriate nature of government often are made under less-than-optimal conditions, usually when the participants are in the throes of passion. Fear drives many choices that Americans make about how much authority their government should exercise, and understandably so. When times are good and exterior threats appear nominal, citizens desire the maximum level of unfettered discretion. To live without constraints imposed by third parties is to exercise one's autonomy without accounting to anyone save God and conscience, a pleasurable condition for many human beings. Yet the citizen is horrified when a seemingly savage force takes advantage of the idyll to inflict harm, especially on innocent civilians.

In the American tradition, individuals frequently denounce "big government" and mistrust centralized authority up until the moment when an exterior threat appears. At precisely that moment, the man who previously espoused his undying allegiance to civil liberties screams recriminations at the top of his lungs. How could this terrible event happen? Where was his great protector in his hour of need? He divorces himself from his prior statements on the illegitimacy of the leviathan and throws his quaking body upon the altar of expediency. He will do whatever it takes to feel safe. If a desire for a bigger, tougher, well-equipped behemoth requires that he forfeit some or all of his heretofore sacrosanct rights of speech and pen, he blanches not a bit. Later, when years have passed and his previous condition of

complacency returns, he will lead the charge to assail the government fat cats who have robbed him of his precious freedoms, but for the time being he is satisfied to embrace his new-found love of a robust, enhanced sovereign.

And so it goes. The pendulum swings back and forth. Some ideologues as well as a coterie of principled men and women will resist such gyrations and stake out a fixed position, but they remain a decided minority. As for the masses, they will swing with the times. So has it ever been, and so will it ever be.

These movements reflect human nature and, taken in moderation, represent a healthy response. Exterior threats cannot be ignored. Governments must meet the challenge or inevitably they lose their utility. Moreover, individuals in times of crisis must be prepared to sacrifice in the name of the collectivity or the burdens necessary to triumph will not be borne—or, if borne, they will be borne disproportionately by the weary few. Fear can be a guide for sound behavior if, after the threat has diminished, the fear diminishes.

A difficulty arises when the fear is connected with exterior events that do not represent a genuine threat to the polity or when the initial fear fails to dissipate after a threat has been eliminated. Instead, the fear spreads and breeds suspicion that strange and alien people and groups are dangerous to the populace. American history is replete with instances where citizens and their leaders reacted to what they perceived to be a threat, but what was little more than an unpopular person or group exercising free speech. The masses, and sometimes their leaders, mistake the "other"—say, ethnic, racial, or religious minorities—for a subversive threat. In these instances, the government response to the supposedly subversive threat damages the regime worse than the original threat. As "Federalist 10" pointed out, in some cases the cure is worse than the disease.[453]

Beware of decisions reached in the heat of the moment. On further reflection, the situation frequently is less damaging than it initially appeared. The government's response, when it is based on fear and public outrage, can exacerbate a crisis or create a crisis where one did not exist. Consider three examples from the annals of American history.

The Hutchinson Letters Affair

The venerable Founding Father Benjamin Franklin was a central figure in one of the first cases of leaked information in American history. Long before Daniel Ellsberg leaked the Pentagon Papers to *The New York Times,* Julian Assange published secret US diplomatic cables on his website WikiLeaks, or Edward Snowden provided a series of classified NSA documents to *The Guardian,* Franklin was living and working in England. In December 1772, he received a packet of letters from an unnamed Member of Parliament. Franklin immediately wrote to Thomas Cushing, a Massachusetts supporter, acknowledging, "There has lately fallen into my hands part of a correspondence that I have reason to believe laid the foundation of most if not all our present grievances." He enclosed the letters in his mailing.[454]

The "present grievances" related to an escalating series of episodes between the English Crown and her colonies in North America. The colonists believed they were English citizens who should be accorded the same rights as anyone living in the Mother Country. The English government had treated the colonies with benign neglect or, more recently, with overt hostility after mistaking the actions of a small group of disaffected colonial leaders as rebelliousness. Each side failed to appreciate the legitimacy of the other side's arguments, and each responded to provocations with provocative acts of its own.

The letters Franklin passed along certainly proved to be provocative, but the good doctor did not intend for them to precipitate a crisis. Thomas Hutchinson, the Royal Governor of Massachusetts, had written six of the thirteen posts, which made the collection especially noteworthy to Franklin and his colleagues. Never intended for public scrutiny, Hutchinson's correspondence outlined a plan for silencing the growing discord among colonists espousing anti-English sentiments. "There must be an abridgement of what are called English liberties," Hutchinson recommended in one especially galling passage. The governor urged his superiors to dispatch more troops to the colonies, as necessary, to ensure compliance with royal edicts.[455]

Franklin later claimed with some credibility that he had not forwarded the letters to inflame public opinion against the English.

Indeed, he asked that Cushing keep the contents private lest the letters fall into the wrong hands, which is precisely what happened. Franklin's goal, he said, was to demonstrate that recent provocations by English forces in the New World did not represent unanimity of opinion within His Majesty's government. Rather, the incidents were the consequence of poor advice passed along by a select few, including Governor Hutchinson.[456]

Franklin's motives did not matter. When the *Boston Gazette* published the contents in June 1773, readers were outraged. They failed to appreciate Franklin's distinction among factions of leaders across the Atlantic. Instead, the colonists saw proof of their suspicions that the English were plotting to curtail the rights of Englishmen. Governor Hutchinson fled to England a step ahead of an incensed citizenry.[457]

As for Franklin, he admitted his role in the affair after learning that two men had accused each other of passing along the purloined letters and had engaged in a duel to preserve their honor. No one was hurt, but Franklin confessed his actions to avoid further misunderstandings. Called before the English Privy Council in January 1774, he was forced to stand mute while the authorities publicly berated him as well as the general American attitude toward the acts of the English royal governors.[458]

The publication of sensitive letters never meant for public consumption undeniably undermined Governor Hutchinson's position in Massachusetts and embarrassed the English government. Yet the Crown's reaction only heightened tensions. Had the king's men announced that the letters contained only recommendations for a course of action the Crown had no intention of pursuing, the affair might have ended with little result. By expressing outrage, dressing down Franklin—a well-regarded representative of the colonies—and denouncing the colonists as rabble-rousers, the English ensured that the affair would become more contentious than it might have been. Even Franklin, a generally moderate man given to diplomatic reserve in public, became radicalized following the incident. If nothing else, the Hutchinson Letters Affairs teaches that a government's response to an incident can defuse a crisis or cause it to become far worse than it otherwise would have been.[459]

The difficulty of dealing with government leaks extends back into history even before the founding of the nation. Benjamin Franklin was involved in the Hutchinson Letters Affair during the 1770s. Courtesy of the Library of Congress.

Eugene V. Debs and the March of Socialism

A second example of government overreaction involves Eugene V. Debs, one of the most unpopular figures in American history. A union leader in the late-nineteenth and early-twentieth centuries, when such views were controversial and thought to be dangerous, Debs also ran for president five times as a candidate of the Socialist Party of America. As recounted in chapter 3, he was arrested and imprisoned during World War I for violating the Espionage Act. The US Supreme Court affirmed his conviction. "That old man with the burning eyes" could be kind and gentle in private, but in public he was a fiery speaker given to using intemperate language as he passionately delivered his sermons on the evils of the day.[460]

To the average American who read about Debs in the partisan press, this charismatic figure voicing his support for socialism while assailing corporate and governmental entities appeared threatening and dangerous. Although Debs never directly participated in acts of violence, he supported doctrines that were used by others to justify violence. In opposing the American military, he seemed to undermine the war effort. If the war was a legitimate defense of American values, a person who opposed the war must also oppose the nation's core values—or so it seemed to many of Debs's detractors.[461]

Socialism, or some variant thereof, appeared to be engulfing the world at the turn of the century. Most Americans possessed only a vague understanding of the concept. They did not see the doctrine the same way Debs did. He was concerned about the power of elites and their abuse of working people in the United States and around the world. In his view, if a more equitable means of distributing wealth could be found, society could be just and American government could be reformed to protect the lower classes from capitalist exploitation.

Americans failed to appreciate the humane side of the socialist credo. When they read about socialism, usually it was in the context of labor disputes that paralyzed industrial output and jeopardized jobs. They learned of alien people with foreign-sounding names uttering threats to the status quo. Although many Americans claimed to be anti-big government, they also were deeply conservative and fearful of

rapid social change. In this context, Eugene V. Debs was a malcontent who would disrupt the order and stability of American life.[462]

Yet Debs believed he was speaking the truth to power in service of a higher ideal—namely the need to step outside of government propaganda and present the average person with a clear alternative to the established policy. He and his larger audience spoke past each other. Citizens who believed in the war effort viewed him as damaging to their interests. It was difficult to understand that the nation's "values" need not require everyone to follow the current presidential administration's party line. Debs could criticize his government as a means of reforming it.

In some ways, the US government's overreaction emboldened Debs and others of a more radical bent. Had the Wilson administration accepted that a certain level of vocal opposition was to be expected and tolerated, Debs might have been characterized as a loud-mouth and a trouble-maker, but nothing more. By jailing him for exercising free speech, the authorities transformed him into a folk hero of sorts. Although many Americans believed he had received a proper comeuppance, civil libertarians believed that Debs had become a symbol of the need to challenge government policy by exercising free speech.[463]

Eugene V. Debs was a self-avowed socialist and perennial presidential candidate. He was a hero to some Americans and a villain to others. Courtesy of the Library of Congress.

Joseph R. McCarthy and the Hunt for Communists

Punishing an irritant such as Eugene Debs is one means of overreacting to perceived subversive threats. Another method is to allow a demagogue to seize control of the institutions of government and subvert them for his own purposes. Typically, he claims to be protecting government and citizens from subversive forces. In reality, however, the demagogue seeks only to enhance his own prestige and consolidate personal power.

American history is filled with demagogues, but few rose as far or fell as quickly as Wisconsin Republican Senator Joseph R. McCarthy. During a four-year-period in the 1950s, McCarthy enjoyed a measure of popular acclaim because, unlike Debs, he rode a tide of public opinion instead of going against it. Before February 1950, "Tail Gunner Joe"—a self-imposed nickname that referred to a fictionalized account of his service record in World War II—had been just another US senator occupying the back benches of that august chamber. After publicly declaring he had obtained a list of 205 employees in the US State Department who were "card-carrying Communists," the legislator previously thought to possess neither character nor ability discovered that a successful public career required no such attributes. He could play on public fears that the world was not a safe place and Communism would soon arrive on America's shores. To capture the limelight, he, Joe McCarthy, assured his supporters he would lead the charge to beat back the enemy and save the day.[464]

Democrats and even a smattering of Republicans denounced McCarthy's tactics as unwholesome and offensive, but they met their match in the wily Wisconsin windbag. Given the hysteria that swept the Western world in the wake of revelations that the Rosenbergs had passed atomic secrets to the Soviet Union, the Soviets had exploded their own nuclear device, and the Communists had taken control of China, Americans were afraid, and their fear made them ripe for a demagogue with McCarthy's skills. McCarthy understood how to stoke citizen fears. Each time he was pressed to substantiate his outrageous allegations, the senator countered by questioning the motives of his enemies. He had come of age as a scrappy, ruthless, socially awkward

boxer and tough-guy wannabe. Now it was this misfit's moment to strut and fret on the national stage, and he would not be shunted into the wings by bit players who failed to appreciate who was starring in the grand production.[465]

Whenever he was attacked, McCarthy blasted his critics unmercifully. After a committee chaired by Maryland Senator Millard E. Tydings investigated McCarthy's claims and issued a scathing report characterizing his charges as "perhaps the most nefarious campaign of half-truths and untruth in the history of the Republic," an incensed and unrepentant McCarthy went on the offensive. He branded the report a "signal to the traitors, Communists, and fellow travelers in our Government that they need have no fear of exposure from the Administration." As far as the red-baiting senator was concerned, even the "most loyal stooges of the Kremlin could not have done a better job" of promoting Communism than the members of the Tydings Committee. McCarthy was following the demagogues' playbook: an attack on his motives and methods was an attack on the nation as well as a deliberate attempt to provide aid and comfort to the enemy.[466]

Numerous elected officials, even members of his own party, saw McCarthy for the blustering buffoon that he was, but his popularity in the hinterlands was so great that they resolved to tread softly. Even Dwight D. Eisenhower, the commanding general who was campaigning for the presidency in 1952, shrank from outright confrontation. McCarthy had attacked the patriotism of General George C. Marshall, a former US army chief of staff, and President Truman's secretary of state and later secretary of defense. Marshall had been instrumental in Eisenhower's rise through the army ranks, and Ike considered the man a friend. Poised to denounce McCarthy for his unfounded assault on Marshall's reputation when Eisenhower and McCarthy shared a speaking engagement, the general caved in to his advisers and excised a paragraph from his speech praising his former mentor. To Eisenhower's critics, it was an unforgivable act of political cowardice, but the decision also demonstrated how powerful the demagogic senator had become.[467]

McCarthy eventually overreached, as blusterers often do. By the mid-1950s, he had slung so many charges against so many supposed villains that he was forced to seek a new set of Communist sympathizers to smear. A few dissenters, notably CBS News's Edward R. Murrow, had criticized the Wisconsin demagogue, but he seemed impervious to serious attack until his would-be victims proved to be remarkably resilient. Unfortunately for McCarthy, his new targets were not helpless individuals who once flirted with the left and could therefore be smeared for their past transgressions. Bullies need weak victims, and McCarthy ignored this crucial factor to his detriment. He found himself face-to-face with a force he could not best: the US army. After it came to light that McCarthy had interfered with the army command structure to secure special treatment for an aide, the senator bellowed to anyone who would listen that he had been framed in retaliation for revealing the presence of disloyal subversives serving in the ranks.

Wisconsin Senator Joseph McCarthy led a witch hunt during the 1950s to root out Communists who had supposedly infiltrated American government. Courtesy of the National Archives & Records Administration.

McCarthy boldly promised that his subcommittee would investigate. Unbeknownst to the demagogue, he had sown the seeds of his own downfall.[468]

The army-McCarthy hearings were televised in 187 hours of coverage stretching over thirty-six days. Americans for the first time saw the demagogue up close, and many people were disgusted by what they saw. The bellicose blowhard showcased his worst attributes. He interrupted speakers, hurled invectives, and acted the part of a spoiled schoolchild. Roy Cohn, McCarthy's ruthless counsel and sidekick, later commented that the senator was the "perfect stock villain" in the little morality play, "with his easily erupting temper, his menacing monotone, his unsmiling mien, his perpetual 5 o'clock shadow."

It helped that McCarthy willingly played his part with such gusto. The dramatic highlight occurred when the senator faced a sixty-three-year old lawyer, Joseph Welch of the renowned Boston law firm of Hale & Dorr. Welch initially appeared to be an unlikely figure to bring down the decade's most effective demagogue. He was short, balding, and folksy—as self-effacing as McCarthy was histrionic.

Their televised exchange became the stuff of legend after McCarthy brought up the fact that Frederick G. Fisher Jr., a young associate working in Welch's law firm, had once associated with a left-wing organization. Roy Cohn had assured Welch before the hearing that Fisher's past associations were immaterial and would not be a subject of discussion. When McCarthy violated this agreement, Welch had reached the end of his tether. His spontaneous defense of a young man unfairly smeared with innuendo devastated McCarthy, finally revealing him as the bully that he was. "Let us not assassinate this lad further, Senator," Welch admonished the man. "Have you no decency, sir, at long last? Have you left no sense of decency?"[469]

In the wake of the hearings, McCarthy's popularity plummeted. Public figures who had embraced him or at least voiced their acquiescence when he bandied about threats to expose lurking Communists in the State Department, the army, or the Voice of America, a pro-America propaganda agency, suddenly were nowhere to be found. Sensing that his hour on the national stage was soon to conclude,

McCarthy screamed about Communist conspiracies aimed at tarnish-ing his good name, but the truth was that he had tarnished it himself without assistance from outside forces. In June 1954, the US Senate passed a resolution "condemning" the man's "contemptuous, contu-macious, and denunciatory" conduct.[470]

Disgraced, the senator became a pariah in Washington. He remained in office, but he delivered his speeches to empty chambers and found that his apocalyptic pronouncements fell on deaf ears. When he died of cirrhosis of the liver brought on by his alcoholism on May 2, 1957, the 48-year-old has-been was mourned by few, and forgiven by fewer still.[471]

Conclusion

Late in the nineteenth century, the political cartoonist Thomas Nast captured the fears that often compel citizens and their leaders to over-react to subversive threats. In two images, Nast contrasted Columbia, a symbol of the United States, in times when the nation is weak and when it is strong. In the first image, Columbia is shown cowering and fearful. Behind her a wooden log replaces a cannon. A skeletal figure lurks in the background, and the American flag hangs upside down, an indication of distress. The caption reads, "Peace insecure—afraid for her life." In the second image, Columbia stands tall, hold-ing an olive branch as she leans on a cannon. Doves of peace are visible while a soldier in the background stands guard beneath an upright American flag. The caption reads: "Peace secure—safe and protected." The image can be interpreted as an illustration of the simultaneous desire for security and liberty in the American repub-lic—with peace enhanced through a balance of governmental author-ity and individual freedom.[472]

Each case explored in this book involves the US government's response to a perceived threat. In responding to the threat, govern-ments must restrict some measure of human freedom. The nature and character of those restrictions must be monitored and altered as con-ditions change. In times of war and imminent national peril, citizens understand the need to surrender a measure of individual freedom in the interest of collective security. Citizens expect the government to

PEACE INSECURE—AFRAID FOR HER LIFE.—[SEE PAGE 135.]

This caption reads "Peace insecure—afraid for her life." Courtesy of the Library of Congress.

PEACE SECURE—SAFE AND PROTECTED.—[See Page 138.]

This caption reads "Peace secure—safe and protected." Courtesy of the Library of Congress.

protect them. Yet that temporary condition must never be allowed to become permanent. The citizenry must be eternally vigilant to ensure that a government based on the consent of the governed remains a reality as well as an ideal. In responding to threats, government must not become the threat itself.[473]

NOTES

1. Quoted in Saul K. Padover, ed., *Thomas Jefferson on Democracy* (New York: The New American Library, 1939), 108.
2. James Roger Sharp, *American Politics in the Early Republic: The New Nation in Crisis* (New Haven: Yale University Press, 1993), 92–97, 263–79; Geoffrey R. Stone, *Perilous Times: Free Speech in Wartime—From the Sedition Act of 1798 to the War on Terrorism* (New York: W.W. Norton & Company, 2004), 16–17; Gordon S. Wood, *Empire of Liberty: A History of the Early Republic, 1789–1815* (New York: Oxford University Press, 2009), 209–10, 230–38.
3. Ron Chernow, *Washington: A Life* (New York: The Penguin Press, 2010), 715–16, 729–31; Jerald A. Combs, *The Jay Treaty: Political Background of the Founding Fathers* (Berkeley: University of California Press, 1970), 4–14; Todd Estes, "Shaping the Politics of Public Opinion: Federalists and the Jay Treaty Debate," *Journal of the Early Republic* 20, no. 3 (2000): 393–422; Arthur H. Garrison, "The Internal Security Acts of 1798: The Founding Generation and the Judiciary during America's First National Security Crisis," *Journal of Supreme Court History* 34, no. 1 (2009): 3.
4. Garrison, "The Internal Security Acts of 1798," 3–4; Stone, *Perilous Times,* 21–22; Wood, *Empire of Liberty,* 239–42.
5. Quoted in Stone, *Perilous Times,* 28. See also David McCullough, *John Adams* (New York: Touchstone Books, 2001), 483–85; Stone, *Perilous Times,* 22; Wood, *Empire of Liberty,* 240.
6. Andrew Burstein and Nancy Isenberg, *Madison and Jefferson* (New York: Random House, 2010), 327–29; Stone, *Perilous Times,* 25–26; Wood, *Empire of Liberty,* 240.
7. Garrison, "The Internal Security Acts of 1798," 4; McCullough, *John Adams,* 489–90; Jean Edward Smith, *John Marshall: Definer of a Nation* (New York: Henry Holt, 1996), 182–84; Stone, *Perilous Times,* 22; Wood, *Empire of Liberty,* 240–42.
8. Burstein and Isenberg, *Madison and Jefferson,* 330, 331; Alan J. Farber, "Reflections on the Sedition Act of 1798," *American Bar Association Journal* 62, no. 3 (1976): 324; Garrison, "The Internal Security Acts of 1798," 4; Stephen John Harnett and Jennifer Rose Mercieca, "'Has Your Courage Rusted?' National Security and the Contested Rhetorical Norms of Republicanism in Post-Revolutionary America, 1798–1801," *Rhetoric & Public Affairs* 9, no. 1 (2006): 87–88; McCullough, *John Adams,* 495–98; Thomas M. Ray, "'Not One Cent for Tribute': The Public Addresses and American Popular Reaction to the XYZ Affair, 1798-1799," *Journal of the Early Republic* 3, no. 4 (1983): 389–412; Smith, *John Marshall,* 204–33; Wood, *Empire of Liberty,* 241–43.
9. Garrison, "The Internal Security Acts of 1798," 4; Stone, *Perilous Times,* 69–70; Wood, *Empire of Liberty,* 245–47.
10. Sharp, *American Politics in the Early Republic,* 92–97, 263–79; Stone, *Perilous Times,* 30–32, 33–38; Wood, *Empire of Liberty,* 248–50.
11. Garrison, "The Internal Security Acts of 1798," 8; Harnett and Mercieca, "'Has Your Courage Rusted?'" 91–92; Stone, *Perilous Times,* 30; Wood, *Empire of Liberty,* 249.
12. Garrison, "The Internal Security Acts of 1798," 8; Harnett and Mercieca, "'Has Your Courage Rusted?'" 92; Wood, *Empire of Liberty,* 249–50.

13. See, for example, Harnett and Mercieca, "'Has Your Courage Rusted?'" 92; James Morton Smith, "The Enforcement of the Alien Friends Act of 1798," *Mississippi Valley Historical Review* 41, no. 1 (1954): 85–104; Wood, *Empire of Liberty*, 250.

14. Quoted in Stone, *Perilous Times*, 44. See also Farber, "Reflections on the Sedition Act of 1798," 324–28; Garrison, "The Internal Security Acts of 1798," 8–9; Harnett and Mercieca, "'Has Your Courage Rusted?'" 93–96. Stone, *Perilous Times*, 36–44.

15. Quoted in Stone, *Perilous Times*, 19. See also James P. Martin, "When Repression Is Democratic and Constitutional: The Federalist Theory of Representation and the Sedition Act of 1798," *University of Chicago Law Review* 66, no. 1 (1999): 122–27; Wood, *Empire of Liberty*, 250–60.

16. Garrison, "The Internal Security Acts of 1798," 2; Erika Pani, "Saving the Nation Through Exclusion: Alien Laws in the Early Republic in the United States and Mexico," *Americas* 65, no. 2 (2008): 221–23; Robert D. Rachlin, "The Sedition Act of 1798 and the Political Divide in Vermont," *Vermont History* 78, no. 2 (2010): 127; Wood, *Empire of Liberty*, 25748.

17. Farber, "Reflections on the Sedition Act of 1798," 324; Garrison, "The Internal Security Acts of 1798," 5–8; Martin, "When Repression Is Democratic and Constitutional," 118–19, 127–28; Wood, *Empire of Liberty*, 246–48.

18. Quoted in Kurt T. Lash and Alicia Harrison, "Minority Report: John Marshall and the Defense of the Alien and Sedition Acts," *Ohio State Law Journal* 68, no. 2 (2007): 448. See also Garrison, "The Internal Security Acts of 1798," 5–6; Jon Meacham, *Thomas Jefferson: The Art of Power* (New York: Random House, 2012), 317–20.

19. Farber, "Reflections on the Sedition Act of 1798," 325–26; Garrison, "The Internal Security Acts of 1798," 8–9; Wood, *Empire of Liberty*, 261.

20. The episode is reported in many sources. See, for example, Garrison, "The Internal Security Acts of 1798," 9; Rachlin, "The Sedition Act of 1798 and the Political Divide in Vermont," 137–38; Stone, *Perilous Times*, 17–19, 20; Wood, *Empire of Liberty*, 229-30.

21. Farber, "Reflections on the Sedition Act of 1798," 325; Garrison, "The Internal Security Acts of 1798," 9–11; Rachlin, "The Sedition Act of 1798 and the Political Divide in Vermont," 135–40; Stone, *Perilous Times*, 48–54; Wood, *Empire of Liberty*, 262.

22. Farber, "Reflections on the Sedition Act of 1798," 325–26; Garrison, "The Internal Security Acts of 1798," 8–9; Stone, *Perilous Times*, 48–64.

23. Garrison, "The Internal Security Acts of 1798," 8–9; Stone, *Perilous Times*, 44–76; Wood, *Empire of Liberty*, 260–62.

24. See, for example, Burstein and Isenberg, *Madison and Jefferson*, 337–41; Adrienne Koch and Harry Ammon, "The Virginia and Kentucky Resolutions: An Episode in Jefferson's and Madison's Defense of Civil Liberties," *William and Mary Quarterly* Third Series, 5, no. 2 (1948): 145–76; Stone, *Perilous Times*, 44–45; Wood, *Empire of Liberty*, 268–71. While the resolutions were important discourses in the evolution of American political theory, some commentators have argued for their centrality as a limitation on the growth of federal power even in later centuries. See, as examples, William J. Watkins Jr., *Reclaiming the American Revolution: The Kentucky and Virginia Resolutions and Their Legacy* (New York: Palgrave, 2004), and Joe Wolverton II, "The Case for Nullification," *New American* 28, no. 9 (2012): 27–30. Few mainstream historians or lawyers would argue that the resolutions were important legal precedents beyond the Civil War era.

25. Both quotes appear in Ron Chernow, *Alexander Hamilton* (New York: The Penguin Press, 2004), 44–45.

26. Quoted in Andrew Jackson, *The Statesmanship of Andrew Jackson as Told in His Writings and Speeches*, ed. Francis Newton Thorpe (New York: The Tandy-Thomas Company, 1909), 235,

238. See also H. W. Brands, *Andrew Jackson: His Life and Times* (New York: Doubleday, 2005), 278–82; Matthew S. Brogdon, "Defending the Union: Andrew Jackson's Nullification Proclamation and American Federalism," *Review of Politics* 73, no. 2 (2011): 245–73; Jon Meacham, *American Lion: Andrew Jackson in the White House,* (New York: Random House, 2008), 227–30; Donald J. Ratcliffe, "The Nullification Crisis, Southern Discontents, and the American Political Process," *American Nineteenth Century History* 1, no. 2 (2000): 1–30.

27. Quoted in James Madison, *The Writings of James Madison,* vol. IX, ed. Gaillard Hunt (New York and London: G. P. Putnam's Sons, 1910), 573, 575. See also William K. Bolt, "Founding Father and Rebellious Son: James Madison, John C. Calhoun, and the Use of Precedents," *American Nineteenth Century History* 5, no. 3 (2004): 1–27; Richard Brookhiser, *James Madison* (New York: Basic Books, 2011), 237–44. Not everyone agrees with this interpretation of Madison's 1835 notes on nullification. See, for example, Michael Maharrey, *Smashing Myths: Understanding Madison's Notes on Nullification* (Los Angeles: Tenth Amendment Center, 2013), 25–28.

28. See, for example, Forrest McDonald, *States' Rights and the Union: Imperium in Imperio, 1776–1876* (Lawrence: University Press of Kansas, 2000).

29. Edward J. Larson, *A Magnificent Catastrophe: The Tumultuous Election of 1800, America's First Presidential Campaign* (New York: The Free Press, 2007), 73–83, 133–37.

30. Michael Shermer cogently discusses Type I and II errors in his book *The Believing Brain: From Ghosts and Gods to Politics and Conspiracies—How We Construct Beliefs and Reinforce Them as Truths* (New York: Times Books, 2011), 59–62.

31. Quoted in Ronald C. White Jr., *The Eloquent President: A Portrait of Lincoln Through His Words* (New York: Random House, 2005), 119.

32. Adam Goodheart, *1861: The Civil War Awakening* (New York: Vintage, 2012), 181–83; James M. McPherson, *Battle Cry of Freedom: The Civil War Era* (New York: Ballantine Books, 1988), 238–40; Stone, *Perilous Times,* 93.

33. McPherson, *Battle Cry of Freedom,* 70–75; Eric H. Walther, *The Shattering of the Union: America in the 1850s* (Wilmington, Del.: SR Books, 2004), xvii–xix, 1–4, 6.

34. Orville Vernon Burton, *The Age of Lincoln* (New York: Hill and Wang, 2007), 145–49; McPherson, *Battle Cry of Freedom,* 237–53.

35. Eric Foner, *The Fiery Trial: Abraham Lincoln and American Slavery* (New York and London: W. W. Norton & Company, 2010), xvi–xx, 339–41; David Waldstreicher, *Slavery's Constitution: From Revolution to Ratification* (New York: Hill and Wang, 2009), 83–101; Walther, *The Shattering of the Union,* xvii–xix.

36. Burton, *The Age of Lincoln,* 113–17; David Herbert Donald, *Lincoln* (New York: Simon & Schuster, 1995), 165–67; McPherson, *Battle Cry of Freedom,* 127–29, 234–35.

37. Richard Carwardine, *Lincoln: A Life of Purpose and Power* (New York: Knopf, 2003), 76–89; Donald, *Lincoln,* 206–9, 227–29; Foner, *The Fiery Trial,* 99–103.

38. Abraham Lincoln, "A House Divided," in *The Complete Works of Abraham Lincoln,* vol. 3, ed. John G. Nicolay and John Hay (New York: The Tandy-Thomas Company, 1905), 2. See also Donald, *Lincoln,* 206–9; McPherson, *Battle Cry of Freedom,* 179–80.

39. LaWanda Fenlason Cox, *Lincoln and Black Freedom: A Study in Presidential Leadership* (Columbia: The University of South Carolina Press, 1994), 183; Foner, *The Fiery Trial,* 228; John Yoo, *Crisis and Command: A History of Executive Power from George Washington to George W. Bush* (New York: Kaplan Publishing, 2009), 219–20.

40. Lincoln, "First Inaugural Address," in *The Complete Works of Abraham Lincoln,* vol. 6, ed. John G. Nicolay and John Hay (New York: The Tandy-Thomas Company, 1905), 184–85. See also Burton, *The Age of Lincoln,* 125–30; Foner, *The Fiery Trial,* 157–61; William Lee Miller, *President Lincoln: The Duty of a Statesman* (New York: Knopf, 2008), 53–54.

41. The definitive book on this time period and the events between the election of 1860 and Lincoln's swearing-in as president is Harold Holzer, *Lincoln President-Elect: Abraham Lincoln and the Great Secession Winter 1860–1861* (New York: Simon & Schuster, 2008). See also Donald, *Lincoln*, 271–84.

42. Donald, *Lincoln*, 416–17; Geoffrey R. Stone, "Free Speech and National Security," *Indiana Law Journal* 84, no. 3 (2009): 942; Ronald C. White Jr., *A. Lincoln: A Biography* (New York: Random House, 2009), 552.

43. Klement, "Copperheads," in *MacMillan Information Now Encyclopedia: The Confederacy*, ed. Richard N. Current (New York: MacMillan Reference USA, 1993), 154–55; White, *A. Lincoln*, 552.

44. Carwardine, *Lincoln*, 253–54; Donald, *Lincoln*, 416–17; Stone, "Free Speech and National Security," 942.

45. Klement, "Copperheads," 154–55; McPherson, *Battle Cry of Freedom*, 493–94, 506–7; Miller, *President Lincoln*, 374; Stone, *Perilous Times*, 89–90.

46. McPherson, *Battle Cry of Freedom*, 288; Justin J. Wert, *Habeas Corpus in America: The Politics of Individual Rights* (Lawrence: University Press of Kansas, 2011), 614.

47. McPherson, *Battle Cry of Freedom*, 288; Stone, "Free Speech and National Security," 942; Stone, *Perilous Times*, 120.

48. Alexander Hamilton and John Jay, "Federalist No. 84," in *The Federalist Papers*, ed. Clinton Rossiter (New York: The New American Library, 1961), 511, 512.

49. Abraham Lincoln, "Order to General Scott," in *The Complete Works of Abraham Lincoln*, vol. 6, ed. John G. Nicolay and John Hay (New York: The Tandy-Thomas Company, 1905), 255–56; Carwardine, *Lincoln*, 164; Donald, *Lincoln*, 299; Stone, *Perilous Times*, 84–85; White, *A. Lincoln*, 416.

50. Donald, *Lincoln*, 299; Abraham Lincoln, "Message to Congress in Special Session, July 4, 1861," in *The Complete Works of Abraham Lincoln*, vol. 6, ed. John G. Nicolay and John Hay (New York: The Tandy-Thomas Company, 1905), 308–10; Wert, *Habeas Corpus*, 31–32.

51. Ex Parte Merryman 17 F. Cas. 144 (C.C.D. Md. 1861) (No. 9487). See also Donald, *Lincoln*, 299; McPherson, *Battle Cry of Freedom*, 287–89; Stone, *Perilous Times*, 85, 87; White, *A. Lincoln*, 416–17.

52. McPherson, *Battle Cry of Freedom*, 287–89; Stone, *Perilous Times*, 85, 87; White, *A. Lincoln*, 416–17.

53. Patrick W. Carey, "Political Atheism: Dred Scott, Roger Brooke Taney, and Orestes A. Brownson," *The Catholic Historical Review* 88, no. 2 (1988): 211; Howard Jones, *Mutiny on the Amistad: The Saga of a Slave Revolt and Its Impact on American Abolition, Law and Diplomacy* (Omaha: The Notable Trials Library, 2014), 170–71, 188–89; Gregory J. Wallance, "The Lawsuit That Started the Civil War," *Civil War Times* 45, no. 2 (2006): 49; John C. Waugh, *One Man Great Enough: Abraham Lincoln's Road to Civil War* (Boston and New York: Houghton Mifflin, 2007), 241.

54. Austin Allen, "The Political Economy of Blackness: Citizenship, Corporations, and Race in *Dred Scott*," *Civil War History* 50, no. 3 (2004): 231–38; Stone, *Perilous Times*, 85; Daniel Walker Howe, *What Hath God Wrought: The Transformation of America, 1815–1848* (Oxford: Oxford University Press, 2007), 387–89.

55. *Ex Parte Merryman*, 17 F. Cas. 144. See also McPherson, *Battle Cry of Freedom*, 288; Stone, *Perilous Times*, 85, 87; Wert, *Habeas Corpus*, 80–83.

56. Donald, *Lincoln*, 304; Stone, *Perilous Times*, 87; White, *A. Lincoln*, 416–17.

57. Lincoln, "Order to General Scott," 255–56.

58. Lincoln, "Message to Congress in Special Session, July 4, 1861," 299, 304. See also McPherson, *Battle Cry of Freedom*, 288–89.

59. Lincoln, "Message to Congress in Special Session, July 4, 1861," 305, 308–9. See also Donald, *Lincoln*, 301–3; Abraham Lincoln, "Proclamation Calling 75,000 Militia, and Convening Congress in Extra Session, April 15, 1861," in *The Complete Works of Abraham Lincoln*, vol. 6, ed. John G. Nicolay and John Hay (New York: The Tandy-Thomas Company, 1905), 246–48; McPherson, *Battle Cry of Freedom*, 276–78, 309.

60. Lincoln, "Message to Congress in Special Session, July 4, 1861," 309–10.

61. Ibid., 310. See also Donald, *Lincoln*, 303–4; Stone, *Perilous Times*, 121–22.

62. Donald, *Lincoln*, 303–304; McPherson, *Battle Cry of Freedom*, 289–90; Stone, *Perilous Times*, 124–25.

63. Klement, "Copperheads," 154–55; McPherson, *Battle Cry of Freedom*, 591; Stone, *Perilous Times*, 89–90.

64. Klement, "Copperheads," 154–55; McPherson, *Battle Cry of Freedom*, 591–92; James M. McPherson, *Tried By War: Abraham Lincoln as Commander in Chief* (New York: The Penguin Press, 2008), 171.

65. Michael Kent Curtis, "Lincoln, Vallandigham, and Anti-War Speech in the Civil War," *William & Mary Bill of Rights Journal* 7, no. 1 (1998): 112–13; Lewis L. Gould, *Grand Old Party: A History of the Republicans* (New York: Random House, 2003), 12–13, 16; Frank L. Klement, *The Limits of Dissent: Clement L. Vallandigham & The Civil War* (New York: Fordham University Press, 1998), 16–20; Bruce Levine, "Conservatism, Nativism, and Slavery: Thomas R. Whitney and the Origins of the Know-Nothing Party," *Journal of American History* 88, no. 2 (2001): 487–88; Christopher Phillips, "'The Crimes Against Missouri' : Slavery, Kansas, and the Cant of Southernness in the Border West," *Civil War History* 48, no. 1 (2002): 72–73; James L. Vallandigham, *A Life of Clement L. Vallandigham* (Baltimore: Turnbull Brothers, 1872), 39–54; White, *A. Lincoln*, 553.

66. Vallandigham, *A Life of Clement L. Vallandigham*, 157–58. See also Klement, *The Limits of Dissent*, 55–56; Klement, "Copperheads," 154–55; Stone, *Perilous Times*, 98–99.

67. Carwardine, *Lincoln*, 141–44; Holzer, *Lincoln President-Elect*, 163–64; Klement, *The Limits of Dissent*, 51–53; McPherson, *Battle Cry of Freedom*, 252–54.

68. Curtis, "Lincoln, Vallandigham, and Anti-War Speech in the Civil War," 113; McPherson, *Battle Cry of Freedom*, 596–97.

69. Klement, *The Limits of Dissent*, 123–27; McPherson, *Tried By War*, 171; Geoffrey Perret, *Lincoln's War: The Untold Story of America's Greatest President as Commander in Chief* (New York: Random House, 2004), 302; White, *A. Lincoln*, 554.

70. Curtis, "Lincoln, Vallandigham, and Anti-War Speech in the Civil War," 113–14; Stone, "Free Speech and National Security," 942; Stone, *Perilous Times*, 113, 115–17.

71. Klement, "Copperheads," 154–55; McPherson, *Battle Cry of Freedom*, 591–92.

72. Quoted in McPherson, *Tried By War*, 177. See also Donald, *Lincoln*, 435–36; John Keegan, *The American Civil War: A Military History* (New York: Knopf, 2009), 185–86.

73. Klement, "Copperheads," 154–55; McPherson, *Battle Cry of Freedom*, 591–92; Stone, *Perilous Times*, 89–90, 98.

74. Donald, *Lincoln*, 418; Klement, "Copperheads," 155; Klement, *The Limits of Dissent*, 271, 281; McPherson, *Battle Cry of Freedom*, 560, 599.

75. Curtis, "Lincoln, Vallandigham, and Anti-War Speech in the Civil War," 119; Doris Kearns Goodwin, *Team of Rivals: The Political Genius of Abraham Lincoln* (New York: Simon & Schuster, 2005), 522; McPherson, *Tried by War*, 172.

76. Curtis, "Lincoln, Vallandigham, and Anti-War Speech in the Civil War," 119; Donald, *Lincoln*, 418; Klement, "Copperheads," 155; McPherson, *Battle Cry of Freedom*, 596; Stone, *Perilous Times*, 94–98.

77. McPherson, *Battle Cry of Freedom*, 596; Stone, "Free Speech and National Security," 942; Stone, *Perilous Times*, 100–101.

78. Ex Parte Vallandigham, 28 F.Cas. 874 (C.C.S.D. Ohio 1863).244. See also Klement, *The Limits of Dissent*, 152–55; McPherson, *Tried by War*, 172; Vallandigham, *A Life of Clement L. Vallandigham*, 248–49; White, *A. Lincoln*, 556.

79. Curtis, "Lincoln, Vallandigham, and Anti-War Speech in the Civil War," 107, 121; Goodwin, *Team of Rivals*, 522–23; Klement, *The Limits of Dissent*, 150–62; *The Trial of the Hon. Clement L. Vallandigham by a Military Commission* (Cincinnati: Rickey and Carroll, 1863), 8; White, *A. Lincoln*, 556–57.

80. *The Trial of the Hon. Clement L. Vallandigham by a Military Commission*, 12. See also Curtis, "Lincoln, Vallandigham, and Anti-War Speech in the Civil War," 121; Goodwin, *Team of Rivals*, 522–23; Klement, *The Limits of Dissent*, 160; McPherson, *Battle Cry of Freedom*, 596–97; Stone, *Perilous Times*, 101–2.

81. *The Trial of the Hon. Clement L. Vallandigham by a Military Commission*, 30. See also Curtis, "Lincoln, Vallandigham, and Anti-War Speech in the Civil War," 122–25.

82. *The Trial of the Hon. Clement L. Vallandigham by a Military Commission*, 32, 33. See also Curtis, "Lincoln, Vallandigham, and Anti-War Speech in the Civil War," 107, 130–31; Stone, "Free Speech and National Security," 943; Stone, *Perilous Times*, 101.

83. Curtis, "Lincoln, Vallandigham, and Anti-War Speech in the Civil War," 131–36; Klement, *The Limits of Dissent*, 168; McPherson, *Battle Cry of Freedom*, 597.

84. *Ex Parte Vallandigham*, 28 F. at 921–22. See also Curtis, "Lincoln, Vallandigham, and Anti-War Speech in the Civil War," 129–31. Lincoln was so happy about the opinion he reputedly said the legal result was equal to three battlefield victories. See Perret, *Lincoln's War*, 303–4.

85. *The Trial of the Hon. Clement L. Vallandigham by a Military Commission*, 40, 41.

86. *The Trial of the Hon. Clement L. Vallandigham by a Military Commission*, 43.

87. Goodwin, *Team of Rivals*, 522–23; McPherson, *Battle Cry of Freedom*, 595–600; Perret, *Lincoln's War*, 303; Stone, *Perilous Times*, 120–32.

88. Quoted in McPherson, *Tried by War*, 172–73. See also Curtis, "Lincoln, Vallandigham, and Anti-War Speech in the Civil War," 131.

89. Donald, *Lincoln*, 420–21; Klement, "Copperheads," 154–55; McPherson, *Battle Cry of Freedom*, 597; Stone, "Free Speech and National Security," 943; Stone, *Perilous Times*, 108–9.

90. Carwardine, *Lincoln*, 274; Klement, "Copperheads," 154–55; McPherson, *Battle Cry of Freedom*, 597–98; Stone, *Perilous Times*, 112.

91. Goodwin, *Team of Rivals*, 523–24; Klement, *The Limits of Dissent*, 183; Perret, *Lincoln's War*, 304–5; White, *A. Lincoln*, 557.

92. Curtis, "Lincoln, Vallandigham, and Anti-War Speech in the Civil War," 107, 132–34; Woodworth, *This Great Struggle*, 239–30.

93. Curtis, "Lincoln, Vallandigham, and Anti-War Speech in the Civil War," 108; Donald, *Lincoln*, 420–21; Klement, "Copperheads," 154–55; Stone, "Free Speech and National Security," 943; Stone, *Perilous Times*, 106–10.

94. McPherson, *Battle Cry of Freedom*, 597; Perret, *Lincoln's War*, 304; Stone, *Perilous Times*, 110.

95. Lincoln, "Letter to Erastus Corning and Others," in *The Complete Works of Abraham Lincoln*, vol. 8, ed. John G. Nicolay and John Hay (New York: The Tandy-Thomas Company, 1905), 304. See also Goodwin, *Team of Rivals*, 524; Klement, *The Limits of Dissent*, 182; McPherson, *Tried by War*, 173–74.

96. Lincoln, "Letter to Erastus Corning and Others," 307–8.

97. Lincoln, "The Case of Vallandigham.; Reply of President Lincoln to the Ohio Committee. Washington, D.C., June 29, 1863," *New York Times*, July 7, 1863. See also Lincoln, "Letter to M. Birchard and Others," in *The Complete Works of Abraham Lincoln*, vol. 9, ed. John G. Nicolay and John Hay (New York: The Tandy-Thomas Company, 1905), 3, 4–5; McPherson, *Tried by War*, 173–74.

98. Quoted in Vallandigham, *A Life of Clement L. Vallandigham*, 300. See also Klement, *The Limits of Dissent*, 193–94, 200; McPherson, *Battle Cry of Freedom*, 597–98; Stone, *Perilous Times*, 109; White, *A. Lincoln*, 557.

99. Klement, "Copperheads," 154–55; McPherson, *Battle Cry of Freedom*, 597–98; Stone, *Perilous Times*, 118–19.

100. Curtis, "Lincoln, Vallandigham, and Anti-War Speech in the Civil War," 135–36; Klement, "Copperheads," 154–55; McPherson, *Battle Cry of Freedom*, 597–98.

101. Ex Parte Vallandigham, 68 US 243, 251–52 (1863). See also Klement, *The Limits of Dissent*, 259; Wert, *Habeas Corpus*, 89.

102. Klement, "Copperheads," 154–55; Klement, *The Limits of Dissent*, 286–88; McPherson, *Battle Cry of Freedom*, 598; Stone, *Perilous Times*, 119.

103. Klement, "Copperheads," 154–55; Klement, *The Limits of Dissent*, 287–88; McPherson, *Battle Cry of Freedom*, 598.

104. Klement, *The Limits of Dissent*, 285–88, 305–8; Stone, *Perilous Times*, 119–20.

105. Klement, *The Limits of Dissent*, 310; Stone, *Perilous Times*, 120; Vallandigham, *A Life of Clement L. Vallandigham*, 520–22.

106. Ex Parte Milligan, 71 US (4 Wall.) 2 (1866). See also Harold H. Burton, "Two Significant Decisions: *Ex Parte Milligan* and *Ex Parte McCardle*," *American Bar Association Journal* 41, No. 2 (1955): 121–24, 176–77; Stone, *Perilous Times*, 126.

107. Stone, "Free Speech and National Security," 942; Stone, *Perilous Times*, 120.

108. Quoted in Robert M. La Follette, *The Political Philosophy of Robert M. La Follette as Revealed in His Speeches and Writings* (Madison: The Robert M. La Follette Company, 1920), 238.

109. For data on casualties, see John Ellis and Michael Cox, *The World War I Data Book* (London: Aurum Press, 2001), 270, especially table 6.1. For American reactions on the eve of war, see Edward M. Coffin, *The War to End All Wars: The American Military Experience in World War I* (Lexington: University of Kentucky Press, 1998), 6–7.

110. Robert Dallek, "Woodrow Wilson: Politician," *Wilson Quarterly* 15, no. 4 (1991): 106–14; Diana Preston, *Lusitania: An Epic Tragedy* (New York: Walker & Company, 2002), 424–25; Jules Witcover, *Party of the People: A History of the Democrats* (New York: Random House, 2003), 17–20.

111. Quoted in Woodrow Wilson, *War Addresses of Woodrow Wilson* (Boston and New York: Ginn and Company, 1918), 32–45. See also Charles Seymour, *Woodrow Wilson and the World War: A Chronicle of Our Own Times* (New Haven: Yale University Press, 1921), 111–15; Robert W. Tucker, *Woodrow Wilson and the Great War: Reconsidering America's Neutrality, 1914–1917* (Charlottesville: University of Virginia Press, 2007), 180–92; Witcover, *Party of the People*, 323–34.

112. Espionage Act of 1917, Act of 1917, ch. 30, 40 Stat. 217. 18 U.S.C. §§ 793 (1917); Robert D. Epstein, "Balancing National Security and Free-Speech Rights: Why Congress Should Revise the Espionage Act," *CommLaw Conspectus: Journal of Communications Law and Policy* 15, no. 2 (2007): 483–516; Stone, "Free Speech and National Security," 944–45; Stone, *Perilous Times*, 146–53.

113. On Lincoln, see, for example, William Blair, *With Malice toward Some: Treason and Loyalty in the Civil War Era* (Chapel Hill: University of North Carolina Press, 2014), 3–5; Holzer, *Lincoln and the Power of the Press*, 343–58, 408–9. See also Stone, *Perilous Times*, 144–45; Stephen I. Vladeck, "Inchoate Liability and the Espionage Act: The Statutory Framework and the Freedom of the Press," *Harvard Law and Policy Review* 1, no. 1 (2007): 221–22.

114. Epstein, "Balancing National Security and Free-Speech Rights," 485–86; Vladeck, "Inchoate Liability and the Espionage Act," 222–23.

115. Quoted in John Bach McMaster, *United States in the World War* (New York and London: D. Appleton and Company, 1918), 193.

116. For a discussion of the congressional reaction, see Epstein, "Balancing National Security and Free-Speech Rights," 486; Stone, *Perilous Times*, 147–49. For the Jefferson quote, see Padover, *Thomas Jefferson on Democracy*, 93.

117. For a discussion of the various provisions, see Geoffrey R. Stone, "Judge Learned Hand and the Espionage Act of 1917: A Mystery Unraveled," *University of Chicago Law Review* 70, no. 1 (2003): 352; Stone, *Perilous Times*, 146–53; Vladeck, "Inchoate Liability and the Espionage Act," 221–27.

118. Epstein, "Balancing National Security and Free-Speech Rights," 484–85; Stone, *Perilous Times*, 151–52.

119. Woodrow Wilson, "Executive Order 2594–Creating Committee on Public Information" 1917, reprinted in *Official Directory, 65th Congress, 3d Session*. Vol. 65. 2nd ed. (Washington, D.C.: Joint Committee on Printing, 1919), 355.

120. Quoted in Richard Rubin, *The Last of the Doughboys: The Forgotten Generation and Their Forgotten World War* (New York: Houghton Mifflin Harcourt, 2013), 175.

121. Chris Hedges, *Death of the Liberal Class* (New York: Nation Books, 2010), 169–78; Rubin, *The Last of the Doughboys*, 174–78.

122. Christopher Capozzola, *Uncle Sam Wants You: World War I and the Making of the Modern American Citizen* (Oxford: Oxford University Press, 2008), 42–44; Rubin, *The Last of the Doughboys*, 237, 254.

123. La Follette, *The Political Philosophy of Robert M. La Follette*, 238. See also Rubin, *The Last of the Doughboys*, 235; Stone, *Perilous Times*, 155–56.

124. Capozzola, *Uncle Sam Wants You*, 43–51; Rubin, *The Last of the Doughboys*, 237.

125. Tiffany Middleton, "Sedition Act of 1918," in *The Social History of Crime and Punishment in America*, ed. Wilbur R. Miller (Thousand Oaks: Sage Publications, Inc., 2012), 1618–19; Rubin, *The Last of the Doughboys*, 236–37; Samuel Walker, *Presidents and Civil Liberties from Wilson to Obama: A Story of Poor Custodians* (Cambridge: Cambridge University Press, 2012), 19.

126. Quoted in Stone, *Perilous Times*, 148–50. See also Rudanko, *Discourses of Freedom of Speech*, 165–70.

127. Middleton, "Sedition Act of 1918," 1618–19; Stone, *Perilous Times*, 184–91, 230–32.

128. Masses Publishing Company v. Patten, 244 F. 535 (S.D.N.Y. 1917). See also Ken I. Kersch, *Freedom of Speech: Rights and Liberties under the Law* (Santa Barbara: ABC-CLIO, 2003), 115–16; Stone, "Judge Learned Hand and the Espionage Act of 1917," 341; Stone, *Perilous Times*, 164–66.

129. The leading source on Judge Hand's life and career is Gerald Gunther, *Learned Hand: The Man and the Judge* (New York: Knopf, 1994). See also Stone, "Judge Learned Hand and the Espionage Act of 1917," 342–44.

130. *Masses Publishing*, at 542–43. See also Stone, "Judge Learned Hand and the Espionage Act of 1917," 342.

131. Quoted in Gunther, *Learned Hand*, 160. See also pages 151–61.

132. *Masses Publishing*, at 540. See also Stone, "Judge Learned Hand and the Espionage Act of 1917," 355–56.

133. Quoted in Gunther, *Learned Hand*, 161.

134. Stone, "Judge Learned Hand and the Espionage Act of 1917," 357–58; Stone, *Perilous Times*, 170.

135. Schenck v. United States, 249 US 47, 49–51 (1919). See also Epstein, "Balancing National Security and Free-Speech Rights," 487; Kersch, *Freedom of Speech*, 115–16; Walker, *Presidents and Civil Liberties from Wilson to Obama*, 33, 42–43.

136. *Schenck*, at 49. See also Chris Demaske, *Modern Power and Free Speech: Contemporary Culture and Issues of Equality* (Lanham: Lexington Books, 2011), 32–33; Epstein, "Balancing National Security and Free-Speech Rights," 487.

137. Schenck, at 52. Demaske, *Modern Power and Free Speech*, 33; Epstein, "Balancing National Security and Free-Speech Rights," 487; Kersch, *Freedom of Speech*, 116.

138. Thomas Healy, *The Great Dissent: How Oliver Wendell Holmes Changed His Mind—And Changed the History of Free Speech in America* (New York: Metropolitan Books, 2013), 156; Kersch, *Freedom of Speech*, 116.

139. Frohwerk v. United States, 249 US 204, 205–6 (1919). See also Healy, *The Great Dissent*, 84–85, 156–57; Kersch, *Freedom of Speech*, 117.

140. *Frohwerk*, at 208–9.

141. Healy, *The Great Dissent*, 85–86; Stone, *Perilous Times*, 196–97.

142. Debs v. United States, 249 US 211, 212–13 (1919). The speech is quoted in Neil A. Hamilton, *Rebels and Renegades: A Chronology of Social and Political Dissent in the United States* (London: Routledge, 2002), 333. See also Healy, *The Great Dissent*, 90–91.

143. Quoted in *Hamilton, Rebels and Renegades*, 335. See also Healy, *The Great Dissent*, 90–91; Kersch, *Freedom of Speech*, 117.

144. Debs at 212–13, 216. See also Healy, *The Great Dissent*, 156–57.

145. Healy, *The Great Dissent*, 154–59; Kersch, *Freedom of Speech*, 118–19.

146. Demaske, *Modern Power and Free Speech*, 33–34; Healy, *The Great Dissent*, 169.

147. Epstein, "Balancing National Security and Free-Speech Rights," 488–89; Healy, *The Great Dissent*, 170–71; Kersch, *Freedom of Speech*, 119.

148. Quoted in Walter Dean Burnham, *Democracy in the Making: American Government and Politics* (Upper Saddle River: Prentice Hall, 1983), 101. See also Stone, *Perilous Times*, 205–6.

149. Abrams v. United States, 250 US 616, 622 (1919). See also Healy, *The Great Dissent*, 212.

150. Abrams, at 627, 628. See also Epstein, "Balancing National Security and Free-Speech Rights," 489; Healy, *The Great Dissent*, 214; Stone, *Perilous Times*, 206.

151. Abrams, at 628. See also Healy, *The Great Dissent*, 244-45; Kersch, *Freedom of Speech*, 119.

152. *Abrams*, at 630. See also Demaske, *Modern Power and Free Speech*, 34; Healy, *The Great Dissent*, 236–37.

153. Epstein, "Balancing National Security and Free-Speech Rights," 490–91; Stone, "Free Speech and National Security," 946; Stone, *Perilous Times*, 208, 210.

154. Schaefer v. United States, 251 US 466, 495 (1920). See also Epstein, "Balancing National Security and Free-Speech Rights," 489–91; Stone, *Perilous Times*, 210.

155. Pierce v. United States, 252 US 239, 267 (1920). See also Epstein, "Balancing National Security and Free-Speech Rights," 491–92.

156. Gilbert v. Minnesota, 254 US 325, 326–27 (1920). Healy, *The Great Dissent*, 297; Stone, *Perilous Times*, 211.

157. *Gilbert*, at 333.

158. *Gilbert*, at 337.

159. Epstein, "Balancing National Security and Free-Speech Rights," 483–84; Stone, "Free Speech and National Security," 944–46.

160. Thomas R. Eddlem, "The Red Scare: When America Was Less Scared Than Today," *New American* 29, no. 20 (2013): 36; Christopher M. Finan, *From the Palmer Raids to the Patriot Act: A History of the Fight for Free Speech in America* (Boston: The Beacon Press, 2007), 2–3; Kersch, *Freedom of Speech*, 121.

161. Finan, *From the Palmer Raids to the Patriot Act*, 13.

162. Stone, *Perilous Times*, 221.

163. Eddlem, "The Red Scare," 36.

164. Eddlem, "The Red Scare," 36; Stone, *Perilous Times*, 222–23.

165. Eddlem, "The Red Scare," 38; Finan, *From the Palmer Raids to the Patriot Act*, 3, 4; Kersch, *Freedom of Speech*, 121.

166. Quoted in Kenneth D. Ackerman, *Young J. Edgar: Hoover and the Red Scare, 1919–1920* (Falls Church: Viral History Press, 2011), 305.

167. Eddlem, "The Red Scare," 37; Stone, *Perilous Times*, 225–26.

168. See, for example, Morton White, *Philosophy, The Federalist, and the Constitution* (New York: Oxford University Press, 1987), 160–61.

169. William Allen Rogers, "Now for a Round-Up," *New York Herald*, May 9, 1918, 5.

170. Capozzola, *Uncle Sam Wants You*, 43–51; Rubin, *The Last of the Doughboys*, 237; Stone, *Perilous Times*, 226–28.

171. West Virginia State Board of Education v. Barnette, 319 US 624, 641 (1943).

172. Epstein, "Balancing National Security and Free-Speech Rights," 483–84; Stone, *Perilous Times*, 192–94.

173. Quoted in Stone, *Perilous Times*, 251–52.

174. Quoted in Willard Hogan, *International Conflict and Collective Security* (Lexington: University of Kentucky Press, 1955), 81. See also Yoram Dinstein, *War, Aggression and Self-Defence* 4th ed. (Cambridge: Cambridge University Press, 2005), 85–87.

175. Howard Ball, *USA Patriot Act of 2001* (Santa Barbara: ABC-CLIO, 2004), 144; William M. Wiecek, *The History of the Supreme Court of the United States Vol. 12: The Birth of the Modern Constitution: The United States Supreme Court, 1941–1953* (Cambridge: Cambridge University Press, 2006), 290.

176. Charles P. Larrowe, *Harry Bridges: The Rise and Fall of Radical Labour in the US* (Chicago: Lawrence Hill & Company, 1972), 222, 227; Kevin Starr, *Endangered Dreams: The Great Depression in California* (New York: Oxford University Press, 1996), 220–22.

177. Michal R. Belknap, "Why Dennis?" *Marquette Law Review* 96, no. 4 (2013): 1014; "To Agree to the Conference Report on H.R. 5138, Alien Registration Act of 1940," GovTrack.Us, accessed February 2015, www.govtrack.us/congress/votes/76-3/h188..; Ira Katznelson, *Fear Itself: The New Deal and the Origins of Our Time* (New York: Liveright Publishing Corporation, 2013), 332–33; Arthur J. Sabin, *In Calmer Times: The Supreme Court and Red Monday* (Philadelphia: University of Pennsylvania Press, 1999), 3–4; Stone, *Perilous Times*, 251–52.

178. Quoted in Katznelson, *Fear Itself*, 333. See also H. W. Brands, *Traitor to His Class: The Privileged Life and Radical Presidency of Franklin Delano Roosevelt* (New York: Doubleday, 2008), 489; Stone, *Perilous Times*, 252.

179. Ball, *USA Patriot Act of 2001*, 144–45; Stone, *Perilous Times*, 251–52.

180. Bridges v. Wixon, 326 US 135, 138–40 (1945); Del Dickson, ed., *The Supreme Court in Conference (1940–1985): The Private Discussions Behind Nearly 300 Supreme Court Decisions* (New York: Oxford University Press, 2001), 199–200.

181. Francis Biddle, *In Brief Authority* (Westport: Praeger, 1976), 302. See also Peter Irons, "Politics and Principle: An Assessment of the Roosevelt Record on Civil Rights and Civil Liberties," in *At War with Civil Rights and Civil Liberties,* ed. Thomas E. Baker and John F. Stack Jr., (Lanham: Rowman & Littlefield, 2006), 63–64; C. P. Larrowe "Did the Old Left Get Due Process? The Case of Harry Bridges," *California Law Review* 60, no. 1 (1972): 80.

182. Stone, *Perilous Times,* 243–44; Patrick S. Washburn, "FDR versus His Own Attorney General: The Struggle Over Sedition, 1941–42," *Journalism Quarterly* 62, no. 4 (1985): 717–18.

183. *Bridges,* at 156. See also Washburn, "FDR versus His Own Attorney General," 720–24.

184. Donna T. Haverty-Stacke, "'Punishment of Mere Political Advocacy': The FBI, Teamsters Local 544, and the Origins of the 1941 Smith Act Case," *Journal of American History* 100, no. 1 (2013): 71, 88–90; Bryan D. Palmer, *Revolutionary Teamsters: The Minneapolis Truckers' Strikes of 1934* (Chicago: Haymarket Books, 2014), 239–48.

185. Haverty-Stacke, "'Punishment of Mere Political Advocacy,'" 90–93; Stone, *Perilous Times,* 255.

186. Christians's discussion of how to stage a *coup d'état* is quoted in Charles Wright Ferguson, *Fifty Million Brothers: A Panorama of American Lodges and Clubs* (New York: Farrar & Rinehart, 1937), 123. See also Jules Archer, *The Plot to Seize the White House: The Shocking True Story of the Conspiracy to Overthrow FDR* (New York: Skyhorse, 2007), 201; High, "Star-Spangled Fascists," 70–71; Allan J. Lichtman, *White Protestant Nation: The Rise of the American Conservative Movement* (New York: Atlantic Monthly Press, 2008), 76.

187. Quoted in "The Law," *Time* 39, no. 19 (1942): 48. See also Lichtman, *White Protestant Nation,* 76.

188. Pelley's background is discussed in several sources, including Scott Beekman, *William Dudley Pelley: A Life in Right-Wing Extremism and the Occult* (Syracuse: Syracuse University Press, 2005); Stanley High, "Star-Spangled Fascists," *Saturday Evening Post* 211, 48 (1939): 7, 70; James Ridgeway, *Blood in the Face: The Ku Klux Klan, Aryan Nations, Nazi Skinheads, and the Rise of a New White Culture,* 2nd. ed. (New York: Thunder's Mouth Press, 1995), 62–64; Stone, *Perilous Times,* 262–63.

189. Beekman, *William Dudley Pelley,* 139; Ridgeway, *Blood in the Face,* 64; Stone, *Perilous Times,* 265.

190. Lawrence Dennis and Maximilian St. George, *A Trial on Trial: The Great Sedition Trial of 1944* (Washington, D.C.: National Civil Rights Committee, 1946), 16–25; Stone, *Perilous Times,* 272–74.

191. Michael, *Confronting Right-Wing Extremism and Terrorism in the USA* (London: Routledge, 2003), 125–26; Walker, *Presidents and Civil Liberties from Wilson to Obama,* 116–17.

192. Dennis v. United States, 341 US 494, 497 (1951).

193. *Dennis,* at 497–99. See also Belknap, "Why Dennis?" 1015–17; Stone, *Perilous Times,* 396–97.

194. Richard M. Fried, *The Russians Are Coming! The Russians Are Coming! Pageantry and Patriotism in Cold-War America* (New York: Oxford University Press, 1998), 10–11, 19–21; Gould, *Grand Old Party,* 310–13.

195. Archie Brown, *The Rise and Fall of Communism* (New York: HarperCollins, 2009), 143, 156–57, 176–78, 204–05; Dallek, *Franklin D. Roosevelt and American Foreign Policy, 1932–1945* (New York: Oxford University Press, 1995), 519–22; Wiecek, *The History of the Supreme Court of the United States*, 551.

196. *Dennis*, at 495; Belknap, "Why Dennis?" 1018–19; Gunther, *Learned Hand*, 523; Wiecek, *The History of the Supreme Court of the United States*, 551–54.

197. Quoted in Belknap, "Cold War in the Courtroom: The Foley Square Communist Trial," in *American Political Trials*, ed. Michal R. Belknap (Westport: Greenwood Press, 1994), 218. See also Harold R. Medina, "The Crime of Conspiracy: Charge to the Jury," *Vital Speeches of the Day* 16, no. 2 (1949): 34–46; Wiecek, *The History of the Supreme Court of the United States*, 554.

198. *Dennis*, at 495; Gunther, *Learned Hand*, 515–28.

199. *Dennis*, at 516–17.

200. *Dennis*, at 581.

201. *Dennis*, at 581.

202. Yates v. United States, 354 US 298 (1957). See also Belknap, "Cold War in the Courtroom," 225–26.

203. Stone is quoted in Walker, *Presidents and Civil Liberties from Wilson to Obama*, 197. See also *Yates*, at 300–01, 332–34; Watkins v. United States, 354 US 178 (1957).

204. *Yates*, at 300–38. See also Stone, *Perilous Times*, 413–14.

205. Stone, *Perilous Times*, 413–15; Walker, *Presidents and Civil Liberties from Wilson to Obama*, 196–97.

206. Quoted in Tetsuden Kashima, *Judgment without Trial: Japanese American Imprisonment During World War II* (Seattle: University of Washington Press, 2003), 214.

207. Roosevelt's speech is quoted in William F. Nimmo, *Stars and Stripes Across the Pacific: The United States, Japan, and the Asia/Pacific Region, 1895–1945* (Westport: Praeger, 2001), 207–08; Rankin is quoted in Molly A. Mayhead and Brenda Devore Marshall, *Women's Political Discourse: a 21st Century Perspective* (Lanham: Rowman & Littlefield, 2005), 23. See also Kashima, *Judgment without Trial*, 46, 51; Richard Reeves, *Infamy: The Shocking Story of the Japanese American Internment in World War II* (New York: Henry Holt, 2015), 3.

208. Kashima, *Judgment without Trial*, 75–76; Reeves, *Infamy*, 9–12; Greg Robinson, *By Order of the President: FDR and the Internment of Japanese Americans* (Cambridge: Harvard University Press, 2001), 75.

209. Knox is quoted in Robinson, *By Order of the President*, 77; Kashima, *Judgment without Trial*, 41, 69, 79–80; Reeves, *Infamy*, 15–16; Robinson, *By Order of the President*, 76–77.

210. Kashima, *Judgment without Trial*, 41, 69; Reeves, *Infamy*, 14–16; Robinson, *By Order of the President*, 78, 79.

211. DeWitt is quoted in Robinson, *By Order of the President*, 86. See also Kashima, *Judgment without Trial*, 58, 129–30; Chris Mead, *The Magicians of Main Street: America and its Chambers of Commerce, 1768–1945* (Oakton: John Cruger Press, 2014), 342–43; Robinson, *By Order of the President*, 84–86.

212. Mead, *The Magicians of Main Street*, 342–43; Robinson, *By Order of the President*, 84–85; Stone, *Perilous Times*, 290–91.

213. Mead, *The Magicians of Main Street*, 343; Robinson, *By Order of the President*, 84–87.

214. Robinson, *By Order of the President*, 90–106; Stone, *Perilous Times*, 291.

215. Quoted in Robinson, *By Order of the President*, 91.

216. Robinson, *By Order of the President*, 92; Stone, *Perilous Times*, 294.

217. The report is quoted in William H. Rehnquist, *All the Laws but One: Civil Liberties in Wartime* (New York: Knopf, 1998), 189.

218. McLemore is quoted in Robinson, *By Order of the President*, 96. Pegler is quoted in Brands, *Traitor to His Class*, 491. See also Joshua Gannis, "The Court, the Constitution and Japanese-American Internment," *Stanford Journal of East Asian Affairs* 11, no. 1 (2011): 90–91.

219. Quoted in Robinson, *By Order of the President*, 96. See also Gannis, "The Court, the Constitution and Japanese-American Internment," 90.

220. United States War Department, *Final Report: Japanese Evacuation from the West Coast* (New York: Arno Press, 1978), 34. See also Jacobus tenBroek, et al., *Prejudice, War and the Constitution: Causes and Consequences of the Evacuation of the Japanese Americans in World War II* (Berkeley: University of California Press, 1970), 109–11.

221. Quoted in Kashima, *Judgment without Trial*, 214.

222. Quoted in Robinson, *By Order of the President*, 105. See also Reeves, *Infamy*, 39, 51; Robinson, *By Order of the President*, 104–06.

223. Reeves, *Infamy*, 51–55; Robinson, *By Order of the President*, 106–24.

224. Gannis, "The Court, the Constitution and Japanese-American Internment," 92; Kashima, *Judgment without Trial*, 72–73; Reeves, *Infamy*, 54–55; Robinson, *By Order of the President*, 125, 130–31; tenBroek, et al., *Prejudice, War and the Constitution*, 111–12.

225. Reeves, *Infamy*, xv; Robinson, *By Order of the President*, 114–24.

226. Robinson, *By Order of the President*, 127–29.

227. Robinson, *By Order of the President*, 128–29; tenBroek, et al., *Prejudice, War and the Constitution*, 121–22, 124.

228. Kashima, *Judgment without Trial*, 9–10; Reeves, *Infamy*, 64–66; tenBroek, et al., *Prejudice, War and the Constitution*, 124–25.

229. Hirabayashi v. United States, 320 US 81, 87 (1943); Kashima, *Judgment without Trial*, 134–35; Reeves, *Infamy*, 64–65, 71; Robinson, *By Order of the President*, 129–31, 230–32; tenBroek, et al., *Prejudice, War and the Constitution*, 122.

230. Robinson, *By Order of the President*, 132–33, 162; Stone, *Perilous Times*, 304.

231. Reeves, *Infamy*, xix; tenBroek, et al., Prejudice, War and the Constitution, 128–30.

232. Robinson, *By Order of the President*, 132–33.

233. Robinson, *By Order of the President*, 192–93.

234. *Hirabayashi*, at 83–84. See also tenBroek, et al., *Prejudice, War and the Constitution*, 233–34.

235. *Hirabayashi*, at 100.

236. *Hirabayashi*, at 101. See also tenBroek, et al., *Prejudice, War and the Constitution*, 234–35.

237. *Hirabayashi*, at 107.

238. Rutledge's concurrence can be found at *Hirabayashi*, at 114. Murphy's dissent is found at *Hirabayashi*, at 109–14.

239. The discussion between Murphy and Frankfurter is reported in Stone, *Perilous Times*, 298.

240. *Hirabayashi*, at 110, 111.

241. *Hirabayashi*, at 105.

242. The case is cited as Korematsu v. United States, 323 US 214 (1944). For the other cases mentioned, see: Yasui v. United States, 320 US 115 (1943); Dred Scott v. Sandford, 60 US 393 (1857); Plessy v. Ferguson, 163 US 537 (1896).

243. *Korematsu*, at 222–23. See also Gannis, "The Court, the Constitution and Japanese-American Internment," 92; tenBroek, et al., *Prejudice, War and the Constitution*, 235–36.

244. *Korematsu*, at 223. See also Gannis, "The Court, the Constitution and Japanese-American Internment," 93–94; tenBroek, et al., *Prejudice, War and the Constitution*, 236–38.

245. *Korematsu*, at 225–226. See also Gannis, "The Court, the Constitution and Japanese-American Internment," 94. Ironically, Justice Roberts headed the commission that issued a report mentioning the possibility of Japanese spies providing intelligence data to the Empire of Japan.

246. *Korematsu*, at 242–43. See also tenBroek, et al., *Prejudice, War and the Constitution*, 240.

247. *Korematsu*, at 233, 234–35.

248. Stone, *Perilous Times*, 302–05.

249. Stone, *Perilous Times*, 304–05.

250. Ex parte Endo, 323 US 283 (1944). See also Stone, *Perilous Times*, 302–03; tenBroek, et al., *Prejudice, War and the Constitution*, 252–54.

251. Oyama v. State of California, 332 US 633 (1948).

252. Takahashi v. Fish and Game Commission, 334 US 410 (1948). See also Evacuation Claims Act of 1948, Pub. L. No. 886, 62 Stat. 1231 (1948); Stone, *Perilous Times*, 303.

253. Duncan v. Kahanamoku, 327 US 304 (1946).

254. Gerald R. Ford, "Proclamation 4417: Confirming the Termination of the Executive Order Authorizing Japanese-American Internment During World War II," in *When Sorry Isn't Enough: The Controversy Over Apologies and Reparations for Human Injustice*, ed. Roy L. Brooks (New York: New York University Press, 1999), 201. See also Reeves, *Infamy*, 275.

255. Ford, "Proclamation 4417," 202.

256. Reeves, *Infamy*, 259–60, 292–93.

257. Quoted in Paul Spickard, *Almost All Aliens: Immigration, Race, and Colonialism in American History and Identity* (London: Routledge, 2007), 401. See also Stone, *Perilous Times*, 307.

258. Bush is quoted in George H. W. Bush, "Remarks on the Fiftieth Anniversary of Pearl Harbor, December 7, 1991," in *Weekly Compilation of Presidential Documents* (Washington, D.C.: Office of the Federal Register, National Archives and Records Service, General Services Administration, 1991): 1791. See also Reeves, *Infamy*, 276–77; Stone, *Perilous Times*, 307.

259. tenBroek, et al., *Prejudice, War and the Constitution*, 235–34.

260. Quoted in James Magee, *Freedom of Expression* (Westport: Greenwood Press, 2002), 166.

261. Blaine T. Browne and Robert C. Cottrell, *Lives and Times: Individuals and Issues in American History Since 1865* (Lanham: Rowman & Littlefield, 2010), 179–80; Theresa S. Hefner-Babb, "Internal Security Act of 1950," in *Social History of Crime and Punishment in America*, ed. Wilbur R. Miller (Thousand Oaks: Sage Publications, Inc., 2012), 845; Stone, *Perilous Times*, 334–35; Samuel Walker, *In Defense of American Liberties: A History of the ACLU*. 2nd. ed. (Carbondale: Southern Illinois University Press, 1999), 198–99; Walker, *Presidents and Civil Liberties from Wilson to Obama*, 140.

262. See especially Tony Perucci, "The Red Mask of Sanity: Paul Robeson, HUAC, and the Sound of Cold War Performance," *TDR: The Drama Review* 53, no. 4 (2009): 18–24.

263. David McCullough, *Truman* (New York: Simon & Schuster, 1992), 743–44, 759–61, 860–61; Stone, *Perilous Times*, 334.

264. Browne and Cottrell, *Lives and Times*, 173–78; Michael J. Ybarra, *Washington Gone Crazy: Senator Pat McCarran and the Great American Communist Witch Hunt* (Hanover: Steerforth Press, 2004), 62.

265. Stephen E. Ambrose, *The Education of a Politician, 1913–1962*, vol. 1 of *Nixon* (New York: Touchstone Books, 1987), 160–64; Conrad Black, *Richard M. Nixon: A Life in Full* (New York: Public Affairs, 2007), 104; John Patrick Diggins, *The Proud Decades: America in War and Peace, 1941–1960* (New York: W. W. Norton & Company, 1988), 117; Robert Justin Goldstein, *Political Repression in Modern America: From 1870 to 1976* (Champaign: University of Illinois Press, 2001), 321–22; Hefner-Babb, "Internal Security Act of 1950," 844; Walker, *In Defense of American Liberties*, 198; Ybarra, *Washington Gone Crazy*, 510, 512, 519.

266. Black, *Richard M. Nixon*, 141; "Caution Needed," *New York Times*, August 31, 1950, 21.

267. Finan, *From the Palmer Raids to the Patriot Act*, 154; Goldstein, *Political Repression in Modern America*, 322–23; Meltzer "Required Records, the McCarran Act, and the Privilege against Self-Incrimination," *University of Chicago Law Review* 18, no. 4 (1951): 719–20; Walker, *In Defense of American Liberties*, 198–99; Walker, *Presidents and Civil Liberties from Wilson to Obama*, 140; Ybarra, *Washington Gone Crazy*, 484, 558–61, 577.

268. Quoted in Meltzer, "Required Records, the McCarran Act, and the Privilege against Self-Incrimination," 720.

269. Goldstein, *Political Repression in Modern America*, 323. See also Meltzer "Required Records, the McCarran Act, and the Privilege against Self-Incrimination," 721–22; Ybarra, *Washington Gone Crazy*, 323.

270. Hefner-Babb, "Internal Security Act of 1950," 844; C. P. Trussell, "Senate Filibuster: Charge Made as Long Truman Message Stirs Debate Into Today," *New York Times*, September 23, 1950 1, 3; Walker, *Presidents and Civil Liberties from Wilson to Obama*, 127.

271. Quoted in "Text of President's Message Vetoing the Communist-Control Bill," *New York Times*, September 23, 1950, 6. See also Browne and Cottrell, *Lives and Times*, 180; Diggins, *The Proud Decades*, 117; Walker, *Presidents and Civil Liberties from Wilson to Obama*, 127; Ybarra, *Washington Gone Crazy*, 527.

272. Diggins, *The Proud Decades*, 117; Finan, *From the Palmer Raids to the Patriot Act*, 155; Hefner-Babb, "Internal Security Act of 1950," 844; C. P. Trussell, "Red Bill Veto Beaten, 57–10, by Senators," *New York Times*, September 24, 1950 1; Walker, *Presidents and Civil Liberties from Wilson to Obama*, 140.

273. Frank B. Ober, "Communism and the Court: An Examination of Recent Developments," *ABA Journal* 44, no. 1 (January 1958): 35; Walker, *Presidents and Civil Liberties from Wilson to Obama*, 129–32; Ybarra, *Washington Gone Crazy*, 283.

274. Communist Party of the United States v. Subversive Activities Control Board, 351 US 115, 118–25 (1956).

275. *Communist Party* 351 US at 125–27. See also Communist Party of the United States v. Subversive Activities Control Board, 367 US 1, 19–21 (1961).

276. *Communist Party* 351 US at 127; *Communist Party* 367 US at 20–22.

277. *Communist Party* 351 US at 124–25. See also Michal R. Belknap, *The Vinson Court: Justices, Rulings, and Legacy* (Santa Barbara: ABC-CLIO, 2004), 171.

278. *Communist Party* 367 US at 19–22.

279. *Communist Party* 367 US at 81–82.

280. *Communist Party* 367 US at 86.

281. *Communist Party* 367 US at 93–94.

282. *Communist Party* 367 US at 107.

283. *Communist Party* 367 US at 113.

284. *Communist Party* 367 US at 115. See also Hefner-Babb, "Internal Security Act of 1950," 844.
285. *Communist Party* 367 US at 137.
286. Albertson v. Subversive Activities Control Board, 382 US 70 (1965).
287. *Albertson* 382 US at 73–74.
288. *Albertson* 382 US at 77.
289. Belknap, *The Vinson Court*, 171; Ed Cray, *Chief Justice: A Biography of Earl Warren* (New York: Simon & Schuster, 1997), 473; Walker, *In Defense of American Liberties*, 246.
290. Hefner-Babb, "Internal Security Act of 1950," 845.
291. Laura Sefton MacDowell, "Paul Robeson in Canada: A Border Story," *Labour/Le Travail* 51, no. 1 (2003): 177; Perucci, "The Red Mask of Sanity," 19.
292. Guenter Lewy, *The Cause That Failed: Communism in American Political Life* (New York and Oxford: Oxford University Press, 1990), 279–84; Walker, *Presidents and Civil Liberties from Wilson to Obama*, 133, 197; Ybarra, *Washington Gone Crazy*, 375. The poster can be found at: Delaware Valley Committee for Democratic Rights, "Will You Register Under the McCarran Act?" accessed March 2015, http://en.wikipedia.org/wiki/File:61-mccarranact-poster.jpg.
293. Dan T. Carter, *Scottsboro: A Tragedy of the American South,* revised edition (Baton Rouge: Louisiana State University Press, 2007), 51–103; James Goodman, *Stories of Scottsboro* (New York: Doubleday, 1995), 101; Perucci, "The Red Mask of Sanity," 23. For a detailed discussion of the uneasy relationship between Communist and blacks in the United States during this period, see Jeff Woods, *Black Struggle, Red Scare: Segregation and Anti-Communism in the South, 1948–1968* (Baton Rouge: Louisiana State University Press, 2004).
294. Browne and Cottrell, *Lives and Times,* 164-69; MacDowell, "Paul Robeson in Canada," 178–81.
295. Browne and Cottrell, *Lives and Times,* 171–73; MacDowell, "Paul Robeson in Canada," 181.
296. The sage is quoted in Perucci, "The Red Mask of Sanity," 19. Robeson is quoted in Virginia Hamilton, *Paul Robeson: The Life and Times of a Free Black Man* (New York: Dell Publishing, 1979), 171.
297. Robeson v. Acheson, 198 F.2d 985, 986–987 (DC Cir. 1952).
298. Quoted in MacDowell, "Paul Robeson in Canada," 186.
299. Hoover is quoted in Perucci, "The Red Mask of Sanity," 36. Canwell is quoted in Tony Perucci, *Paul Robeson and the Cold War Performance Complex: Race, Madness, Activism* (Ann Arbor: University of Michigan Press, 2012), 48. See also Richard M. Fried, *Nightmare in Red: The McCarthy Era in Perspective* (New York and Oxford: Oxford University Press, 1990), 107–08.
300. Browne and Cottrell, *Lives and Times,* 172–73; Perucci, "The Red Mask of Sanity," 20–29.
301. Quoted in Ambrose, *The Education of a Politician*, 195.
302. John Braeman, "House Un-American Activities Committee," in *Conspiracy Theories in American History: An Encyclopedia*, ed. Peter Knight (Santa Barbara: ABC-CLIO, 2003), 325. The Committee was named the House Committee on Un-American Activities, but it became known almost universally as the House Un-American Activities Committee (HUAC). Accordingly, the latter term is used here.
303. Stone, *Perilous Times,* 353.

304. Kilbourn v. Thompson, 103 US 168 (1880).

305. McGrain v. Daugherty, 273 US 135 (1927).

306. Braeman, "House Un-American Activities Committee," 325; Carol Richey, "House Committee on Un-American Activities," *History Magazine* 15, no. 2 (December 2013/ January 2014): 45–46.

307. Braeman, "House Un-American Activities Committee," 325; Richard Gid Powers, *Not Without Honor: The History of American Communism* (New Haven: Yale University Press, 1998), 124.

308. Braeman, "House Un-American Activities Committee," 325; Kenneth Heineman, "Media Bias in Coverage of the Dies Committee on Un-American Activities, 1938–1940," *Historian* 50, no. 1 (1992): 37–38; Richey, "House Committee on Un-American Activities," 45–46.

309. Quoted in Stone, *Perilous Times*, 354. See also Powers, *Not Without Honor*, 124–25; Richey, "House Committee on Un-American Activities," 46.

310. Powers, *Not Without Honor*, 126–28; Stone, *Perilous Times*, 246.

311. Powers, *Not Without Honor*, 128–29.

312. Powers, *Not Without Honor*, 129, 187.

313. Braeman, "House Un-American Activities Committee," 325.

314. The incident is recounted in Gerald Meyer, *Vito Marcantonio: Radical Politician, 1902–1954* (Albany: SUNY Press, 1989), note 7, 221.

315. Braeman, "House Un-American Activities Committee," 325; Powers, *Not Without Honor*, 216.

316. Blackwell, *Notorious New Jersey*, 199–203.

317. Braeman, "House Un-American Activities Committee," 325; Stone, *Perilous Times*, 355.

318. Ambrose, *The Education of a Politician*, 146–47; Stone, *Perilous Times*, 356–59.

319. Black, *Richard M. Nixon*, 91–92; Braeman, "House Un-American Activities Committee," 326; Richey, "House Committee on Un-American Activities," 47–48.

320. Bernard K. Dick, *Radical Innocence: a Critical Study of the Hollywood Ten* (Lexington: University of Kentucky Press, 1989); Richey, "House Committee on Un-American Activities," 47–48.

321. Dick, *Radical Innocence*, 135–65. For a detailed discussion of the issue, see especially Edward Dmytryk, *Odd Man Out: A Memoir of the Hollywood Ten* (Carbondale: Southern Illinois University Press, 1996).

322. United States House of Representatives, Committee on Un-American Activities, *Hearings Regarding Communist Espionage in the United States Government. Hearings Before the Committee on Un-American Activities, House of Representatives*, 80th Cong., 2d sess., Public Law 601 (Washington, D.C.: Government Printing Office, 1948), 539–40. See also Ambrose, *The Education of a Politician*, 167, 168; Braeman, "House Un-American Activities Committee," 326; Kathryn S. Olmsted, *Red Spy Queen: A Biography of Elizabeth Bentley* (Chapel Hill: University of North Carolina Press, 2002), 1–16.

323. Braeman, "House Un-American Activities Committee," 326; Olmsted, *Red Spy Queen*, 45–47.

324. United States House of Representatives, Committee on Un-American Activities, *Hearings Regarding Communist Espionage in the United States Government*, 540. See also Olmsted, *Red Spy Queen*, 61–62, 63, 64.

325. Olmsted, *Red Spy Queen*, 105.

326. Olmsted, *Red Spy Queen*, 140–41; Edward G. White, *Alger Hiss's Looking-Glass Wars: The Covert Life of a Soviet Spy* (New York and Oxford: Oxford University Press, 2004), 195, 288.

327. Gary May, *Un-American Activities: The Trials of William Remington* (New York: Gryphon Editions, 1999), 98–100.
328. Braeman, "House Un-American Activities Committee," 326.
329. Ambrose, *The Education of a Politician*, 168–70; Powers, *Not Without Honor*, 171.
330. Ambrose, *The Education of a Politician*, 170–71; Braeman, "House Un-American Activities Committee," 326.
331. White, *Alger Hiss's Looking-Glass Wars*, 3–19.
332. Ambrose, *The Education of a Politician*, 170; Powers, *Not Without Honor*, 222.
333. Ambrose, *The Education of a Politician*, 170–71; Black, *Richard M. Nixon*, 111–12.
334. Ambrose, *The Education of a Politician*, 172–74; Black, *Richard M. Nixon*, 112–14; Braeman, "House Un-American Activities Committee," 326.
335. Ambrose, *The Education of a Politician*, 174–87; White, *Alger Hiss's Looking-Glass Wars*, 60.
336. Ambrose, *The Education of a Politician*, 180–85; Black, *Richard M. Nixon*, 117–19.
337. Ambrose, *The Education of a Politician*, 189–90.
338. Ambrose, *The Education of a Politician*, 187–88; Black, *Richard M. Nixon*, 125–27.
339. Ambrose, *The Education of a Politician*, 189–91; Black, *Richard M. Nixon*, 127–30.
340. Ambrose, *The Education of a Politician*, 191–92; Black, *Richard M. Nixon*, 129–32; White, *Alger Hiss's Looking-Glass Wars*, 63–64.
341. Ambrose, *The Education of a Politician*, 192–93; Black, *Richard M. Nixon*, 132–36; White, *Alger Hiss's Looking-Glass Wars*, 63–66.
342. Ambrose, *The Education of a Politician*, 192–95; Black, *Richard M. Nixon*, 138.
343. Quoted in Ambrose, *The Education of a Politician*, 195. See also Black, *Richard M. Nixon*, 135–37; White, *Alger Hiss's Looking-Glass Wars*, 64-71.
344. Ambrose, *The Education of a Politician*, 199–205; Black, *Richard M. Nixon*, 137–39.
345. Acheson is quoted in Black, *Richard M. Nixon*, 139. See also Ambrose, *The Education of a Politician*, 205–06; Black, *Richard M. Nixon*, 139–40.
346. Ambrose, *The Education of a Politician*, 206–07; Black, *Richard M. Nixon*, 141–42.
347. Braeman, "House Un-American Activities Committee," 327.
348. Richey, "House Committee on Un-American Activities," 45–48; Stone, *Perilous Times*,
349. Stone, *Perilous Times*, 372–74; White, *Alger Hiss's Looking-Glass Wars*, 221–36.
350. White, *Alger Hiss's Looking-Glass Wars*, 224–35, 237–38.
351. Stone, *Perilous Times*, 372–74; White, *Alger Hiss's Looking-Glass Wars*, xiii.
352. Quoted in the United States Senate Select Committee to Study Governmental Operations with Respect to Intelligence Activities, *Final Report of the Select Committee to Study Governmental Operations with Respect to Intelligence Activities, United States Senate, Together with Additional, Supplemental, and Separate Views*, Book II. Report No. 94-755 (Washington, D.C.: US Government Printing Office, 1976), 14.
353. Ronald Kessler, *The Bureau: The Secret History of the FBI* (New York: St. Martin's Press, 2003), 9–10; Tim Weiner, *Enemies: A History of the FBI* (New York: Random House, 2012), 12.
354. Burton Hersh, *Bobby and J. Edgar: the Historic Face-off Between the Kennedys and J. Edgar Hoover That Transformed America* (New York: Carroll & Graf, 2007), 513–15; Kessler, *The Bureau*, 9–11, 172–75, 187; Weiner, *Enemies*, 121.
355. David M. Chalmers, *Hooded Americanism: The History of the Ku Klux Klan,* third edition. (Durham: Duke University Press, 1987), 398–99; David Cunningham, *There's Something Happening Here: The New Left, the Klan, and FBI Counterintelligence,* (Berkeley: University of California Press, 2004), 27, 181–85; Todd Gitlin, *The Sixties: Years of Hope, Days of*

Rage (New York: Bantam Books, 1989), 413; Ron Jacobs, *The Way the Wind Blew: A History of the Weather Underground* (New York: Verso Books, 1997), 74; Ronald Kessler, *The FBI* (New York: Pocket Books, 1993), 80; United States Senate Select Committee to Study Governmental Operations with Respect to Intelligence Activities, *Final Report*, Book II, 40; Wyn Craig Wade, *The Fiery Cross: The Ku Klux Klan in America* (New York: Oxford University Press, 1987), 361–63.

356. Nelson Blackstock, *COINTELPRO: The FBI's Secret War on Political Freedom* (New York: Pathfinder, 1988), 91–92, 111; William C. Sullivan with Bill Brown, *The Bureau: My Thirty Years in Hoover's FBI* (New York: W. W. Norton & Company, 1979), 135–38; Weiner, *Enemies*, 198–99.

357. Kessler, *The Bureau*, 155; Weiner, *Enemies*, 198.

358. Taylor Branch, *Parting the Waters: America in the King Years, 1954–63* (New York: Simon & Schuster, 1988), 857–62; Hersh, *Bobby and J. Edgar*, 372–74; Richard D. Mahoney, *The Kennedy Brothers: The Rise and Fall of Jack and Bobby* (New York: Arcade Publishing, 2011), 334; Weiner, *Enemies*, 199–200.

359. Quoted in Kessler, *The Bureau*, 157. See also Hersh, *Bobby and J. Edgar*, 370–71; Weiner, *Enemies*, 235.

360. Blackstock, *COINTELPRO*, 109–11; Manning Marable, *Malcolm X: A Life of Reinvention* (New York: Viking, 2011), 212; Weiner, *Enemies*, 199.

361. Blackstock, *COINTELPRO*, 110; Marable, *Malcolm X*, 298–99, 341–42, 356–58.

362. Taylor Branch, *Pillar of Fire: America in the King Years, 1963–65* (New York: Simon & Schuster, 1998), 243; Blackstock, *COINTELPRO*, 110–11; Marable, *Malcolm X*, 293–96.

363. Blackstock, *COINTELPRO*, 110–11, 116–18; Marable, *Malcolm X*, 436–49.

364. Branch, *Parting the Waters*, 291–92; Weiner, *Enemies*, 199, 271–74.

365. Kessler, *The Bureau*, 174–75, Weiner, *Enemies*, 271, 274, 329–30.

366. Quoted in John Drabble, "Fighting Black Power-New Left Coalitions: Covert FBI Media Campaigns and American Cultural Discourse," *European Journal of American Culture* 27, no. 2 (2008): 66–67. See also Blackstock, *COINTELPRO*, 119–25, 142–46; Cunningham, *There's Something Happening Here*, 12, 42–43.

367. Quoted in Blackstock, *COINTELPRO*, 129, 130.

368. Bill Ayers, *Fugitive Days: A Memoir* (Boston: Beacon Press, 2001), 144; Dan Berger, *Outlaws of America: The Weather Underground and the Politics of Solidarity* (San Francisco: AK Press, 2006), 91–94; Blackstock, *COINTELPRO*, 120; Jacobs, "The New History of the Weather Underground," *Monthly Review* 58, no. 2 (2006): 59–61.

369. Cunningham, *There's Something Happening Here*, 97-98; Gitlin, *The Sixties*, 180–85, 242, 385–400.

370. Gitlin, *The Sixties*, 411–12; Cunningham, *There's Something Happening Here*, 151; Sullivan with Brown, *The Bureau*, 147–59

371. Blackstock, *COINTELPRO*, 124–25; Weiner, *Enemies*, 266–72.

372. Blackstock, *COINTELPRO*, 137, 144–45.

373. Drabble, "Fighting Black Power-New Left Coalitions," 79; Stone, *Perilous Times*, 489–90.

374. Blackstock, *COINTELPRO*, 145; Drabble, "Fighting Black Power-New Left Coalitions," 86–87; Gitlin, *The Sixties*, 347–49; Weiner, *Enemies*, 284.

375. Cunningham, *There's Something Happening Here*, 77–78, 181; Kessler, *The FBI*, 410; Stone, *Perilous Times*, 494–95; Wade, *The Fiery Cross*, 363.

376. Cunningham, *There's Something Happening Here*, 333; Kessler, *The FBI*, 410, 440.

377. Kessler, *The Bureau*, 210; Stone, *Perilous Times*, 495–96.

378. United States Senate Select Committee to Study Governmental Operations with Respect to Intelligence Activities, *Final Report*, Book II, 5, 6.

379. Hersh, *Bobby and J. Edgar*, 41, 42, 51; Mahoney, *The Kennedy Brothers*, 156–65.

380. Drabble, "Fighting Black Power-New Left Coalitions," 89–91; Stone, *Perilous Times*, 496–97.

381. Bjelopera and Randol, *The Federal Bureau of Investigation and Terrorism Investigations* (Darby: Diane Publishing, 2011), 13–14; Stone, *Perilous Times*, 555–56.

382. United States Department of Justice, Office of the Inspector General, *A Review of the FBI's Investigations of Certain Domestic Advocacy Groups*, (Washington, D.C.: Oversight and Review Division, Office of the Inspector General, September 2010), 190. See also Ivan Greenberg, *The Dangers of Dissent: The FBI and Civil Liberties Since 1965* (Lanham: Lexington Books, 2010), 199–200.

383. Blackstock, *COINTELPRO*, 201–03; United States Senate Select Committee to Study Governmental Operations with Respect to Intelligence Activities, *Final Report*, Book II, 289–93.

384. George W. Bush, "Address before a Joint Session of the Congress on the United States Response to the Terrorist Attacks of September 11," *Public Papers of the Presidents of the United States* (Washington, D.C.: Office of the Federal Register, 2004), 1140.

385. Editors of Life, *Brought to Justice: Osama Bin Laden's War on America and the Mission That Stopped Him* (New York: Little, Brown and Company, 2011), 19; Rohan Gunaratna, *Inside Al-Qaeda: Global Network of Terror* (New York: Columbia University Press, 2002), 16; National Commission on Terrorist Attacks Upon the United States, *The 9/11 Commission Report* (New York: W. W. Norton & Company, 2004), 55; Lawrence Wright, *The Looming Tower: Al-Qaeda and the Road to 9/11* (New York: Knopf, 2006), 72.

386. Editors of Life, *Brought to Justice*, 19, 21; Gunaratna, *Inside Al-Qaeda*, 17; Wright, *The Looming Tower*, 72–74.

387. Zachary Abuza, "Tentacles of Terror: Al Qaeda's Southeast Asian Network," *Contemporary Southeast Asia* 24, no. 3 (2002): 432; Charles Allen, "The Hidden Roots of Wahhabism in British India," *World Policy Journal* 22, no. 2 (2005): 88; G. H. Jansen, *Militant Islam* (New York: Harper & Row, 1979), 87–88.

388. Michael Doran, "The Pragmatic Fanaticism of al-Qaeda: An Anatomy of Extremism in Middle Eastern Politics," *Political Science Quarterly* 117, no. 2 (2002): 180–82; Fawaz Gerges, *The Rise and Fall of Al-Qaeda* (New York: Oxford University Press, 2011), 31–33, 40; Henzel, "The Origins of al-Qaeda's Ideology: Implications for US Strategy," *Parameters* 35, no. 1 (2005): 74–75; Wright, *Looming Tower*, 7–31.

389. Editors of Life, *Brought to Justice*, 21, 23; National Commission on Terrorist Attacks Upon the United States, *The 9/11 Commission Report*, 55; Wright, *The Looming Tower*, 74–83.

390. Editors of Life, *Brought to Justice*, 23; Ann M. Lesch, "Osama bin Laden: Embedded in the Middle East Crises," *Middle East Policy* 9, no. 2 (2002): 82–83; Wright, *The Looming Tower*, 94–98.

391. Editors of Life, *Brought to Justice*, 38; Pervez Hoodbhoy, "Afghanistan and the Genesis of Global Jihad," *Peace Research* 37, no. 1 (2005): 27–29; National Commission on Terrorist Attacks Upon the United States, *The 9/11 Commission Report*, 55; Wright, *The Looming Tower*, 95–96, 99–100; Robin Wright, *Rock the Casbah: Rage and Rebellion Across the Islamic World* (New York: Simon & Schuster, 2011), 49–50.

392. Henzel, "The Origins of al-Qaeda's Ideology," 75–76; Hoodbhoy, "Afghanistan and the Genesis of Global Jihad," 25–26; Lesch, "Osama bin Laden," 82–84; Wright, *The Looming Tower*, 101–02.

393. Abuza, "Tentacles of Terror," 429; Editors of Life, *Brought to Justice*, 35, 37, 38, 43; Gunaratna, *Inside Al-Qaeda*, 21–23; Sohail Abdul Nasir, "Al-Qaeda, Two Years On," *Bulletin of the Atomic Scientists* 59, no. 5 (2003): 34; National Commission on Terrorist Attacks Upon the United States, *The 9/11 Commission Report*, 56; Wright, *The Looming Tower*, 129–33.

394. Abuza, "Tentacles of Terror," 429–31; Gerges, *The Rise and Fall of Al-Qaeda*, 40-43; Editors of Life, *Brought to Justice*, 35; Gunaratna, *Inside Al-Qaeda*, 25–26; Nasir, "Al-Qaeda, Two Years On," 34; National Commission on Terrorist Attacks Upon the United States, *The 9/11 Commission Report*, 56; Wright, *The Looming Tower*, 141–44.

395. Editors of Life, *Brought to Justice*, 35, 46; Bruce Hoffman, "The Global Terrorist Threat: Is Al-Qaeda on the Run or on the March?" *Middle East Policy* 14, no. 2 (2007): 45–53; Hoodbhoy, "Afghanistan and the Genesis of Global Jihad," 26; Nasir, "Al-Qaeda, Two Years On," 32; National Commission on Terrorist Attacks Upon the United States, *The 9/11 Commission Report*, 56–57; Wright, *The Looming Tower*, 32–59, 95, 124-26; Wright, *Rock the Casbah*, 6.

396. Editors of Life, *Brought to Justice*, 43, 45; Lesch, "Osama bin Laden," 84–85; National Commission on Terrorist Attacks Upon the United States, *The 9/11 Commission Report*, 57–58; Wright, *The Looming Tower*, 164–66.

397. National Commission on Terrorist Attacks Upon the United States, *The 9/11 Commission Report*, 57; Wright, *The Looming Tower*, 194–97; Wright, *Rock the Casbah*, 171.

398. Djamchid Assadi and Britta Lorünser, "Strategic Management Analysis of al-Qaeda: The Role of Worldwide Organization for a Worldwide Strategy," *Problems and Perspectives in Management* 5, no. 4 (2007): 65–67; Jason Burke, "Al-Qaeda," *Foreign Policy* 142, no. 1 (2004): 18–19; National Commission on Terrorist Attacks Upon the United States, *The 9/11 Commission Report*, 57–59; Wright, *The Looming Tower*, 133–34, 168–69.

399. Lesch, "Osama bin Laden," 85; National Commission on Terrorist Attacks Upon the United States, *The 9/11 Commission Report*, 59–60.

400. National Commission on Terrorist Attacks Upon the United States, *The 9/11 Commission Report*, 59–60; Wright, *The Looming Tower*, 188–89.

401. Editors of Life, *Brought to Justice*, 45, 48–49; Lesch, "Osama bin Laden," 85; National Commission on Terrorist Attacks Upon the United States, *The 9/11 Commission Report*, 60; Wright, *The Looming Tower*, 237–39.

402. Editors of Life, *Brought to Justice*, 45; Joseph T. McCann, *Terrorism on American Soil: A Concise History of Plots and Perpetrators from the Famous to the Forgotten* (Boulder: Sentient Publications, 2006), 187–88; National Commission on Terrorist Attacks Upon the United States, *The 9/11 Commission Report*, 71; Wright, *The Looming Tower*, 177–78.

403. Abuza, "Tentacles of Terror," 441–42; McCann, *Terrorism on American Soil*, 188–91; National Commission on Terrorist Attacks Upon the United States, *The 9/11 Commission Report*, 71–72; Wright, *The Looming Tower*, 177–78.

404. McCann, *Terrorism on American Soil*, 189; National Commission on Terrorist Attacks Upon the United States, *The 9/11 Commission Report*, 72.

405. McCann, Terrorism on American Soil, 189; National Commission on Terrorist Attacks Upon the United States, *The 9/11 Commission Report*, 72; Wright, *The Looming Tower*, 177–78.

406. Editors of Life, *Brought to Justice*, 45, 46; McCann, *Terrorism on American Soil*, 190–92; National Commission on Terrorist Attacks Upon the United States, *The 9/11 Commission Report*, 71–73.

407. McCann, *Terrorism on American Soil*, 190–92; National Commission on Terrorist Attacks Upon the United States, *The 9/11 Commission Report*, 73.

408. CBS News, *What We Saw: The Events of September 11, 2001—In Words. Pictures, and Video* (New York: Simon & Schuster, 2002), 9; Editors of Life, *Brought to Justice*, 9–10; McCann, *Terrorism on American Soil*, 274–75; National Commission on Terrorist Attacks Upon the United States, *The 9/11 Commission Report*, 1–46.

409. Quoted in Benjamin Runkle, *Wanted Dead or Alive: Manhunts from Geronimo to Bin Laden* (New York: Palgrave-MacMillan, 2011), 158. See also McCann, *Terrorism on American Soil*, 191–92; National Commission on Terrorist Attacks Upon the United States, *The 9/11 Commission Report*, 108–09.

410. McCann, *Terrorism on American Soil*, 277; National Commission on Terrorist Attacks Upon the United States, *The 9/11 Commission Report*, 126–34; Runkle, *Wanted Dead or Alive*, 158–59; Wright, *The Looming Tower*, 265–66.

411. Lesch, "Osama bin Laden," 86; Runkle, *Wanted Dead or Alive*, 158–59; Wright, *The Looming Tower*, 262–65; Wright, *Rock the Casbah*, 69.

412. Lesch, "Osama bin Laden," 87; McCann, *Terrorism on American Soil*, 276–77; National Commission on Terrorist Attacks Upon the United States, *The 9/11 Commission Report*, 69; Runkle, *Wanted Dead or Alive*, 160; Richard Sale, *Clinton's Secret Wars: The Evolution of a Commander in Chief* (New York: Thomas Dunne Books, 2009), 295; Wright, *The Looming Tower*, 259–61.

413. Bill Clinton, *My Life* (New York: Knopf, 2004), 797; Doran, "The Pragmatic Fanaticism of al-Qaeda," 183; Editors of Life, *Brought to Justice*, 48–49; Lesch, "Osama bin Laden," 87; National Commission on Terrorist Attacks Upon the United States, *The 9/11 Commission Report*, 70, 115–16; Runkle, *Wanted Dead or Alive*, 160–61; Sale, *Clinton's Secret Wars*, 295–96; Wright, *The Looming Tower*, 270–72.

414. National Commission on Terrorist Attacks Upon the United States, *The 9/11 Commission Report*, 117–18; Runkle, *Wanted Dead or Alive*, 161–62; Wright, *The Looming Tower*, 283.

415. National Commission on Terrorist Attacks Upon the United States, *The 9/11 Commission Report*, 115–19; Runkle, *Wanted Dead or Alive*, 162; Sale, *Clinton's Secret Wars*, 298–301.

416. Doran, "The Pragmatic Fanaticism of al-Qaeda," 183; Editors of Life, *Brought to Justice*, 52; Gerges, *The Rise and Fall of Al-Qaeda*, 68; Lesch, "Osama bin Laden," 87; McCann, Terrorism on American Soil, 277; National Commission on Terrorist Attacks Upon the United States, *The 9/11 Commission Report*, 190–91; Runkle, *Wanted Dead or Alive*, 166–67; Wright, *The Looming Tower*, 319–20.

417. Abuza, "Tentacles of Terror," 441–43; McCann, *Terrorism on American Soil*, 277–79; National Commission on Terrorist Attacks Upon the United States, *The 9/11 Commission Report*, 153–54; Wright, *The Looming Tower*, 307–08.

418. McCann, *Terrorism on American Soil*, 277–78; National Commission on Terrorist Attacks Upon the United States, *The 9/11 Commission Report*, 153–56; Wright, *The Looming Tower*, 307–11.

419. Editors of Life, *Brought to Justice*, 58–59; McDermott, "A Perfect Soldier: Mohamed Atta, Whose Hard Gaze Has Stared from a Billion Television Screens and Newspaper Pages, Has Become, for Many, the Face of Evil Incarnate," *Los Angeles Times*, January 27, 2002, A1; National Commission on Terrorist Attacks Upon the United States, *The 9/11 Commission Report*, 160–63; Philip Shenon, "Report Claims That 9/11 Terrorists

were Identified Before Attacks," *New York Times*, September 22, 2006, A15; Wright, *The Looming Tower*, 308–10.

420. Editors of Life, *Brought to Justice*, 58–59; McDermott, "A Perfect Soldier," A1; National Commission on Terrorist Attacks Upon the United States, *The 9/11 Commission Report*, 165–67; Shenon, "Report Claims That 9/11 Terrorists were Identified Before Attacks," A15; Wright, *The Looming Tower*, 307–08.

421. McDermott, "A Perfect Soldier," A1; National Commission on Terrorist Attacks Upon the United States, *The 9/11 Commission Report*, 167–69; Shenon, "Report Claims That 9/11 Terrorists were Identified Before Attacks," A15.

422. McCann, *Terrorism on American Soil*, 278; National Commission on Terrorist Attacks Upon the United States, *The 9/11 Commission Report*, 163–67; Shenon, "Report Claims That 9/11 Terrorists were Identified Before Attacks," A15.

423. McDermott, "A Perfect Soldier," A1; National Commission on Terrorist Attacks Upon the United States, *The 9/11 Commission Report*, 248–53; Shenon, "Report Claims That 9/11 Terrorists were Identified Before Attacks," A15.

424. Editors of Life, *Brought to Justice*, 58–59; Yosri Fouda and Nick Fielding, *Masterminds of Terror: The Truth Behind the Most Devastating Terrorist Attack the World Has Ever Seen* (New York: Arcade, 2003), 110. Most of the details for the descriptions of what happened on board the airplanes come from *The 9/11 Commission Report*. See, for example, National Commission on Terrorist Attacks Upon the United States, *The 9/11 Commission Report*, 1–2.

425. National Commission on Terrorist Attacks Upon the United States, *The 9/11 Commission Report*, 4–8.

426. National Commission on Terrorist Attacks Upon the United States, *The 9/11 Commission Report*, 2, 7–8. See also Fouda and Fielding, *Masterminds of Terror*, 110–11.

427. National Commission on Terrorist Attacks Upon the United States, *The 9/11 Commission Report*, 2–4, 8–10.

428. McCann, *Terrorism on American Soil*, 276; Phil Mole, "9/11 Conspiracy Theories: The 9/11 Truth Movement in Perspective," *Skeptic* 12, no. 4 (2006): 37–38; National Commission on Terrorist Attacks Upon the United States, *The 9/11 Commission Report*, 314–15.

429. National Commission on Terrorist Attacks Upon the United States, *The 9/11 Commission Report*, 4. See also Editors of Life, *Brought to Justice*, 58–59; John Rosenthal, "Doing Justice to Zacarias Moussaoui," *Policy Review* 146, no. 1 (December 2007/January 2008): 47–57.

430. Jim Dwyer and Kevin Flynn, *102 Minutes: The Untold Story of the Fight to Survive Inside the Twin Towers* (New York: Times Books, 2005), 19; National Commission on Terrorist Attacks Upon the United States, *The 9/11 Commission Report*, 285–86.

431. CBS News, *What We Saw*, 14–15; Dwyer and Flynn, *102 Minutes*, xxi–xxiv; Editors of Life, *Brought to Justice*, 9–10; Brigitte L. Nacos, "Terrorism as Breaking News: Attack on America," *Political Science Quarterly* 118, no. 1 (2003): 45–52.

432. National Commission on Terrorist Attacks Upon the United States, *The 9/11 Commission Report*, 289; John P. Pryor, "The 2001 World Trade Center Disaster: Summary and Evaluation of Experiences," *European Journal of Trauma and Emergency Surgery* 35, no. 3 (2009): 213–14, 216–18.

433. Dwyer and Flynn, *102 Minutes*, 120–25; National Commission on Terrorist Attacks Upon the United States, *The 9/11 Commission Report*, 298–301; Pryor, "The 2001 World Trade Center Disaster," 221–22.

434. Dwyer and Flynn, *102 Minutes*, 255–63; National Commission on Terrorist Attacks Upon the United States, *The 9/11 Commission Report*, 311.

435. Giovanna Borradori, "Beyond the Culture of Terrorism," *Philosophy Today* 49, no. 4 (2005): 397–98; Editors of Life, *Brought to Justice*, 6, 9–10; N. R. Kleinfield, "Getting Here From There: In the Years Since 2001, Neither Our Worst Fears Nor Our Highest Hopes Have Been Realized, But What Passes for Normal Has Exacted a Price," *New York Times—Supplement: The Reckoning*, September 11, 2011, 1–2; Waler Laqueur, "The Terrorism to Come," *Policy Review* 126, no. 1 (2004): 49–51; McCann, *Terrorism on American Soil*, 275–75; Ariel Merari, "Deterring Fear: Government Responses to Terrorist Attacks," *Harvard International Review* 23, no. 4 (2002): 26; National Commission on Terrorist Attacks Upon the United States, *The 9/11 Commission Report*, 339–60; Runkle, *Wanted Dead or Alive*, 2–4; Bret Stephens, "9/11 and the Struggle for Meaning," *Wall Street Journal*, September 6, 2011, A19; Norman K. Swazo, "'My Brother is My King': Evaluating the Moral Duty of Global Jihad," *International Journal on World Peace* 25, no. 4 (2008): 9–13; "Ten Years On," *Economist* 400, no. 8749 (2011): 11–12.

436. Bush, "Address before a Joint Session," p. 1140.

437. Zbigniew Brzezinski, "Right Cause, Wrong Response," *Wall Street Journal*, September 9, 2011, A19; Mark Helprin, "We Can't Reform the Arab World," *Wall Street Journal*, September 9, 2011, A19; Robert C. McFarlane, "Afghanistan Should Have Been the Focus," *Wall Street Journal*, September 9, 2011, A19; National Commission on Terrorist Attacks Upon the United States, *The 9/11 Commission Report*, 328, 330–38; Runkle, *Wanted Dead or Alive*, 167–70; Anne-Marie Slaughter, "Resilience vs. Revenge," *Wall Street Journal*, September 9, 2011, A19; Leon Wieseltier, "Even Obama Embraces Drones," *Wall Street Journal*, September 9, 2011, A19; Paul Wolfowitz, "We Had to Address State Sponsors of Terror," *Wall Street Journal*, September 9, 2011, A19; John Yoo, "Ten Years Without an Attack," *Wall Street Journal*, September 6, 2011, A21.

438. Samuel Estreicher and Diarmuid O'Scannlain, "*Hamdan*'s Limits and the Military Commissions Act," *Constitutional Commentary* 23, no. 3 (2006): 403–407; Margaret Kohn, "Due Process and Empire's Law: *Hamdan v. Rumsfeld*," *Dissent* 54, no. 1 (2007): 5; Amy Quimby, "*Hamdan v. Rumsfeld*: Reviewing the Geneva Convention Rights of the Unlawful Enemy Combatants Detained at Gitmo," *Widener Law Journal* 17, no. 1 (2010): 318–19.

439. Editors of Life, *Brought to Justice*, 78; Runkle, *Wanted Dead or Alive*, 224.

440. Editors of Life, *Brought to Justice*, 84; Runkle, *Wanted Dead or Alive*, 222–25.

441. Roger Berkowitz, "Assassinating Justly: Reflections on Justice and Revenge in the Osama Bin Laden Killing," *Law, Culture and the Humanities* 7, no. 3 (2011): 346–48; John Crook, "U.S. Special Operations Personnel Raid Compound in Pakistan, Kill Osama bin Laden," *American Journal of International Law* 105, no. 3 (2011): 602–604; Editors of Life, *Brought to Justice*, 84; "The President Reports the Death of Osama bin Laden," *Army* 61, no. 6 (2011): 6–7; Runkle, *Wanted Dead or Alive*, 206–207.

442. Quoted in J. Michael Martinez, *Terrorist Attacks on American Soil: From the Civil War Era to the Present* (Lanham: Rowman & Littlefield, 2012), 402–03. See also Editors of Life, *Brought to Justice*, 91.

443. Robert P. Abele, *A User's Guide to the Patriot Act and Beyond* (Lanham: University Press of America, 2004), 74; Cary Stacy Smith and Li-Ching Hung, *The Patriot Act: Issues and Controversies* (Springfield: Charles C. Thomas, 2010), 133–34, 172–78; Stone, *Perilous Times*, 553.

444. Abele, *A User's Guide to the Patriot Act and Beyond*, 25, 46–47; Smith and Hung, *The Patriot Act*, 98–99.

445. Abele, *A User's Guide to the Patriot Act and Beyond*, 22, 27, 71; Richard Henry Seamon and William Dylan Gardner, "The Patriot Act and the Wall Between Foreign Intelligence and Law Enforcement," *Harvard Journal of Law & Public Policy* 28, no. 1 (2005): 338; Smith and Hung, *The Patriot Act*, 33–38.

446. Abele, *A User's Guide to the Patriot Act and Beyond*, 33; Smith and Hung, *The Patriot Act*, 173.

447. Abele, *A User's Guide to the Patriot Act and Beyond*, 19–28; Francoise Gilbert, "Demystifying the United States Patriot Act," *Journal of Internet Law* 16, no. 8 (2013): 4, 5–6; Seamon and Gardner, "The Patriot Act and the Wall Between Foreign Intelligence and Law Enforcement," 449–55.

448. Abele, *A User's Guide to the Patriot Act and Beyond*, 26, 46; Smith and Hung, *The Patriot Act*, 41, 102–03, 165–66, 174–78.

449. Abele, *A User's Guide to the Patriot Act and Beyond*, 45; Smith and Hung, *The Patriot Act*, 74, 83, 92, 174, 177.

450. See, for example, "Edward Snowden: Whistle-Blower," *New York Times*, January 2, 2014, A18; Kara Hackett, "Edward Snowden: The New Brand of Whistleblower?" *Quill* 101, no. 5 (2013): 26–31; Luke Harding, *The Snowden Files: The Inside Story of the World's Most Wanted Man* (New York: Vintage, 2014); Peter Maas, "Snowden's People," *New York Times Magazine* (2013): 22–29, 49; Charlie Savage, "Snowden Denies That He Was a Spy for Russia," *New York Times*, January 22, 2014, A9.

451. Ambrose Bierce, *The Devil's Dictionary of Ambrose Bierce* (El Paso: El Paso Norte Press, 2010), 63.

452. Hackett, "Edward Snowden," 26–31; Harding, *The Snowden Files*.

453. James Madison, "Federalist 10" in *The Federalist Papers*, ed. Clinton Rossiter (New York: The New American Library, 1961), 77–84.

454. Quoted in Benjamin Franklin and William Templeton Franklin, *Memoirs of the Life and Writings of Benjamin Franklin* (London: Henry Colburn, 1818), 191. See also Bernard Bailyn, *The Ordeal of Thomas Hutchinson* (Cambridge: Harvard University Press, 1974), 238–39; Walter Isaacson, *Benjamin Franklin: An American Life* (New York: Simon & Schuster, 2003), 271–72; Edmund S. Morgan, *Benjamin Franklin* (New Haven: Yale University Press, 2002), 187.

455. Quoted in David Edwin Harrell, et al., *Unto a Good Land: A History of the American People*, vol. 1 (Cambridge: William B. Eerdmans Publishing Company, 2005), 144. See also Bailyn, *The Ordeal of Thomas Hutchinson*, 239–40; Isaacson, *Benjamin Franklin*, 272; Morgan, *Benjamin Franklin*, 185–87.

456. Bailyn, *The Ordeal of Thomas Hutchinson*, 239; Isaacson, *Benjamin Franklin*, 272; Morgan, *Benjamin Franklin*, 196.

457. Isaacson, *Benjamin Franklin*, 272; Morgan, *Benjamin Franklin*, 198–99.

458. Isaacson, *Benjamin Franklin*, 277–78; Morgan, *Benjamin Franklin*, 199–203.

459. Isaacson, *Benjamin Franklin*, 276–78.

460. Kersch, *Freedom of Speech*, 117; Anthony Lewis, *Freedom for the Thought We Hate: A Biography of the First Amendment* (New York: Basic Books, 2007), 27; John Nichols, *The "S" Word: A Shirt History of an American Tradition...Socialism* (London and Brooklyn: Verso, 2011), 147–48.

461. Nichols, *The "S" Word*, 60.

462. Nichols, *The "S" Word*, xiii; Stone, *Perilous Times*, 141.

463. Lewis, *Freedom for the Thought We Hate*, 27; Nichols, *The "S" Word*, 106.

464. Thomas C. Reeves, *The Life and Times of Joe McCarthy: A Biography* (Ontario: Madison Press Books, 1997), 50–52, 224–26; Richard H. Rovere, *Senator Joe McCarthy* (Berkeley,

Los Angeles: University of California Press, 1996), 94–98, 126–30; Stephen W. Stathis, *Landmark Debates in Congress: From the Declaration of Independence to the War in Iraq* (Washington, D.C.: CQ Press, 2009), 357.

465. John Lewis Gaddis, *The Cold War: A New History* (New York: Penguin, 2005), 5–6, 37–38, 40; James McCormick, *American Foreign Policy and Process* (Boston: Wadsworth Cengage, 2010), 74–78.

466. Reeves, *The Life and Times of Joe McCarthy*, 304; Rovere, *Senator Joe McCarthy*, 156–59; McCarthy is quoted in Stathis, *Landmark Debates in Congress*, 357.

467. Reeves, *The Life and Times of Joe McCarthy*, 437–40; Rovere, *Senator Joe McCarthy*, 15–16, 163; Stathis, *Landmark Debates in Congress*, 357.

468. Reeves, *The Life and Times of Joe McCarthy*, 564–76; Stathis, *Landmark Debates in Congress*, 357.

469. Reeves, *The Life and Times of Joe McCarthy*, 596–99; Rovere, *Senator Joe McCarthy*, 213, 215–18; Stathis, *Landmark Debates in Congress*, 357–59, Welch is quoted on page 359.

470. Reeves, *The Life and Times of Joe McCarthy*, 641–57; Rovere, *Senator Joe McCarthy*, 232–43; Stathis, *Landmark Debates in Congress*, 359.

471. Reeves, *The Life and Times of Joe McCarthy*, 660; Rovere, *Senator Joe McCarthy*, 247, 251–52.

472. Peter Hayes Gries, *The Politics of American Foreign Policy: How Ideology Divides Liberals and Conservatives over Foreign Affairs* (Stanford: Stanford University Press, 2014), 107–108.

473. Stone, *Perilous Times*, 530–58.

REFERENCES

Abele, Robert P. *A User's Guide to the Patriot Act and Beyond*. Lanham: University Press of America, 2004.

Abrams v. United States, 250 US 616 (1919).

Abuza, Zachary. "Tentacles of Terror: Al Qaeda's Southeast Asian Network." *Contemporary Southeast Asia* 24, no. 3 (December 2002): 427–65.

Ackerman, Kenneth D. *Young J. Edgar: Hoover and the Red Scare, 1919–1920*. Falls Church: Viral History Press, 2011.

Albertson v. Subversive Activities Control Board, 382 US 70 (1965).

Allen, Austin. "The Political Economy of Blackness: Citizenship, Corporations, and Race in *Dred Scott*." *Civil War History* 50, no. 3 (September 2004): 229–60.

Allen, Charles. "The Hidden Roots of Wahhabism in British India." *World Policy Journal* 22, no. 2 (Summer 2005): 87–93.

Ambrose, Stephen E. *The Education of a Politician, 1913–1962*. Vol. 1 of *Nixon*. New York: Touchstone Books, 1987.

Archer, Jules. *The Plot to Seize the White House: The Shocking True Story of the Conspiracy to Overthrow FDR*. New York: Skyhorse, 2007.

Assadi, Djamchid, and Britta Lorünser "Strategic Management Analysis of al Qaeda: The Role of Worldwide Organization for a Worldwide Strategy." *Problems and Perspectives in Management* 5, no. 4 (2007): 57–71.

Ayers, Bill. *Fugitive Days: A Memoir*. Boston: Beacon Press, 2001.

Bailyn, Bernard. *The Ordeal of Thomas Hutchinson*. Cambridge: Harvard University Press, 1974.

Ball, Howard. *USA Patriot Act of 2001*. Santa Barbara: ABC-CLIO, 2004.

Beekman, Scott. *William Dudley Pelley: A Life in Right-Wing Extremism and the Occult*. Syracuse: Syracuse University Press, 2005.

Belknap, Michal R. "Cold War in the Courtroom: The Foley Square Communist Trial." In *American Political Trials*, edited by Michal R. Belknap, 207–32. Westport: Greenwood Press, 1994.

———. *The Vinson Court: Justices, Rulings, and Legacy*. Santa Barbara: ABC-CLIO, 2004.

———. "Why Dennis?" *Marquette Law Review* 96, no. 4 (Summer 2013): 1013-34.

Berger, Dan. *Outlaws of America: The Weather Underground and the Politics of Solidarity*. San Francisco: AK Press, 2006.

Berkowitz, Roger. "Assassinating Justly: Reflections on Justice and Revenge in the Osama Bin Laden Killing." *Law, Culture and the Humanities* 7, no. 3 (October 2011): 346–51.

Bjelopera, Jerome P., and Mark A. Randol. *The Federal Bureau of Investigation and Terrorism Investigations*. Darby: Diane Publishing, 2011.

Biddle, Francis. *In Brief Authority*. Westport: Praeger, 1976.

Bierce, Ambrose. *The Devil's Dictionary of Ambrose Bierce*. El Paso: El Paso Norte Press, 2010.

Black, Conrad. *Richard M. Nixon: A Life in Full*. New York: Public Affairs, 2007.

Blackstock, Nelson. *COINTELPRO: The FBI's Secret War on Political Freedom*. New York: Pathfinder, 1988.

Blackwell, Jon. *Notorious New Jersey: 100 True Tales of Murders and Mobsters, Scandals and Scoundrels.* New Brunswick: Rutgers University Press, 2008.

Blair, William. *With Malice toward Some: Treason and Loyalty in the Civil War Era.* Chapel Hill: University of North Carolina Press, 2014.

Bolt, William K. "Founding Father and Rebellious Son: James Madison, John C. Calhoun, and the Use of Precedents." *American Nineteenth Century History* 5, no. 3 (Fall 2004): 1–27.

Borradori, Giovanna. "Beyond the Culture of Terrorism." *Philosophy Today* 49, no. 4 (Winter 2005): 397–407.

Braeman, John. "House Un-American Activities Committee." In *Conspiracy Theories in American History: An Encyclopedia,* edited by Peter Knight, 325–28. Santa Barbara: ABC-CLIO, 2003.

Branch, Taylor. *Parting the Waters: America in the King Years, 1954–63.* New York: Simon & Schuster, 1988.

———. *Pillar of Fire: America in the King Years, 1963–65.* New York: Simon & Schuster, 1998.

Brands, H. W. *Andrew Jackson: His Life and Times.* New York: Doubleday, 2005.

———. *Traitor to His Class: The Privileged Life and Radical Presidency of Franklin Delano Roosevelt.* New York: Doubleday, 2008.

Bridges v. Wixon, 326 US 135 (1945).

Brogdon, Matthew S. "Defending the Union: Andrew Jackson's Nullification Proclamation and American Federalism." *The Review of Politics* 73, no. 2 (March 2011): 245–73.

Brookhiser, Richard. *James Madison.* New York: Basic Books, 2011.

Brown, Archie. *The Rise and Fall of Communism.* New York: HarperCollins, 2009.

Browne, Blaine T., and Robert C. Cottrell. *Lives and Times: Individuals and Issues in American History Since 1865.* Lanham: Rowman & Littlefield, 2010.

Brzezinski, Zbigniew. "Right Cause, Wrong Response." *Wall Street Journal,* September 9, 2011.

Burke, Jason. "Al Qaeda." *Foreign Policy* 142, no. 1 (May/June 2004): 18–26.

Burnham, Walter Dean. *Democracy in the Making: American Government and Politics.* Upper Saddle River: Prentice Hall, 1983.

Burstein, Andrew, and Nancy Isenberg. *Madison and Jefferson.* New York: Random House, 2010.

Burton, Harold H. "Two Significant Decisions: *Ex Parte Milligan* and *Ex Parte McCardle.*" *American Bar Association Journal* 41, No. 2 (February 1955): 121–24, 176–77.

Burton, Orville Vernon. *The Age of Lincoln.* New York: Hill and Wang, 2007.

Bush, George H. W. "Remarks on the Fiftieth Anniversary of Pearl Harbor, December 7, 1991." In *Weekly Compilation of Presidential Documents.* Washington, D.C.: Office of the Federal Register, National Archives and Records Service, General Services Administration, 1991: 1791.

Bush, George W. "Address before a Joint Session of the Congress on the United States Response to the Terrorist Attacks of September 11." *Public Papers of the Presidents of the United States.* Washington, D.C.: Office of the Federal Register, 2004.

Capozzola, Christopher. *Uncle Sam Wants You: World War I and the Making of the Modern American Citizen.* Oxford: Oxford University Press, 2008.

Carey, Patrick W. "Political Atheism: Dred Scott, Roger Brooke Taney, and Orestes A. Brownson." *The Catholic Historical Review* 88, no. 2 (April 1988): 207–29.

Carter, Dan T. *Scottsboro: A Tragedy of the American South.* Revised Edition. Baton Rouge: Louisiana State University Press, 2007.

Carwardine, Richard. *Lincoln: A Life of Purpose and Power.* New York: Knopf, 2003.

"Caution Needed." *New York Times,* August 31, 1950.

CBS News. *What We Saw: The Events of September 11, 2001—In Words, Pictures, and Video.* New York: Simon & Schuster, 2002.

Chalmers, David M. *Hooded Americanism: The History of the Ku Klux Klan.* 3rd ed. Durham: Duke University Press, 1987.

Chernow, Ron. *Alexander Hamilton.* New York: The Penguin Press, 2004.

———. *Washington: A Life.* New York: The Penguin Press, 2010.

Clinton, Bill. *My Life.* New York: Knopf, 2004.

Coffin, Edward M. *The War to End All Wars: The American Military Experience in World War I.* Lexington: University of Kentucky Press, 1998.

Combs, Jerald A. *The Jay Treaty: Political Background of the Founding Fathers.* Berkeley: University of California Press, 1970.

Communist Party of the United States v. Subversive Activities Control Board, 351 US 115 (1956).

Communist Party of the United States v. Subversive Activities Control Board, 367 US 1 (1961).

Cox, LaWanda Fenlason. *Lincoln and Black Freedom: A Study in Presidential Leadership.* Columbia: The University of South Carolina Press, 1994.

Cray, Ed. *Chief Justice: A Biography of Earl Warren.* New York: Simon & Schuster, 1997.

Crook, John. "US Special Operations Personnel Raid Compound in Pakistan, Kill Osama bin Laden." *The American Journal of International Law* 105, no. 3 (July 2011): 602–605.

Cunningham, David. *There's Something Happening Here: The New Left, the Klan, and FBI Counterintelligence.* Berkeley: University of California Press, 2004.

Curtis, Michael Kent. "Lincoln, Vallandigham, and Anti-War Speech in the Civil War." *William & Mary Bill of Rights Journal* 7, no. 1 (December 1998): 105–91.

Dallek, Robert. *Franklin D. Roosevelt and American Foreign Policy, 1932–1945.* New York: Oxford University Press, 1995.

Dallek, Robert. "Woodrow Wilson: Politician." *The Wilson Quarterly* 15, no. 4 (Autumn 1991): 106–114.

Delaware Valley Committee for Democratic Rights. "Will You Register Under the McCarran Act?" Accessed March 2015. http://en.wikipedia.org/wiki/File:61-mccarranact-poster.jpg.

Demaske, Chris. *Modern Power and Free Speech: Contemporary Culture and Issues of Equality.* Lanham: Lexington Books, 2011.

Debs v. United States, 249 US 211 (1919).

Dennis v. United States, 341 US 494 (1951).

Dennis, Lawrence, and Maximilian St. George. *A Trial on Trial: The Great Sedition Trial of 1944.* Washington, D.C.: National Civil Rights Committee, 1946.

Dick, Bernard K. *Radical Innocence: a Critical Study of the Hollywood Ten.* Lexington: University of Kentucky Press, 1989.

Dickson, Del, ed. *The Supreme Court in Conference (1940–1985): The Private Discussions Behind Nearly 300 Supreme Court Decisions.* New York: Oxford University Press, 2001.

Diggins, John Patrick. *The Proud Decades: America in War and Peace, 1941–1960.* New York: W. W. Norton & Company, 1988.

Dinstein, Yoram. *War, Aggression and Self-Defence.* 4th ed. Cambridge: Cambridge University Press, 2005.

Dmytryk, Edward. *Odd Man Out: A Memoir of the Hollywood Ten.* Carbondale: Southern Illinois University Press, 1996.

Donald, David Herbert. *Lincoln.* New York: Simon & Schuster, 1995.

Doran Michael. "The Pragmatic Fanaticism of al Qaeda: An Anatomy of Extremism in Middle Eastern Politics." *Political Science Quarterly* 117, no. 2 (Summer 2002): 177–90.

Drabble, John. "Fighting Black Power-New Left Coalitions: Covert FBI Media Campaigns and American Cultural Discourse." *European Journal of American Culture* 27, no. 2 (June 2008): 65–91.

Dred Scott v. Sandford, 60 US 393 (1857).

Duncan v. Kahanamoku, 327 US 304 (1946).

Dwyer, Jim, and Kevin Flynn. *102 Minutes: The Untold Story of the Fight to Survive Inside the Twin Towers.* New York: Times Books, 2005.

Eddlem, Thomas R. "The Red Scare: When America Was Less Scared Than Today." *The New American* 29, no. 20 (October 21, 2013): 35–39.

Editors of Life. *Brought to Justice: Osama Bin Laden's War on America and the Mission That Stopped Him.* New York: Little, Brown and Company, 2011.

"Edward Snowden: Whistle-Blower." *New York Times*, January 2, 2014.

Ellis, John, and Michael Cox. *The World War I Data Book.* London: Aurum Press, 2001.

Epstein, Robert D. "Balancing National Security and Free-Speech Rights: Why Congress Should Revise the Espionage Act." *CommLaw Conspectus: Journal of Communications Law and Policy* 15, no. 2 (2007): 483–516.

Espionage Act of 1917. Act of June 15, 1917, ch. 30, 40 Stat. 217. Codified as amended at 18 U.S.C. §§ 793 *et seq.*

Estes, Todd. "Shaping the Politics of Public Opinion: Federalists and the Jay Treaty Debate" *Journal of the Early Republic* 20, no. 3 (Autumn 2000): 393–422.

Estreicher, Samuel, and Diarmuid O'Scannlain. "*Hamdan's* Limits and the Military Commissions Act." *Constitutional Commentary* 23, no. 3 (Winter 2006): 403–21.

Evacuation Claims Act of 1948, Pub. L. No. 886, 62 Stat. 1231 (1948).

Ex parte Endo, 323 US 283 (1944).

Ex Parte Merryman, 17 F. Cas. 144 (C.C.D. Md. 1861) (No. 9487).

Ex Parte Milligan, 71 US (4 Wall.) 2 (1866).

Ex Parte Vallandigham, 28 F.Cas. 874 (C.C.S.D. Ohio 1863).

Ex Parte Vallandigham, 68 US 243 (1863).

Farber, Alan J. "Reflections on the Sedition Act of 1798." *American Bar Association Journal* 62, no. 3 (March 1976): 324–28.

Ferguson, Charles Wright. *Fifty Million Brothers: A Panorama of American Lodges and Clubs.* New York: Farrar & Rinehart, 1937.

Field, N. R. "Getting Here From There: In the Years Since 2001, Neither Our Worst Fears Nor Our Highest Hopes Have Been Realized, But What Passes for Normal Has Exacted a Price." *New York Times—Supplement: The Reckoning*, September 11, 2011.

Finan, Christopher M. *From the Palmer Raids to the Patriot Act: A History of the Fight for Free Speech.* Boston: The Beacon Press, 2007.

Foner, Eric. *The Fiery Trial: Abraham Lincoln and American Slavery.* New York: W. W. Norton & Company, 2010.

Ford, Gerald R. "Proclamation 4417: Confirming the Termination of the Executive Order Authorizing Japanese-American Internment During World War II." In *When Sorry Isn't Enough: The Controversy Over Apologies and Reparations for Human Injustice*, edited by Roy L. Brooks, 201–02. New York: New York University Press, 1999.

Fouda, Yosri, and Nick Fielding. *Masterminds of Terror: The Truth Behind the Most Devastating Terrorist Attack the World Has Ever Seen.* New York: Arcade, 2003.

Franklin, Benjamin, and William Templeton Franklin. *Memoirs of the Life and Writings of Benjamin Franklin*. London: Henry Colburn, 1818.

Fried, Richard M. *Nightmare in Red: The McCarthy Era in Perspective*. New York: Oxford University Press, 1990.

Fried, Richard M. *The Russians Are Coming! The Russians Are Coming! Pageantry and Patriotism in Cold-War America*. New York: Oxford University Press, 1998.

Frohwerk v. United States, 249 US 204 (1919).

Gaddis, John Lewis. *The Cold War: A New History*. New York: Penguin, 2005.

Gannis, Joshua. "The Court, the Constitution and Japanese-American Internment." *Stanford Journal of East Asian Affairs* 11, no. 1 (Summer 2011): 87–96.

Garrison, Arthur H. "The Internal Security Acts of 1798: The Founding Generation and the Judiciary during America's First National Security Crisis." *Journal of Supreme Court History* 34, no. 1 (2009): 1–27.

Gerges, Fawaz A. *The Rise and Fall of Al-Qaeda*. New York: Oxford University Press, 2011.

Gilbert v. Minnesota, 254 US 325 (1920).

Gilbert, Francoise. "Demystifying the United States Patriot Act." *Journal of Internet Law* 16, no. 8 (February 2013): 3–7.

Gitlin, Todd. *The Sixties: Years of Hope, Days of Rage*. New York: Bantam Books, 1989.

Goldstein, Robert Justin. *Political Repression in Modern America: From 1870 to 1976*. Champaign: University of Illinois Press, 2001.

Goodheart, Adam. *1861: The Civil War Awakening*. New York: Vintage, 2012.

Goodman, James. *Stories of Scottsboro*. New York: Doubleday, 1995.

Goodwin, Doris Kearns. *Team of Rivals: The Political Genius of Abraham Lincoln*. New York: Simon & Schuster, 2005.

Gould, Lewis L. *Grand Old Party: A History of the Republicans*. New York: Random House, 2003.

GovTrack.us. "To Agree to the Conference Report on H.R. 5138, Alien Registration Act of 1940." Accessed February 2015. www.govtrack.us/congress/votes/76-3/h188.

Greenberg, Ivan. *The Dangers of Dissent: The FBI and Civil Liberties Since 1965*. Lanham: Lexington Books, 2010.

Gries, Peter Hayes. *The Politics of American Foreign Policy: How Ideology Divides Liberals and Conservatives over Foreign Affairs*. Stanford: Stanford University Press, 2014.

Gunaratna, Rohan. *Inside Al Qaeda: Global Network of Terror*. New York: Columbia University Press, 2002.

Gunther, Gerald. *Learned Hand: The Man and the Judge*. New York: Knopf, 1994.

Hackett, Kara. "Edward Snowden: The New Brand of Whistleblower?" *Quill* 101, no. 5 (September/October 2013): 26–31.

Hamilton, Alexander, James Madison, and John Jay. *The Federalist Papers*. Edited by Clinton Rossiter. New York: The New American Library, 1961.

Hamilton, Neil A. *Rebels and Renegades: A Chronology of Social and Political Dissent in the United States*. London: Routledge, 2002.

Hamilton, Virginia. *Paul Robeson: The Life and Times of a Free Black Man*. New York: Dell Publishing, 1979.

Harding, Luke. *The Snowden Files: The Inside Story of the World's Most Wanted Man*. New York: Vintage, 2014.

Harnett, Stephen John, and Jennifer Rose Mercieca. "'Has Your Courage Rusted?' National Security and the Contested Rhetorical Norms of Republicanism in Post-Revolutionary America, 1798-1801." *Rhetoric & Public Affairs* 9, no. 1 (Spring 2006): 79–112.

Harrell, David Edwin, and Edwin S. Gaustad, John B. Boles, Sally Foreman Griffith, Randall M. Miller, and Randall B. Woods. *Unto a Good Land: A History of the American People.* Vol. 1. Cambridge: William B. Eerdmans Publishing Company, 2005.

Haverty-Stacke, Donna T. "'Punishment of Mere Political Advocacy': The FBI, Teamsters Local 544, and the Origins of the 1941 Smith Act Case." *The Journal of American History* 100, no. 1 (June 2013): 68–93.

Healy, Thomas. *The Great Dissent: How Oliver Wendell Holmes Changed His Mind—And Changed the History of Free Speech in America.* New York: Metropolitan Books, 2013.

Hedges, Chris. *Death of the Liberal Class.* New York: Nation Books, 2010.

Hefner-Babb, Theresa S. "Internal Security Act of 1950." In *The Social History of Crime and Punishment in America,* edited by Wilbur R. Miller, 844-45. Thousand Oaks: Sage Publications, Inc., 2012.

Heineman, Kenneth. "Media Bias in Coverage of the Dies Committee on Un-American Activities, 1938–1940." *Historian* 50, no. 1 (Autumn 1992): 37–52.

Helprin, Mark. "We Can't Reform the Arab World." *Wall Street Journal,* September 9, 2011.

Henzel, Christopher. "The Origins of al Qaeda's Ideology: Implications for US Strategy." *Parameters* 35, no. 1 (Spring 2005): 69–80.

Hersh, Burton. *Bobby and J. Edgar: the Historic Face-off Between the Kennedys and J. Edgar Hoover That Transformed America.* New York: Carroll & Graf, 2007.

High, Stanley. "Star-Spangled Fascists." *Saturday Evening Post* 211, 48 (May 27, 1939): 5–7, 70–73.

Hirabayashi v. United States, 320 US 81 (1943).

Hoffman, Bruce. "The Global Terrorist Threat: Is Al-Qaeda on the Run or on the March?" *Middle East Policy* 14, no. 2 (Summer 2007): 44–58.

Hogan, Willard N. *International Conflict and Collective Security.* Lexington: University of Kentucky Press, 1955.

Holzer, Harold. *Lincoln and the Power of the Press.* New York: Simon & Schuster, 2014.

———. *Lincoln President-Elect: Abraham Lincoln and the Great Secession Winter 1860–1861.* New York: Simon & Schuster, 2008.

Hoodbhoy, Pervez. "Afghanistan and the Genesis of Global Jihad." *Peace Research* 37, no. 1 (May 2005): 15–30.

Howe, Daniel Walker. *What Hath God Wrought: The Transformation of America,* 1815–1848. Oxford: Oxford University Press, 2007.

Irons, Peter. "Politics and Principle: An Assessment of the Roosevelt Record on Civil Rights and Civil Liberties." In *At War with Civil Rights and Civil Liberties,* edited by Thomas E. Baker and John F. Stack Jr., 49–79. Lanham: Rowman & Littlefield, 2006.

Isaacson, Walter. *Benjamin Franklin: An American Life.* New York: Simon & Schuster, 2003.

Jackson, Andrew. *The Statesmanship of Andrew Jackson as Told in His Writings and Speeches.* Edited by Francis Newton Thorpe. New York: The Tandy-Thomas Company, 1909.

———. "The New History of the Weather Underground." *Monthly Review* 58, no. 2 (June 2006): 59–64.

Jacobs, Ron. *The Way the Wind Blew: A History of the Weather Underground.* New York: Verso Books, 1997.

Jansen, G. H. *Militant Islam.* New York: Harper & Row, 1979.

Jenkins, David. "The Sedition Act of 1798 and the Incorporation of Seditious Libel into First Amendment Jurisprudence." *American Journal of Legal History* 45, no. 2 (April 2001): 154–213.

Jones, Howard. *Mutiny on the Amistad: The Saga of a Slave Revolt and Its Impact on American Abolition, Law and Diplomacy.* Omaha: The Notable Trials Library, 2014.

Kashima, Tetsuden. *Judgment without Trial: Japanese American Imprisonment During World War II*. Seattle: University of Washington Press, 2003.

Katznelson, Ira. *Fear Itself: The New Deal and the Origins of Our Time*. New York: Liveright Publishing Corporation, 2013.

Keegan, John. *The American Civil War: A Military History*. New York: Knopf, 2009.

Kersch, Ken I. *Freedom of Speech: Rights and Liberties under the Law*. Santa Barbara: ABC-CLIO, 2003.

Kessler, Ronald. *The Bureau: The Secret History of the FBI*. New York: St. Martin's Press, 2003.

———. *The FBI*. New York: Pocket Books, 1993.

Kilbourn v. Thompson, 103 US 168 (1880).

Klement, Frank L. "Copperheads." In *MacMillan Information Now Encyclopedia: The Confederacy*. Edited by Richard N. Current, 154–55. New York: MacMillan Reference USA, 1993.

———. *The Limits of Dissent: Clement L. Vallandigham & The Civil War*. New York: Fordham University Press, 1998.

Kleinfield, N. R. "Getting Here From There: In the Years Since 2001, Neither Our Worst Fears Nor Our Highest Hopes Have Been Realized, But What Passes for Normal Has Exacted a Price." *New York Times—Supplement: The Reckoning*, September 11, 2011.

Koch, Adrienne, and Harry Ammon. "The Virginia and Kentucky Resolutions: An Episode in Jefferson's and Madison's Defense of Civil Liberties." *William and Mary Quarterly* Third Series, 5, no. 2 (April 1948): 145–76.

Kohn, Margaret. "Due Process and Empire's Law: *Hamdan v. Rumsfeld*." *Dissent* 54, no. 1 (Winter 2007): 5–8.

Korematsu v. United States, 323 US 214 (1944).

La Follette, Robert M. *The Political Philosophy of Robert M. La Follette as Revealed in His Speeches and Writings*. Madison: The Robert M. La Follette Company, 1920.

Laqueur, Walter. "The Terrorism to Come." *Policy Review* 126, no. 1 (August/September 2004): 49–64.

Larrowe, C. P. "Did the Old Left Get Due Process? The Case of Harry Bridges." *California Law Review* 60, no. 1 (January 1972): 39–83.

Larrowe, Charles P. *Harry Bridges: The Rise and Fall of Radical Labour in the US*. Lawrence Hill & Company, 1972.

Larson, Edward J. *A Magnificent Catastrophe: The Tumultuous Election of 1800, America's First Presidential Campaign*. New York: The Free Press, 2007.

Lash, Kurt T., and Alicia Harrison. "Minority Report: John Marshall and the Defense of the Alien and Sedition Acts." *Ohio State Law Journal* 68, no. 2 (2007): 435–516.

"The Law." *Time* 39, no. 19 (May 11, 1942): 48.

Lesch, Ann M. "Osama Bin Laden: Embedded in the Middle East Crises." *Middle East Policy* 9, 2 (June 2002): 82–91.

Levine, Bruce. "Conservatism, Nativism, and Slavery: Thomas R. Whitney and the Origins of the Know-Nothing Party." *Journal of American History* 88, no. 2 (September 2001): 455–88.

Lewis, Anthony. *Freedom for the Thought We Hate: A Biography of the First Amendment*. New York: Basic Books, 2007.

Lewy, Guenter. *The Cause That Failed: Communism in American Political Life*. New York: Oxford University Press, 1990.

Lichtman, Allan J. *White Protestant Nation: The Rise of the American Conservative Movement*. New York: Atlantic Monthly Press, 2008.

Lincoln, Abraham. "The Case of Vallandigham.; Reply of President Lincoln to the Ohio Committee. Washington, D.C., June 29, 1863." *New York Times*, July 7, 1863.

Lincoln, Abraham. *The Complete Works of Abraham Lincoln*. Vols. III, VI, VIII, IX. Edited by John G. Nicolay and John Hay. New York: The Tandy-Thomas Company, 1905.

Maas, Peter. "Snowden's People." *New York Times Magazine* (2013): 22–29, 49.

MacDowell, Laura Sefton. "Paul Robeson in Canada: A Border Story." *Labour/Le Travail* 51, no. 1 (Spring 2003): 171–221.

Madison, James. *The Writings of James Madison*. Vol. IX: 1819–1836. Edited by Gaillard Hunt. New York: G.P. Putnam's Sons, 1910.

Magee, James. *Freedom of Expression*. Westport: Greenwood Press, 2002.

Maharrey, Michael. *Smashing Myths: Understanding Madison's Notes on Nullification*. Los Angeles: Tenth Amendment Center, 2013.

Mahoney, Richard D. *The Kennedy Brothers: The Rise and Fall of Jack and Bobby*. New York: Arcade Publishing, 2011.

Marable, Manning. *Malcolm X: A Life of Reinvention*. New York: Viking, 2011.

Martin, James P. "When Repression Is Democratic and Constitutional: The Federalist Theory of Representation and the Sedition Act of 1798." *University of Chicago Law Review* 66, no. 1 (Winter 1999): 117–82.

Martinez, J. Michael. *Terrorist Attacks on American Soil: From the Civil War Era to the Present*. Lanham: Rowman & Littlefield, 2012.

Masses Publishing Company v. Patten, 244 F. 535 (S.D.N.Y. 1917).

May, Gary. *Un-American Activities: The Trials of William Remington*. New York: Gryphon Editions, 1999.

Mayhead, Molly A., and Brenda Devore Marshall. *Women's Political Discourse: a 21st Century Perspective*. Lanham: Rowman & Littlefield, 2005.

McCann, Joseph T. *Terrorism on American Soil: A Concise History of Plots and Perpetrators from the Famous to the Forgotten*. Boulder: Sentient Publications, 2006.

McCormick, James. *American Foreign Policy and Process*. Boston: Wadsworth Cengage, 2010.

McCullough, David. *John Adams*. New York: Touchstone Books, 2001.

———. New York: Simon & Schuster, 1992.

McDermott, Terry. "A Perfect Soldier: Mohamed Atta, Whose Hard Gaze Has Stared from a Billion Television Screens and Newspaper Pages, Has Become, for Many, the Face of Evil Incarnate." *Los Angeles Times*, January 27, 2002.

McDonald, Forrest. *States' Rights and the Union: Imperium in Imperio, 1776–1876*. Lawrence: University Press of Kansas, 2000.

McFarlane, Robert C. "Afghanistan Should Have Been the Focus." *Wall Street Journal*, September 9, 2011.

McGrain v. Daugherty, 273 US 135 (1927).

McMaster, John Bach. *United States in the World War*. New York: D. Appleton and Company, 1918.

McPherson, James M. *Battle Cry of Freedom: The Civil War Era*. New York: Ballantine Books, 1988.

———. *Tried By War: Abraham Lincoln as Commander in Chief*. New York: The Penguin Press, 2008.

Meacham, Jon. *American Lion: Andrew Jackson in the White House*. New York: Random House, 2008.

———. *Thomas Jefferson: The Art of Power*. New York: Random House, 2012.

Mead, Chris. *The Magicians of Main Street: America and its Chambers of Commerce, 1768–1945*. Oakton: John Cruger Press, 2014.

Medina, Harold R. "The Crime of Conspiracy: Charge to the Jury." *Vital Speeches of the Day* 16, no. 2 (November 1, 1949): 34–46.

Meltzer, Bernard D. "Required Records, the McCarran Act, and the Privilege against Self-Incrimination." *University of Chicago Law Review* 18, no. 4 (Summer 1951): 687–728.

Merari, Ariel. "Deterring Fear: Government Responses to Terrorist Attacks." *Harvard International Review* 23, no. 4 (Winter 2002): 26–31.

Meyer, Gerald. *Vito Marcantonio: Radical Politician, 1902–1954.* Albany: SUNY Press, 1989.

Michael, George. *Confronting Right-Wing Extremism and Terrorism in the USA.* London: Routledge, 2003.

Miller, William Lee. *President Lincoln: The Duty of a Statesman.* New York: Knopf, 2008.

Middleton, Tiffany. "Sedition Act of 1918." In *The Social History of Crime and Punishment in America,* edited by Wilbur R. Miller. Thousand Oaks: Sage Publications, Inc., 2012.

Mole, Phil. "9/11 Conspiracy Theories: The 9/11 Truth Movement in Perspective." *Skeptic* 12, no. 4 (2006): 30–42.

Morgan, Edmund S. *Benjamin Franklin.* New Haven: Yale University Press, 2002.

Nacos, Brigitte L. "Terrorism as Breaking News: Attack on America." *Political Science Quarterly* 118, no. 1 (Spring 2003): 23–52.

Nasir, Sohail Abdul. "Al Qaeda, Two Years On." *Bulletin of the Atomic Scientists* 59, no. 5 (September/October 2003): 32–41.

National Commission on Terrorist Attacks Upon the United States. *The 9/11 Commission Report.* New York: W. W. Norton & Company, 2004.

Nichols, John. *The "S" Word: A Short History of an American Tradition...Socialism.* London: Verso, 2011.

Nimmo, William F. *Stars and Stripes Across the Pacific: The United States, Japan, and the Asia/Pacific Region, 1895–1945.* Westport: Praeger, 2001.

Ober, Frank B. "Communism and the Court: An Examination of Recent Developments." *ABA Journal* 44, no. 1 (January 1958): 35–38, 84–89.

Olmsted, Kathryn S. *Red Spy Queen: A Biography of Elizabeth Bentley.* Chapel Hill: University of North Carolina Press, 2002.

Oyama v. State of California, 332 US 633 (1948).

Padover, Saul K., ed. *Thomas Jefferson on Democracy.* New York: The New American Library, 1939.

Palmer, Bryan D. *Revolutionary Teamsters: The Minneapolis Truckers' Strikes of 1934.* Chicago: Haymarket Books, 2014.

Pani, Erika. "Saving the Nation Through Exclusion: Alien Laws in the Early Republic in the United States and Mexico." *Americas* 65, no. 2 (October 2008): 217–46.

Perret, Geoffrey. *Lincoln's War: The Untold Story of America's Greatest President as Commander in Chief.* New York: Random House, 2004.

Perucci, Tony. *Paul Robeson and the Cold War Performance Complex: Race, Madness, Activism.* Ann Arbor: University of Michigan Press, 2012.

Perucci, Tony. "The Red Mask of Sanity: Paul Robeson, HUAC, and the Sound of Cold War Performance." *TDR: The Drama Review* 53, no. 4 (Winter 2009): 18–48.

Phillips, Christopher. "'The Crimes Against Missouri': Slavery, Kansas, and the Cant of Southernness in the Border West." *Civil War History* 48, no. 1 (March 2002): 60–81.

Pierce v. United States, 252 US 239 (1920).

Plessy v. Ferguson, 163 US 537 (1896).

Powers, Richard Gid. *Not Without Honor: The History of American Communism.* New Haven: Yale University Press, 1998.

"The President Reports on the Death of Osama bin Laden." *Army* 61, no. 6 (June 2011): 6–7.

Preston, Diana. *Lusitania: An Epic Tragedy.* New York: Walker & Company, 2002.

Pryor, John P. "The 2001 World Trade Center Disaster: Summary and Evaluation of Experiences." *European Journal of Trauma and Emergency Surgery* 35, no. 3 (June 2009): 212–24.

Quimby, Amy. "*Hamdan v. Rumsfeld*: Reviewing the Geneva Convention Rights of the Unlawful Enemy Combatants Detained at Gitmo." *Widener Law Journal* 17, no. 1 (Spring 2010): 317–53.

Rachlin, Robert D. "The Sedition Act of 1798 and the Political Divide in Vermont." *Vermont History* 78, no. 2 (Summer/Fall 2010): 123–50.

Ratcliffe, Donald J. "The Nullification Crisis, Southern Discontents, and the American Political Process." *American Nineteenth Century History* 1, no. 2 (Summer 2000): 1–30.

Ray, Thomas M. "'Not One Cent for Tribute': The Public Addresses and American Popular Reaction to the XYZ Affair, 1798–1799." *Journal of the Early Republic* 3, no. 4 (Winter 1983): 389–412.

Reeves, Richard. *Infamy: The Shocking Story of the Japanese American Internment in World War II*. New York: Henry Holt, 2015.

Reeves, Thomas C. *The Life and Times of Joe McCarthy: A Biography*. Ontario: Madison Press Books, 1997.

Rehnquist, William H. *All the Laws but One: Civil Liberties in Wartime*. New York: Knopf, 1998.

Richey, Carol. "House Committee on Un-American Activities." *History Magazine* 15, no. 2 (December 2013/January 2014): 45–48.

Ridgeway, James. *Blood in the Face: The Ku Klux Klan, Aryan Nations, Nazi Skinheads, and the Rise of a New White Culture*. 2nd. ed. New York: Thunder's Mouth Press, 1995.

Robeson v. Acheson, 198 F.2d 985 (DC Cir. 1952).

Robinson, Greg. *By Order of the President: FDR and the Internment of Japanese Americans*. Cambridge: Harvard University Press, 2001.

Rogers, William Allen. "Now for a Round-Up." *New York Herald*, May 9, 1918.

Rosenthal, John. "Doing Justice to Zacarias Moussaoui." *Policy Review* 146, no. 1 (December 2007/January 2008): 39–61.

Rovere, Richard H. *Senator Joe McCarthy*. Berkeley: University of California Press, 1996.

Rubin, Richard. *The Last of the Doughboys: The Forgotten Generation and Their Forgotten World War*. New York: Houghton Mifflin Harcourt, 2013.

Rudanko, Juhani. *Discourses of Freedom of Speech: From the Enactment of the Bill of Rights to the Sedition Act of 1918*. New York and London: Palgrave MacMillan, 2012.

Runkle, Benjamin. *Wanted Dead or Alive: Manhunts from Geronimo to Bin Laden*. New York: Palgrave-MacMillan, 2011.

Sabin, Arthur J. *In Calmer Times: The Supreme Court and Red Monday*. Philadelphia: University of Pennsylvania Press, 1999.

Sale, Richard. *Clinton's Secret Wars: The Evolution of a Commander in Chief*. New York: Thomas Dunne Books, 2009.

Savage, Charlie. "Snowden Denies That He Was a Spy for Russia." *New York Times*, January 22, 2014.

Schaefer v. United States, 251 US 466 (1920).

Schenck v. United States, 249 US 47 (1919).

Seamon, Richard Henry, and William Dylan Gardner. "The Patriot Act and the Wall Between Foreign Intelligence and Law Enforcement." *Harvard Journal of Law & Public Policy* 28, no. 1 (April 2005): 319–463.

Seymour, Charles. *Woodrow Wilson and the World War: A Chronicle of Our Own Times*. New Haven: Yale University Press, 1921.

Sharp, James Roger. *American Politics in the Early Republic: The New Nation in Crisis*. New Haven: Yale University Press, 1993.

Shenon, Philip. "Report Claims That 9/11 Terrorists were Identified Before Attacks." *New York Times*, September 22, 2006.

Shermer, Michael. *The Believing Brain: From Ghosts and Gods to Politics and Conspiracies—How We Construct Beliefs and Reinforce Them as Truths*. New York: Times Books, 2011.

Slaughter, Anne-Marie. "Resilience vs. Revenge." *Wall Street Journal, September 9, 2011*.

Smith, Cary Stacy, and Li-Ching Hung. *The Patriot Act: Issues and Controversies*. Springfield: Charles C. Thomas, 2010.

Smith, James Morton. "The Enforcement of the Alien Friends Act of 1798." *Mississippi Valley Historical Review* 41, no. 1 (June 1954): 85–104.

Smith, Jean Edward. *John Marshall: Definer of a Nation*. New York: Henry Holt, 1996.

Spickard, Paul. *Almost All Aliens: Immigration, Race, and Colonialism in American History and Identity*. London: Routledge, 2007.

Starr, Kevin. *Endangered Dreams: The Great Depression in California*. New York: Oxford University Press, 1996.

Stathis, Stephen W. *Landmark Debates in Congress: From the Declaration of Independence to the War in Iraq*. Washington, D.C.: CQ Press, 2009.

Stephens, Bret. "9/11 and the Struggle for Meaning." *Wall Street Journal*, September 6, 2011.

Stone, Geoffrey R. "Free Speech and National Security." *Indiana Law Journal* 84, no. 3 (Summer 2009): 939–62.

———. "Judge Learned Hand and the Espionage Act of 1917: A Mystery Unraveled." *University of Chicago Law Review* 70, no. 1 (Winter 2003): 335–58.

———. *Perilous Times: Free Speech in Wartime—From the Sedition Act of 1798 to the War on Terrorism*. New York: W. W. Norton & Company, 2004.

Sullivan, William C., with Bill Brown. *The Bureau: My Thirty Years in Hoover's FBI*. New York: W. W. Norton & Company, 1979.

Swazo, Norman K. "'My Brother is my King': Evaluating the Moral Duty of Global Jihad." *International Journal on World Peace* 25, no. 4 (December 2008): 7–47.

Takahashi v. Fish and Game Commission, 334 US 410 (1948).

"Ten Years On." *Economist* 400, no. 8749 (September 3, 2011): 11–12.

tenBroek, Jacobus, Edward N. Barnhart, and Floyd W. Matson. *Prejudice, War and the Constitution: Causes and Consequences of the Evacuation of the Japanese Americans in World War II*. Berkeley: University of California Press, 1970.

"Text of President's Message Vetoing the Communist-Control Bill." *New York Times*, September 23, 1950.

The Trial of the Hon. Clement L. Vallandigham by a Military Commission: And the Proceedings Under His Application for a Writ of Habeas Corpus in the Circuit Court of the United States for the Southern District of Ohio. Cincinnati: Rickey and Carroll, 1863.

Trussell, C. P. "Red Bill Veto Beaten, 57–10, by Senators." *New York Times*, September 24, 1950.

———. "Senate Filibuster: Charge Made as Long Truman Message Stirs Debate Into Today." *New York Times*, September 23, 1950.

Tucker, Robert W. *Woodrow Wilson and the Great War: Reconsidering America's Neutrality, 1914–1917*. Charlottesville: University of Virginia Press, 2007.

United States Department of Justice, Office of the Inspector General. *A Review of the FBI's Investigations of Certain Domestic Advocacy Groups*. Washington, D.C.: Oversight and Review Division, Office of the Inspector General, September 2010.

United States House of Representatives, Committee on Un-American Activities. *Hearings Regarding Communist Espionage in the United States Government. Hearings Before the Committee on Un-American Activities, House of Representatives, 80th Congress, Second Session, Public Law 601.* Washington, D.C.: Government Printing Office, 1948.

United States Senate Select Committee to Study Governmental Operations with Respect to Intelligence Activities. *Final Report of the Select Committee to Study Governmental Operations with Respect to Intelligence Activities, United States Senate, Together with Additional, Supplemental, and Separate Views.* Book II. Report No. 94-755. Washington, D.C.: US Government Printing Office, 1976.

United States War Department. *Final Report: Japanese Evacuation from the West Coast.* New York: Arno Press, 1978.

Vallandigham, James L. *A Life of Clement L. Vallandigham.* Baltimore: Turnbull Brothers, 1872.

Vladeck, Stephen I. "Inchoate Liability and the Espionage Act: The Statutory Framework and the Freedom of the Press." *Harvard Law and Policy Review* 1, no. 1 (2007): 219–237.

Wade, Wyn Craig. *The Fiery Cross: The Ku Klux Klan in America.* New York: Oxford University Press, 1987.

Waldstreicher, David. *Slavery's Constitution: From Revolution to Ratification.* New York: Hill and Wang, 2009.

Walker, Samuel. *In Defense of American Liberties: A History of the ACLU.* 2nd ed. Carbondale: Southern Illinois University Press, 1999.

Walker, Samuel. *Presidents and Civil Liberties from Wilson to Obama: A Story of Poor Custodians.* Cambridge: Cambridge University Press, 2012.

Wallance, Gregory J. "The Lawsuit That Started the Civil War." *Civil War Times* 45, no. 2 (March/April 2006): 46–52.

Walther, Eric H. *The Shattering of the Union: America in the 1850s.* Wilmington: SR Books, 2004.

Washburn, Patrick S. "FDR versus His Own Attorney General: The Struggle Over Sedition, 1941–42." *Journalism Quarterly* 62, no. 4 (Winter 1985): 717–24.

Watkins v. United States, 354 US 178 (1957).

Watkins, William J., Jr. *Reclaiming the American Revolution: The Kentucky and Virginia Resolutions and Their Legacy.* New York: Palgrave, 2004.

Waugh, John C. *One Man Great Enough: Abraham Lincoln's Road to Civil War.* Boston and New York: Houghton Mifflin, 2007.

Weiner, Tim. *Enemies: A History of the FBI.* New York: Random House, 2012.

Wert, Justin J. *Habeas Corpus in America: The Politics of Individual Rights.* Lawrence: University Press of Kansas, 2011.

West Virginia State Board of Education v. Barnette, 319 US 624 (1943).

White, G. Edward. *Alger Hiss's Looking-Glass Wars: The Covert Life of a Soviet Spy.* New York: Oxford University Press, 2004.

White, Morton. *Philosophy, The Federalist, and the Constitution.* New York: Oxford University Press, 1987.

White, Ronald C. Jr. *A. Lincoln: A Biography.* New York: Random House, 2009.

———. *The Eloquent President: A Portrait of Lincoln Through His Words.* New York: Random House, 2005.

Wiecek, William M. *The History of the Supreme Court of the United States. Vol. 12: The Birth of the Modern Constitution: The United States Supreme Court, 1941–1953.* Cambridge: Cambridge University Press, 2006.

Wieseltier, Leon. "Even Obama Embraces Drones." *Wall Street Journal*, September 9, 2011.

Wilson, Woodrow. "Executive Order 2594–Creating Committee on Public Information" 1917. Reprinted in *Official Directory, 65th Congress, 3d Session*. Vol. 65. 2nd ed. Washington, D.C.: Joint Committee on Printing, 1919.

Wilson, Woodrow. *War Addresses of Woodrow Wilson*. Boston: Ginn and Company, 1918.

Witcover, Jules. *Party of the People: A History of the Democrats*. Random House: New York, 2003.

Wolfowitz, Paul. "We Had to Address State Sponsors of Terror." *Wall Street Journal*, 9 September 2011.

Wolverton, Joe II. "The Case for Nullification." *New American* 28, no. 9 (May 7, 2012): 27–30.

Wood, Gordon S. *Empire of Liberty: A History of the Early Republic, 1789–1815*. New York: Oxford University Press, 2009.

Woods, Jeff. *Black Struggle, Red Scare: Segregation and Anti-Communism in the South, 1948–1968*. Baton Rouge: Louisiana State University Press, 2004.

Woodworth, Steven E. *This Great Struggle: America's Civil War*. Lanham: Rowman & Littlefield, 2011.

Wright, Lawrence. *The Looming Tower: Al-Qaeda and the Road to 9/11*. New York: Knopf, 2006.

Wright, Robin. *Rock the Casbah: Rage and Rebellion across the Islamic World*. New York: Simon & Schuster, 2011.

Yasui v. United States, 320 US 115 (1943).

Yates v. United States, 354 US 298 (1957).

Ybarra, Michael J. *Washington Gone Crazy: Senator Pat McCarran and the Great American Communist Witch Hunt*. Hanover: Steerforth Press, 2004.

Yoo, John. *Crisis and Command*. New York: Kaplan Publishing, 2009.

—— "Ten Years without an Attack." *Wall Street Journal*, September 6, 2011.

INDEX

ABOUT THE AUTHOR

J. Michael Martinez works in Monroe, Georgia, as corporate counsel with a manufacturing company. He also teaches political science as a part-time faculty member at Kennesaw State University in Kennesaw, Georgia. He is the author of eight previous books, including *Terrorist Attacks on American Soil: From the Civil War Era to the Present* (2012) and *The Greatest Criminal Cases: Changing the Course of American Law* (2014). Visit him on the Internet at www.jmichaelmartinez.com.